LLEWELLYN'S
2013
Magical Almanac

D1012190
B

Featuring
Chandra Alexandre, Barbara Ardinger,
Blake Octavian Blair, Deborah Blake, Boudica,
Calantirniel, Emily Carlin, Andrea Chavez,
Dallas Jennifer Cobb, Autumn Damiana,
Raven Digitalis, Ellen Dugan, Emyme, Sybil Fogg,
Ember Grant, Magenta Griffith, James Kambos,
Alan Lucia, Lupa, Kristin Madden,
Melanie Marquis, Lisa McSherry, Mickie Mueller,
Sharynne MacLeod NicMhacha,
Susan Pesznecker, Marion Sipe,
Charlynn Walls, and Tess Whitehurst

Llewellyn's 2013 Magical Almanac

ISBN 978-0-7387-1515-5. Copyright © 2012 by Llewellyn. All rights reserved. Printed in the United States. Llewellyn is a registered trademark of Llewellyn Worldwide Ltd.

Editor/Designer: Ed Day

Cover Illustration: © Tammy Shane

Calendar Pages Design: Michael Fallon

Calendar Pages Illustrations: © Fiona King

Interior Illustrations © Carol Coogan: pages 13, 37, 41, 79, 108, 113, 141, 215, 257, 260, 289, 304, 309, 333, 335; © Chris Down: pages 27, 31, 34, 80, 87, 131, 134, 136, 250, 254, 299, 302, 339, 342, 345; © Kathleen Edwards: pages 45, 49, 97, 100, 143, 144, 146, 264, 267, 312, 314, 349; © Don Higgins: pages 23, 24, 75, 117, 121, 243, 245, 246, 283, 286; © Wen Hsu: pages 15, 18, 65, 68, 73, 123, 127, 129, 235, 239, 291, 294, 296; © Mickie Mueller: pages 59, 63, 90, 93, 226, 228, 231, 275, 279, 317, 322, 357; © Amber Zoellner: pages 53, 54, 103, 217, 221, 269, 272, 325, 329.

Clip Art Illustrations: Dover Publications

Special thanks to Amber Wolfe for the use of daily color and incense correspondences. For more detailed information, please see *Personal Alchemy* by Amber Wolfe.

You can order Llewellyn annuals and books from *New Worlds,* Llewellyn's catalog. To request a free copy of the catalog, call toll-free 1-877-NEW-WRLD or visit our website: www.llewellyn.com

Astrological data compiled and programmed by Rique Pottenger. Based on the earlier work of Neil F. Michelsen.

Llewellyn Worldwide Ltd.
2143 Wooddale Drive
Woodbury, MN 55125

About the Authors

CHANDRA ALEXANDRE is an initiated Tantrika and hereditary Witch. Since 1998, she has worked to create a vehicle for those seeking to embrace the ancient (yet living) embodied and goddess-centered spiritual traditions of India. This resulted in SHARANYA (www.sharanya.org), a goddess temple run by a community in San Francisco, and the Sha'can tradition, a syncretism based on Hindu Tantra and witchcraft. She holds a Ph.D. in philosophy and religion, a doctorate of ministry, and an MBA in sustainable management.

BARBARA ARDINGER, PH.D., (www.barbaraardinger.com) is the author of *Secret Lives*, a novel about a circle of crones, mothers, and maidens, plus goddesses, a talking cat, and the Green Man. Her earlier books include *Pagan Every Day*, *Goddess Meditations*, *Finding New Goddesses* (a parody of goddess encyclopedias), and *Quicksilver Moon* (a realistic novel … except for the vampire). Her day job is freelance editing for people who have good ideas but don't want to embarrass themselves in print. To date, she has edited more than 250 books, both fiction and nonfiction, on a wide range of topics. Barbara lives in Southern California with her two rescued Maine coon cats, Heisenberg and Schroedinger.

BLAKE OCTAVIAN BLAIR (Carrboro, N.C.) is an Eclectic IndoPagan Witch, psychic, tarot reader, freelance writer, energy worker, and a devotee of Lord Ganesha. He holds a degree in English and Religion from the University of Florida. Blake lives in the Piedmont Region of North Carolina with his beloved husband, an aquarium full of fish, and an indoor jungle of houseplants. Visit him at www.blakeoctavianblair.com or write to blake@blakeoctavianblair.com.

DEBORAH BLAKE is a Wiccan High Priestess who has been leading Blue Moon Circle for many years. She is the author of *Circle, Coven and Grove*, *Everyday Witch A to Z*, *The Goddess is in the Details*, and *The*

Everyday Witch A to Z Spellbook, all from Llewellyn. She was a finalist in the Pagan Fiction Award Contest and her short story, "Dead and (Mostly) Gone," is in *The Pagan Anthology of Short Fiction*. She is also working on a number of novels. When not writing, Deborah runs The Artisans' Guild and works as a jewelry maker, a tarot reader, an ordained minister, and an Intuitive Energy Healer. She lives in a hundred-year-old farmhouse in rural upstate New York with five cats who supervise all her activities, both magickal and mundane.

BOUDICA is reviews editor and co-owner of *The Wiccan/Pagan Times* and owner of *The Zodiac Bistro*. A former New Yorker, she now resides with her husband and eight cats in Ohio.

LISA ALLEN/CALANTIRNIEL has been published in many Llewellyn annuals and has practiced many forms of natural spirituality since the early 1990s. She currently lives in western Montana with her husband, teenage daughter, and three young cats, while her older son is in college. She is a professional astrologer, tarot card reader, dowser, flower essence creator and practitioner, a ULC Reverend, Usui Reiki II, and a certified Master Herbalist. She has an organic garden, crochets professionally, and is co-creating Tië eldaliéva, "the Elven Path," a spiritual practice based on J. R. R. Tolkien's Middle-Earth stories. www.myspace.com/aartiana.

EMILY CARLIN is an eclectic witch, mediator, and attorney, based in Seattle, Washington. She specializes in shadow work and defensive magick. Emily teaches extensively online at the Grey School, and at Pagan events around the Puget Sound area. Her book, *Defense Against the Dark*, a guide to all things that go bump in the night and what to do about them, is available online and at major retailers.

ANDREA CHAVEZ, a.k.a. Sapphire Soleil, started down the pagan path over twelve years ago. Her studies have allowed her to explore many areas of paganism and she calls herself "an eclectic pagan with kitchen witch tendencies." Born and raised among the

peas, lentils, and wheat of northern Idaho, this rural Pagan has two university degrees in telecommunications and journalism and is a proud graduate from the Grey School of Wizardry, where she is currently on faculty and associate Dean of Magickal Practices. You can reach her at sapphiresoleil@greyschool.com.

DALLAS JENNIFER COBB lives a magical life. She conjures meaningful and flexible work, satisfying relationships and abundant gardens. She has manifested a balance of time and money which support her deepest desires: a loving family, time in nature, self-expression, and a healthy home. She lives in paradise, in a waterfront village in rural Ontario. jennifer.cobb@live.com.

AUTUMN DAMIANA is a writer, artist, crafter, and amateur photographer, and has been a mostly solitary eclectic Witch for fourteen years. She is passionate about eco-friendly living, and writes about this and her day-to-day walk on the Pagan path in her blog, "Sacred Survival in a Mundane World" at http://autumndamiana.blogspot.com/. When not writing or making art, you can find her outside enjoying nature or investigating local history in her hometown of San Jose, California. Contact her at autumndamiana@gmail.com.

RAVEN DIGITALIS (Montana) is the author of *Planetary Spells & Rituals, Shadow Magick Compendium,* and *Goth Craft,* all from Llewellyn. He is a Neopagan Priest, cofounder of the "disciplined eclectic" tradition and training coven Opus Aima Obscuræ, and is a DJ. Also trained in Georgian Witchcraft and Buddhist philosophy, Raven is a Witch, Priest, and Empath. He holds a degree in anthropology and is also an animal rights activist, photographic artist, Tarot reader, and the co-owner of Twigs & Brews Herbs. www.ravendigitalis.com, www.myspace.com/oakraven.

ELLEN DUGAN, the "Garden Witch," is an award-winning author and psychic-clairvoyant. A practicing Witch for more than twenty-seven years, she is the author of many Llewellyn books; her newest are

A Garden Witch's Herbal and *Book of Witchery*. Ellen encourages folks to personalize their spellcraft, to go outside and get their hands dirty, so they can discover the wonder and magick of the natural world. Ellen and her family live in Missouri. www.ellendugan.com.

EMYME is a solitary practitioner who resides in a multigenerational, multicat household in southern New Jersey. Hobbies that renew her are: gardening, sewing and crafts, and home care and repair. Emyme has self-published a children's book about mending families after divorce and remarriage. She is an avid diarist; dabbles in poetry; creates her own blessings, incantations, and spells; and is currently writing a series of fantasy fiction stories set in the twenty-fifth century. Her personal mantra is summed up in four words: Curiosity, Objectivity, Quality, Integrity. catsmeow24@verizon.net.

SYBIL FOGG, also known as Sybil Wilen, has been a practicing Witch for more than twenty years. She chose to use her mother's maiden name in Pagan circles to honor her grandparents. She's also a wife, mother, writer, teacher, and belly dancer. She lives in Portland, Maine, with her husband and their plethora of children. www.sybilwilen.com.

EMBER GRANT is a poet and freelance writer and has been contributing to the Llewellyn Annuals for ten years. Her first book from Llewellyn, *Magical Candle Crafting*, was published in March 2011.

MAGENTA GRIFFITH has been a Witch for more than thirty years and a High Priestess for more than twenty. She is a founding member of the coven Prodea, which has been celebrating rituals since 1980, as well as being a member of various Pagan organizations such as Covenant of the Goddess. She presents classes and workshops at a variety of events around the Midwest. She shares her home with a small black cat and a large collection of books.

JAMES KAMBOS is a regular contributor to Llewellyn's annuals. Born and raised in Appalachia, his magical traditions have been

influenced by the folk magic ways of Appalachia and by his Greek heritage. When not writing, he enjoys painting and cooking. He currently lives in the beautiful hill country of southeastern Ohio.

ALAN LUCIA joined the human race in January of 1959. Born in Rockville, Connecticut, this avid student of world religions and global mysteries studied Christian theology and eventually became ordained as a Christian minister. Later, he set these credentials aside and took on the role of Priest and overseer for a home-based nonprofit Interfaith Temple for eight years. While completing degrees in sociology, music, and education (M.Ed.) through New York State University (Regents College) and Old Dominion University, Virginia, Alan served his country as an active-duty member of the U.S. Armed Forces. After retiring, Alan taught high school science and conducted private music lessons while publishing his first two books: *Ufology: The New Religion*, and the fictional work, *Nomadic Wizards*. Alan and his wife live in the United States, and have raised their three children to adulthood.

LUPA is a (neo)shaman, author, artist, and professional mental health counselor living in Portland, Oregon. She earned her master's degree in counseling psychology, with an emphasis on ecopsychology, from Lewis and Clark College. She is the author of several books on neoshamanism and related topics, including *New Paths to Animal Totems* (Llewellyn, 2012). When she isn't attacking the computer keyboard or making ritual tools out of dead things, she hikes, camps, runs, and occasionally sits down long enough to read. She may be found online at www.thegreen-wolf.com, www.therioshamanism.com, and www.antlerrunes.com.

MARY PAT LYNCH explores the realms of dreams, astrology, the Tarot and shamanic journeying, and loves writing about her explorations. Life is a magical story, lived across many dimensions, and wonderful to share.

KRISTIN MADDEN is the author of several books, including *The Book of Shamanic Healing* and the 2009 COVR Visionary Award finalist, *Magick, Mystery, and Medicine*. Raised in a shamanic home, Kristin has had ongoing experience with both Eastern and Western mystic paths since 1972. In her other life, she works as a wildlife biologist and wildlife rehabilitator.

MELANIE MARQUIS is a full-time Witch and writer. She's the founder of United Witches global coven, and she also organizes a Pagan group in Denver. She's written for many New Age and Pagan publications. A nondenominational Witch, she specializes in practical spellwork, tarot, and spirit communication, teaching a personalized approach to the magickal arts. Her first book with Llewellyn, *The Witch's Bag of Tricks: Personalize your Magic & Kickstart Your Craft*, was released in July 2011. injoyart@yahoo.com.

LISA MCSHERRY is a priestess and author living outside of Seattle with her husband, dog, and cats. She runs a review site (www.FacingNorth.net), a coven, and more of her work is on her website, cybercoven.org. Contact her at: lisa@cybercoven.org.

MICKIE MUELLER is an award-winning and critically acclaimed Pagan spiritual artist. She is Co-High Priestess of Coven of the Greenwood, an ordained Pagan Minister. She is also a Reiki healing master/teacher in the Usui Shiki Royoho tradition. Mickie is the illustrator of *The Well Worn Path* and *The Hidden Path* and the illustrator/writer of *The Voice of the Trees: A Celtic Divination Oracle*. She is a regular article contributor to Llewellyn's publications, and her art is published internationally. www.mickiemuellerart.com.

SHARYNNE MACLEOD NICMHACHA is a Celtic shaman-priestess, writer, teacher, and bard of Scottish, Irish, and Welsh ancestry, and a direct descendant of "Fairy Clan" MacLeod. She trained in Celtic Studies through Harvard University and has taught Celtic myth and religion at the university level, at holistic centers and Pagan festivals.

She is an award-winning singer and musicians (The Moors, Devand-aurae) and a published author (*Queen of the Night, Celtic Myth and Religion*). Dun na Sidhe website: www.mobiusbandwidth.com/dns

SUSAN PESZNECKER is a mother, writer, nurse, hearth Pagan, and Druid living in northwest Oregon. In her spare time, Sue is an organic gardener and herbalist and she loves to read, take long walks with her wonder poodle, camp, play with rocks, and look up at the stars. Sue teaches green magick and astronomy in the online Grey School (www.greyschool.com) and is the author of three books: *Gargoyles* (New Page, 2007), *Crafting Magick with Pen and Ink* (Llewellyn, 2009), and *The Magickal Retreat: Making Time for Solitude, Intention, and Rejuvenation* (Llewellyn, 2012). Contact Sue via Facebook or through her web page (www.susanpesznecker.com).

MARION SIPE is a New Orleanian at heart and a traveler by nature. She has been a writer for eleven years and a practicing Witch for seventeen. A devotee of Hekate, she's served as a priestess, leading rituals with both private covens and public churches. She also teaches classes, writes about paganism for several publications, and publishes poetry and speculative fiction.

CHARLYNN WALLS is an active member of the St. Louis Pagan Community. Driven toward community service, she works on the St. Louis Pagan Picnic and St. Louis Witches Ball Committees. She is a member of two covens and she has written articles for *Witches and Pagans* magazine and is pursuing other writing opportunities.

TESS WHITEHURST is an advocate of self-love, self-expression, and personal freedom. She's a Llewellyn author, columnist for *newWitch* magazine, intuitive counselor, and feng shui practitioner. Her website and e-newsletter *Good Energy* include simple rituals, meditations, and musings for everyday magical living. Tess lives in Venice Beach, California, with two magical cats, one musical boyfriend, and a constant stream of visiting hummingbirds. www.tesswhitehurst.com.

Table of Contents

Earth Magic

Spring Garden Magic

by James Kambos

The precise date is always a little unpredictable, but suddenly on a warm sunny afternoon you know the change has begun. Winter has turned to spring! You can feel it, see it, hear it, and smell it. You begin by feeling that sense of quickening in yourself and in your garden. You can see it in the green daffodils thrusting their tips from the soil, reaching for the strengthening Sun. You can hear it; birdsong is more melodious now. And you can smell it, that unmistakable fragrance of spring. It's a combination of scents—the earthy scent of the soil shaking off the icy grip of winter, the scent of damp cool moss, and the faint woodsy smell of tree bark.

More than anything you can simply sense it. I call it the "promise." If you look around your spring garden closely, you can see the promise—it's the future that every garden holds. You can "see" June, July, August—and eventually the autumn harvest. You're surrounded by the promise of life and rebirth.

The spring garden is a magical place, and you can turn it into a sacred space. With the magical ideas I'd like to share with you, you'll be able to transform your spring garden into an outdoor altar. It can become a place where you can connect with the Earth and perform simple rituals and magic.

Let's begin by experiencing the magic of the soil.

Earth and Soil Magic

If you ever have a chance, watch a farmer approach a field for the first time in the spring. They show a deep reverence for the soil. First, they'll drag the heel of their boot across the soil, then silently they'll reach down and form a clump of soil with their hand—a sort of mini-Earth—and with a gesture resembling a ritual, they'll raise their hand skyward as they crumble the soil through their fingers. They touch the Earth not only with their hands, but also with their hearts.

If you want to develop a magical connection with your spring garden, you must also show a similar respect for the Earth and soil. When you do, you'll be richly rewarded spiritually and physically.

This begins by thanking Mother Earth for the gifts she bestows upon us. Here are some magical ways to do this. On a warm spring day, kneel directly on the ground. Crumble the soil in your hands and release its earthy scent. To purify your garden and to create a ritual space, sprinkle vinegar lightly over the soil. To welcome the Goddess into your garden, press three apple slices into the soil. This not only draws fertility and abundance, it also honors the three aspects of the Goddess—Maiden, Mother, and Crone.

To protect your garden or property from any negativity, try this spell. Place your cauldron or a terra cotta flowerpot in the garden. In it, combine a handful of garden soil, a generous dash of pepper, and a pinch of dried basil. Tap the cauldron three times and stir the ingredients with a rusty nail. Sprinkle this mixture around your garden's perimeter as you say: "Basil cleanse, pepper sting, this garden is sealed with a protective ring." Bury the nail on the edge of your garden.

Fertility and abundance were important magical goals for early farmers. To ensure a good harvest in the fall, fertility magic was usually performed in the spring. Here is a ritual based on these old magical practices. Cut some grasses, stems, or branches from spring-blooming plants, shrubs, or trees; honeysuckle, forsythia, grapevine, hawthorn, dogwood, or even lawn grass are just a few ideas. Tie your bundle with willow branches or jute twine. If you're artistic, you may shape your bundle into a human form. Hide your bundle in your garden or bury it. As the bundle decays, its magical powers of fertility will be released, renewing the vitality of both plant and soil. This belief dates back to the fertility rites involving nature deities such as Pan and the Green Man.

As you begin your spring garden chores, you should treat your gardening tools with the same respect you show your other magical tools. This way, as you plant and tend your garden, each task becomes a form of ritual. Begin by blessing each tool; you may do this by simply anointing each shovel, hoe, or trowel with a drop of olive oil. Rub each handle and visualize your magical intent.

The Earth and the soil are the foundation of the spring garden, but to perform its miracle of rebirth, the soil must be nourished by another sacred element—water.

Rain and Water Magic

The wonder of rebirth and rejuvenation in the spring garden wouldn't take place without water. The seed would never sprout and the bud would shrivel and die if not for the magic of rain. The soil may be the backbone of the spring garden, but rain is its blood. It cleanses a winter-weary world. It polishes every stone and nourishes the most humble blade of grass. Even the sound of a spring rain is magical. It doesn't pound the earth like it does during a summer thunderstorm, nor does it have an icy sting to it like autumn rains often do. Instead, it sings a soft magical song. It murmurs softly in the eaves and in the rocky streams. It patters gently on young foliage and perfumes the spring garden with subtle earthy scents.

By being aware of the importance of water's role in the spring garden, as a purifier and as a form of renewal, you'll be able to turn every watering task into a sacred rite.

You can begin by using your watering can as a magical tool. Like the cauldron, it holds water and can symbolize the womb or represent the Goddess. And, like the cauldron, it is also a vessel of renewal, from which flows the life-giving element, water. To make watering even more magical, try this. Bring peaceful vibrations to your garden by adding a bit of rose water to your watering can prior to watering. To attract fertility, love, or even encourage a marriage, add a few drops of orange flower water to garden water.

To ease tensions in your life, here is a spring garden ritual that may help. During a waning Moon, fill a birdbath with clean water. Drop a rock into the water and watch as the ripples subside. Exhale, and think of your tensions lessening as the water becomes still. As an offering to the water element, leave flowers or foliage from plants associated with protection floating on the water. Dogwood petals, tulips, or hyacinth are a few ideas.

Another form of water that contains magical properties is morning dew. Most occultists believe the dew of a spring morning to be the most magically potent. Lightly rub dew on the blade of a ceremonial knife to purify it, or anoint your forehead with it to increase psychic abilities.

For the ultimate in spring garden or water magic, catch rain in a jar or your cauldron. Use it as you water your plants during the growing season. Use it to cleanse magical tools. Add it to your bath water, or mix a drop with shampoo. To make rainwater holy, pray over it.

Above all, let the spring rain rejuvenate your own spirit. During a warm spring rain, stand in your garden and be a kid again—make mud pies or jump in a puddle.

Spring gently creeps into the garden. Delicate shades of green begin to appear, and soon we'll be able to work magic with the flowers of spring.

Spring Flower Magic

Suddenly, the spring garden begins to bloom. Purple and yellow crocuses, creamy-yellow daffodils, and pink crab apple blossoms are some of the flowers that delight the eye. The flowering plants found in the spring garden aren't only beautiful, they possess ancient magical powers that enchant the garden and home. Here are some spring-blooming plants and their magical associations.

Among the earliest flowers to bloom are crocuses. These small, cup-shaped flowers come in yellow, purple, and white; they're grown to attract love. Burn the petals and stamens with incense to draw money that is owed to you. Along with crocus, early daffodils begin to bloom. Use daffodils in love and fertility spells. Include them in fertility spells during Ostara.

By April, crab apple trees and hyacinths begin to blossom. Use their flower petals in love sachets and to petition Athena or Venus. To relieve depression and lift your spirits, place a few fragrant hyacinths in a vase.

Spring garden magic wouldn't be complete without planting the cheerful pansy. They come in an array of colors, tolerate cool temperatures, and draw love. Given in bouquets, they show affection.

If you can plant only one spring blooming shrub, let it be the lilac. Lilacs bloom in white, purple, pink, and now, yellow. They're known to repel all evil. White and purple varieties were cut for bouquets to cleanse negative spirits from the home. It's no coincidence that these charming shrubs were planted in many New England and Midwestern dooryards during the eighteenth and nineteenth centuries.

~

The spring garden should be a place to celebrate magic. Let it be a place to experience the joy of rebirth and the promise of tomorrow.

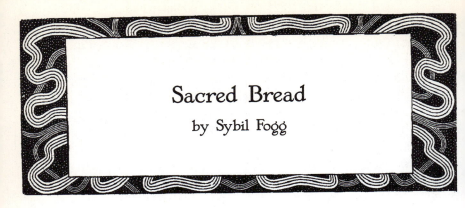

Sacred Bread
by Sybil Fogg

Making bread is an ancient way to get in touch with our magical cores. There are such things as magical bread-machine recipes, but this method of baking does not really add our beings as a sacred ingredient, so occasionally we must put away the machine and get down and dirty with the business of crafting bread.

Here are a few recipes that all contain a magical essence. Because these are hallowed recipes, remember to cast a circle and call on the quarters as well as the God and Goddess for blessings before beginning.

Easy Moon Goddess Bread

Sometimes, even the witchiest of us are pressed for time when there's a Full Moon on the rise. This bread is perfect for those occasions when we want to give thanks but cannot spend a day baking.

1½ cups warm water
2¼ teaspoons of active yeast
1 teaspoon sugar
3¼ cups all-purpose unbleached flour, plus a bit more for dusting
¾ tablespoon sea salt
Coarse salt, dried rosemary, thyme, oregano, and marjoram (topping)
Olive oil

Directions: Mix ¼ cup of the warm water with the yeast and sugar. Let stand for about ten minutes until yeast bubbles.

Add remaining warm water. Mix flour and salt in until well incorporated. This dough is pretty sticky, but don't be afraid to get your hands in it, as that is the best way to touch the spirit.

Place dough in lightly oiled bowl and cover with a damp dish towel. Let rise for two hours in a warm, draft-free area.

After the dough rises, place it on a bread board or table lightly dusted with flour. Divide dough into two small rounds. Work flour into your hands and more into the dough as you shape it into a round, moonlike shape. Place dough on a lightly oiled cookie sheet and sprinkle with coarse salt and dried herbs. Allow the dough to rest for about 40 minutes.

Preheat oven to 450 degrees F. For best results, fill a roasting pan halfway with water and slide onto the bottom rack.

Bake on upper rack for approximately 40 minutes or until golden brown. Bread should sound hollow when you tap it.

Leave a piece outside in honor of the Moon goddess.

Brigid's Inspiring Soda Bread

This bread is perfect for any Imbolc celebration or when our creativity needs a nudge. I find that I can mix the ingredients while thinking about what I want to do artistically and then get working while the bread is in the oven.

2 tablespoons ground flax
3 ounces water
¾ cup plain almond milk
1 tablespoon white vinegar
1½ cups whole wheat flour
½ teaspoon baking powder
1 tablespoon baking soda
1½ tablespoons margarine
¾ cup dried currants
1 tablespoon caraway seeds

Directions: Preheat oven to 375 degrees F and grease a loaf pan.

In a small bowl, stir together flax and water. Let stand for 10 minutes.

Combine the almond milk and vinegar, and let stand to curdle.

In a large bowl, sift together flour, baking powder, and baking soda. Work the margarine in with your hands while thinking of what artistic endeavors you would like to pursue or complete.

Whisk the flax and the almond milk mixtures together. Add to the flour mixture, stirring clockwise just until moist.

Stir in currants and caraway seeds and transfer to the prepared loaf pan.

Bake for one hour. Let cool in pan for a bit, and then invert onto a wire rack or cutting board.

Set a portion aside for Brigid's inspiration.

Radha-Krishna Love Bread

This bread calls upon the eternal love of the divine couple. Use in love spells or to celebrate love. It is perfect alongside a romantic meal complete with candles, incense, and soft music.

1 (15-ounce) can coconut milk, shaken well before opening
½ cup molasses
¼ cup margarine, cut into pieces
2¼ teaspoons active dry yeast
3 cups all-purpose flour
2 cups wheat flour
1 teaspoon salt
2 teaspoons ground cardamom
1½ teaspoons fennel seed
2 tablespoons finely grated citrus zest (I prefer a mixture
    of orange, lemon, and lime)

Directions: Combine coconut milk, molasses, and margarine in a saucepan over medium heat. Stir frequently until margarine is melted and liquids are well-combined. Set aside to cool to room temperature.

Sprinkle yeast onto the coconut milk mixture and set aside until yeast begins to bubble, about 10 minutes.

Sift flours, mix with salt, cardamom, fennel seed, and citrus zest.

Combine dry and wet ingredients and stir in a clockwise direction while meditating on your sacred lover.

Turn dough out onto a lightly floured surface and knead until the dough is smooth and elastic, about 10 to 15 minutes. Use this time to really feel the dough and become one with it as you are focusing your essence into the bread.

Grease a large bowl with oil. Form dough into a ball and place in the bowl, turning a few times to coat with oil. Cover with a towel and set in a warm, draft-free area until doubled in size, about 2½ hours.

Uncover bowl and focusing your love into your arm, punch down using your fist, releasing your desires into the dough. Turn dough onto a lightly floured surface and divide in half. One mound will be sacred to Radha and one to Krishna. Knead a few times and form one half into a female shape and the other into a male shape.

Place loaves on a baking sheet and cover with a damp towel. Let rise until loaves have doubled in size, approximately one hour.

Using a sharp knife, slash love symbols into each loaf (hearts, lotus shapes, a flute). Brush with melted margarine. Place loaves on the baking stone or place baking sheet in the oven.

Bake for 20 minutes at 375 degrees F. Lower heat to 350 degrees F and bake an additional 15 minutes or until loaves sound hollow when tapped.

Leave a portion of each loaf out for the eternal lovers.

Demeter's Wheat Bread

Although bread is a sacred part of the first harvest, this loaf is a perfect accompaniment to a Lammas feast because it honors the feminine principle.

2½ cups warm water
2 tablespoons active yeast
½ cup molasses, divided
3 cups whole-wheat flour
¼ cup vegetable oil
¼ cup almond milk
1 teaspoon salt
3 to 4 cups unbleached white flour, divided

Directions: Mix water, yeast, and 1 tablespoon of the molasses together in a large bowl. Let sit for about 10 minutes, until the yeast bubbles. Pour in the 3 cups wheat flour and mix well, stirring clockwise. Send wishes for abundance into the bowl. When finished, cover the bowl with a towel that has been purchased or crafted for sacred baking. Let the dough sit for 15 to 20 minutes.

Pull back the towel and give thanks. Pour in the rest of the molasses, oil, milk, and salt. Mix together. Begin adding white flour, ½ cup at a time while kneading the bread. I like to begin kneading in the bowl. I once had a beautiful wooden bowl that was shallow and a bit porous, so that it absorbed the essence of my baking. It was handcrafted by a close friend who disappeared

from my life not too long after presenting me with his art. Years later, the bowl passed from my hands to my eldest daughter's when she set off into the world. I would like to think she still uses it to bake bread.

Knead until the dough is smooth and elastic, about 15 to 20 minutes. This is where you will fully work your desires into the dough. Do you want a new house? A new job? Visualize your desire. Cut the dough into two equal parts.

Grease two bread pans, shape the bread pieces into loaves, and place them in prepared pans. Cover pans with a towel, set in a warm place, and let the dough double in size. This will take up to 1½ hours.

Bake loaves at 350 degrees F for about 35 to 40 minutes, until they sound hollow when you tap them.

Leave a bit for the grain goddess as thanks.

Osiris Beer Bread

This works well at either a Lammas or Mabon gathering. At this time, drink and eat to the God and be merry!

2 cups all-purpose flour
1 tablespoon baking powder
1 teaspoon salt
3 tablespoons sugar
1 12-ounce can or bottle of your favorite beer
Olive oil

Directions: Drizzle olive oil into a loaf pan and work it in with your fingers while giving thanks to Osiris for all that you are fortunate for.

Sift together flour, baking powder, and salt. Add sugar and beer. Pour into loaf pan and bake for 20 minutes at 350 degrees F.

Remove bread and brush top of loaf with olive oil. Return to oven and bake for an additional 15 minutes or until loaf is golden brown.

Set aside a piece to honor Osiris.

Hecate's Pumpkin Bread

As the year comes to a close, don't forget to honor the dark goddess. This bread works well as part of a Samhain feast or in the ritual of cakes and ale.

3½ cups all-purpose flour
2 teaspoons baking soda
1 teaspoon salt
1 teaspoon ground nutmeg
¼ teaspoon ground cloves
1½ teaspoons ground cinnamon
2 cups packed dark brown sugar
⅔ cup white sugar
2 cups pumpkin puree
1 cup canola oil
⅔ cup coconut milk

Directions: Preheat oven to 350 degrees F. Grease and flour two loaf pans.

In a small bowl, sift together the flour, baking soda, salt, nutmeg, cloves, and cinnamon.

In a large bowl, whisk together the brown sugar, white sugar, pumpkin puree, oil, and coconut milk. Slowly add the flour mixture, slowly stirring counterclockwise. Imagine your troubles being banished as the lumps disappear. Meditate on Hecate and the forks in the road we all encounter.

Divide the batter evenly between the prepared pans. Bake in the preheated oven for 75 minutes or until a toothpick inserted in the center comes out clean.

Leave out a portion for Hecate.

∼

Remember to always bless your working space and thank any spirits that might have joined in the process. Blessed be.

Writing and Casting Spells for the Best Results

by Deborah Blake

There are a lot of great spellbooks out there for the modern Witch to use—spellbooks dedicated to specific goals like love or prosperity or more general ones like my *Everyday Witch A to Z Spellbook* (Llewellyn, 2010) that cover almost every situation for which a spell might come in handy. But I advise the Witches I know to occasionally write their own spells, no matter how handy it is to use ones written by others.

There are a couple of reasons for this. For one thing, words are power, so words that come from your own heart and spirit will have the most power for you. Under many circumstances, a spell written by someone else will do just fine, but if the need is great, consider writing one of your own. Additionally, there are sometimes specific circumstances that just don't fall into the usual categories, and it can be hard to find a prewritten spell that is "just right." More than this, for many of us, spellcasting is an integral part of being a Witch. By writing your own spells, you are practicing the art of the Craft.

But many people find the thought of writing their own spells a little intimidating. Some folks don't think they use words well enough. Others are worried that they might get it wrong, and create a spell that either doesn't work or causes unintentional problems. Both of these are understandable concerns, but don't let them stand in your way. Everyone can write spells that are both safe and effective, and here's how.

Spell-Writing Basics

Don't worry if you are not the world's greatest writer. Spells don't have to be long and complicated in order to work, and the gods don't care if you can spell correctly! The most common complaint I get is from people who can't get their spells to rhyme. But that's okay—they don't have to.

Rhyming is nice for some spells. Traditionally, rhyming is used to give the spells a little more power through the rhythms of the words and to make them easier to memorize. But it certainly isn't necessary. I'll give you an example of a prosperity spell done both ways, just to make it clear.

Prosperity Spell 1 – Rhyming
God and goddess hear my plea
Rain prosperity down on me
Bring in monies large and small
To pay my bills one and all

Money earned and gifts for free
As I will, so mote it be

(Originally published in *Circle, Coven & Grove: A Year of Magickal Practice.* Llewellyn, 2007.)

Prosperity Spell 2 – Not Rhyming
Money I need and money I want
So let it come to me
In positive ways, at perfect times
As I need it, as I want it
As I will it so it is

As you can see, both spells ask for the same thing—they just do it in a slightly different way. The second spell is simpler; it doesn't rhyme, it is shorter, and it doesn't get as specific—but there's no reason it couldn't work. You could write a spell like that even if writing isn't your thing.

So the first thing to know about writing spells is that it is fine to do so in whatever style or manner you are comfortable with.

Clarifying Your Goals

Before you ever sit down to write your spell, you want to make sure you have a clear idea of the goal you are working toward. Your spell will be more effective if you are specific—although you don't want to be *so* specific that you don't leave the universe some wiggle room to grant your desires in ways you might not have thought of.

In the first prosperity spell above, you will notice that I use the phrase "Money earned and gifts for free." That was to allow for the possibility that something might come to me in a fashion I didn't expect—and it has happened that way pretty often. For instance, I might do a prosperity spell before taking the jewelry I make to a craft show in hopes of good sales. But instead, I might get connections to people who want to sell my work in their store, thereby making more money in the long run. It is better if I don't specify something like "lots of sales at the show," when I might end up with even better results if I leave the prosperity spell open-ended.

If you know exactly what you need, such as money to pay for a new car, you can ask for that thing specifically. But keep in mind that if you are a little less specific, the gods might send you someone with a car they need to get rid of cheaply, so try to leave them a little space to gift you with an unexpected but positive solution.

If you don't know exactly what you need, it is a good idea to sit down before writing the spell and make a list of what it is you want—and what you don't. Remember that *intent* is a major component of magick, and make sure you have your intent clear in your head before you write or perform any spell. This can save you a lot of trouble later, or keep you from wasting your time and energy on a spell that simply won't work.

Casting the Spell

Focus, Will, and Intent

We've already talked about writing your spell with your intent firmly in mind. Two other major components of spellwork are focus and will. Your will is your own personal power and desire, and focus is how you direct that will into your magickal work. How well you apply both of these elements to casting your spell can make the difference between a spell that is successful and one that is not.

Will can be built up in a number of ways, including meditating on your goal and its importance to you, drumming, chanting, dancing, etc. It is crucial that you *believe* in your own power as strongly as possible and put any lingering self-doubt (which we all have) out of your mind if you can. It is also important to believe that you are deserving of receiving the magickal bounty you are asking for. If you need to, you can start your work by saying out loud, "I am strong and worthy," or any other assertive statement that feels right to you.

Focus is as necessary as will to the process of spellcasting. An unfocused spell rarely works because the energy simply isn't sent out into the universe strongly enough to be heard or acted on.

Tools as an Aid to Focus

One of the simplest ways to create more or stronger focus when casting a spell is to add in some tools that will help you with your task. Witches use many different items to aid them in building focus during ritual, including candles, crystals, incense, herbs, wands, athames, and the like. Each of these tools has a different purpose or purposes, and if you use them correctly, they can heighten and strengthen your spell.

Of course, the trick is to know which tool to use. Sometimes that will depend on the spell itself. For instance, if you write a spell that calls on the four elements, you will probably want tools to represent them. Here is an example from my *Everyday Witch A to Z Spellbook* (Llewellyn, 2010):

Spell for Ambiance

Supplies: Small candles in red, yellow, blue, green and/or a candle (any color), a feather, a rock/salt, a bowl of water

Notes: As you call on fire, light the red candle or whatever candle you are using. As you call on air, light the yellow candle and/or waft the feather gently through the air. As you call on earth, light the green candle and/or hold up the rock or sprinkle the salt. As you call on water, light the blue candle and/or sprinkle some water. When you call on spirit, you can lift your hands to the sky or place them over your heart.

> *I call on fire to set the mood*
> *The perfect style and attitude*
> *To serve my purpose and meet my goal*
> *And cast me in the perfect role*
> *I call on air to set the pace*
> *All obstacles shall it erase*
> *Wafting in the perfect breeze*
> *So I might play my role with ease*
> *I call on earth to set the scene*
> *And ground me so I stay serene*
> *No matter what might come my way*
> *Supporting me through night and day*
> *I call on water to set me free*
> *To be the best most perfect me*
> *Smoothly flowing through the hour*
> *All aspects of my self empower*
> *I call on spirit for success*
> *For confidence and lack of stress*
> *On this occasion let me shine*
> *And touch me with a gift divine*

You can see that in the case of this particular spell, it will deepen your focus if you have tools that help you to call on the powers of the elements. If you write a spell for health, you may want to use some items that are sometimes associated with this quality, including a blue candle, a gemstone with healing properties like lapis or bloodstone, and/or an herb or incense associated with healing (lemon balm, eucalyptus, or rosemary, for example).

It can be useful when writing a spell to have some knowledge of these associations, called "correspondences," and there are many wonderful books that will tell you what they are. But keep in mind that your instincts and intuition are the best sources you have; if it feels right to use a green candle when all the books say to use yellow, you should probably go with your gut.

Timing Your Spell

Many spells have an optimum time for you to cast them. For instance, spells for increase (more of something) should generally be done under a waxing Moon, so that your spell grows stronger as the Moon gets larger. Or else under the light of the Full Moon, which is very powerful. Spells for decrease (letting go of something, banishing, etc.) are usually done during a waning Moon.

Additionally, some days of the week are associated with particular aspects of magick, so you might wish to perform a spell for prosperity on a Thursday, and a spell for love on a Friday. Is this strictly necessary? Of course not. If you have trouble focusing, or the occasion is important, or if you worry that your spell isn't strong enough, you may want to use more tools to help you focus, and purposely cast the spell on a day and time that might give your magickal work an extra boost. But sometimes the timing just doesn't work out that way, and this alone doesn't mean your spell won't turn out as intended.

Things that Weaken or Ruin Spellcasting

If you follow all the instructions above, you should be able to write and cast a powerful spell that will work for you in positive ways. But there are some circumstances that can weaken or even destroy the spell you have worked so hard to cast, so you want to be aware of and avoid the following:

Drug or alcohol use: You should never cast a spell with anything other than a clear head. For one thing, it is insulting to the gods to come into sacred space under the influence of mind-altering substances. For another, it interferes with focus. (Yes, there are some folks who believe in the use of drugs to deepen spiritual practice; they are entitled to their opinions, and I would never argue with them, but it has been

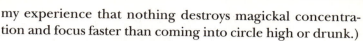

my experience that nothing destroys magickal concentration and focus faster than coming into circle high or drunk.)

Extreme emotional states: As I said above, you need to have a clear head in order to do your best spellcasting. Coming in to your sacred space filled with anger or fear or any other very strong emotion will not only stand in the way of clarity and focus, but you may cast a spell you later wished you hadn't. This doesn't mean that you can't do spellwork when things are bad—sometimes this is when we need magick the most. But try to achieve as calm a state as possible before starting the work. Do some meditation, take a long bath or walk, repeat some calming affirmations. At the very least, take slow, deep breaths and concentrate on the light and love of the gods until your head is in a better place.

Mixed feelings about the spellwork: If you're not sure whether the spell you are casting is the right thing to do or not, that doubt may undermine the will you need to feed the spell. Never cast a spell unless you are certain of your path in that instance. This is also true of the times when you are uncertain of your goal. That confusion will sap your spell of strength, so it is better to wait until you have a solid goal in mind, and the will to back it up.

Negative intent: This is not to say that you can't cast a spell that would have a negative impact on someone else; for better or for worse, free will allows for this. However, you should bear in mind that not only do the powers of the universe often not allow these types of spells to work, it is not unusual for them to rebound on the one what casts them—either immediately, or sometime down the line.

Lack of focus: This is the main reason for not coming into circle under the influence of drugs, alcohol, or heavy emotions; they will simply make it too difficult to maintain the focus needed to create a powerful spell and send it out into the world. But other things can get in the way of focus, too. If you can't find a quiet, private place to cast your spell (the kids are running around screaming, the dog is barking, the neighbors are arguing at the top of their lungs) you are better off waiting for a different time. It is almost impossible to get good results when you cast a spell in the midst of chaos.

The Spell Is Cast

Don't let any of these cautions discourage you, though. Writing and casting your own spells can be a fun and empowering part of a well-balanced witchcraft practice. If you follow the few simple suggestions laid out above, and sidestep the (easily avoidable) pitfalls that can stand in the way of successful spellcasting, all Witches can create spells to enhance and entrance their lives.

Valerian
(Valeriana officinalis)

VALERIAN ROOT

Valerian aeth.

Herbal Constituents

by Susan Pesznecker

If you're doing serious work or study in the field of herbalism—especially medicinal herbalism—it's only a matter or time before you encounter the idea of herbal constituents.

A "constituent" is part of a whole. In herbalist terms, a constituent is the component of the plant that contributes to its unique properties and characteristics.

We typically speak of constituents in terms of medicinal herbalism; however, the magickal, culinary, or spa herbalist should also be aware of these effects, as they may interact with what one is trying to accomplish in the *sanctum*, spa, or kitchen. Even more importantly, understanding the nature of an herb's constituents shows respect for the plant material and helps one avoid the "fluff versus science" conundrum. In other words, a practitioner should thoroughly understand her materials and what she's working with, rather than simply following a recipe from a book.

When using different types of herbal preparations, such as infusions, decoctions, or tinctures, the goal is to extract the plant's constituents efficiently while retaining the greatest percentage of active constituents possible. Each herbal technique is therefore matched to the type of material and the desired result. For example:

Infusions are used to extract constituents from soft or fragile materials, such as leaves, flowers, and light stems—collectively known as aerial parts. If these delicate materials are treated too aggressively, most of the constituents will be lost. Thus, infusions of water or oil are used to gently coax the constituents from the herbs.

Decoctions are used to extract constituents from hard or woody material, such as roots, heavy stems, seeds, and bark, with the herbal parts being simmered or even gently boiled in water for twenty to thirty minutes or longer. Straining a decoction while it's still warm is important in order to capture the beneficial constiutents in the precipitate (like the excess salt that cannot be dissolved into the saltwater solution), which typically settles as the mixture cools. Once it settles, the precipitate often could be lost in the sediment. Straining while warm will result in a potion that-may be a little cloudy, but it will be much more effective.

Dried herbs have had their water removed, so their constituents tend to be more concentrated than those of fresh herbs. When using fresh herbs, we compensate by chopping or crushing them to release their constituents, and also by doubling the quantity.

When working seriously with herbal materials and constituents, accuracy is critical, and it's also very important to use a plant's scientific name. This creates clarity and ensures that both practitioner and source material are referring to the same plant. For instance, there are at least half a dozen "bluebell" species in the continental United States. Instead of just calling a plant a bluebell, referring to it as *Hyacinthoides non-scripta* makes it clear you're talking about the common bluebell rather than the Scottish bluebell or the English bluebell. Obviously, this could make a tremendous difference in the end product.

There are hundreds of known constituents. Some—like minerals and volatile oils—are common and more or less harmless, while others—like coumarins and alkaloids—are less well understood and can be dangerous or even lethal, especially if used incorrectly. This is yet another reason to always use the scientific name when referring to any plant.

Let's look at some of the more common constituents:

Alkaloids: Organic compounds that contain nitrogen molecules, these bond easily with other compounds, and this makes alkaloids especially active and potent. The classic alkaloid reduces spasm, relieves pain, and dries up secretions. Alkaloids, however, may be extremely dangerous and should be used only by expert herbalists. One of the most common and powerful alkaloids, atropine, is found in the deadly nightshade plant (*Atropa belladonna*). Another strong alkaloid, vincristine, comes from a rare periwinkle and is used to treat leukemia.

Bitters: When taken by mouth, these substances taste bitter, stimulate salivation and digestive secretion, and whet the appetite. Orange peel, wormwood (*Artemesia absinthum*), and hops (*Humulus lupulus*) contain high levels of bitters.

Cardiac glycosides: These substances stimulate the heart and improve its contraction; they also improve urinary output, removing the edema associated with heart failure. Cardiac glycosides are extremely dangerous—even lethal—if used incorrectly. The best-known herb containing these constituents is foxglove (*Digitalis purpurea*).

Coumarin: A substance that tends to thin the blood, i.e., acting as an anticoagulant (anti-clotting agents). Coumarins tend to have a sweet, vanilla, or "fresh-mown hay" smell. Plants that contain coumarins include sweet grass (*Hierochloe odorata*), mullein (*Verbascum species*), and woodruff (also called sweet woodruff, *Galium odoratum*).

Flavonoids: Rich in antioxidant chemicals, flavonoids help repair cell and tissue damage and slow down the effects of aging. They are strongly flavored and often associated with yellow and white fruits or flowers: lemon (*Citrus limon*) is a good example. One type of flavonoid—the isoflavone—is found in red clover (*Trifolium pratense*) and has estrogen-like effects.

Minerals: Organic substances—calcium, sodium, iron, potassium, etc.—that help the body carry out various cellular activities. For example, potassium is essential to a healthy heartbeat and normal blood pressure, while calcium is needed for strong bones and teeth. Mineral-containing herbs often have a gritty texture, as in dandelion greens (*Taraxicum officinale*) and the common horsetail (*Equisetum arvense*).

Mucilage: A polysaccharide substance extracted as a viscous or gelatinous solution from plant roots, seeds, etc., and used in medicines and adhesives. Mucilages soothe and heal the digestive tract. Slippery elm (*Ulmus rubra*) and flaxseed (*Linum usitatissimum*) are often used for their mucilaginous properties.

Phenols: A group of strong compounds that tend to reduce inflammation and protect against infection. These herbs tend to have a strong or sharp smell. Examples include the mint and thyme families (various species), wintergreen (*Galutheria procumbens*), and willow (*Salix alba*, and its cousin compound, acetylsalicylic acid, aka aspirin).

Proanthocyanins: Closely related to flavonoids, these compounds also work as strong antioxidants and tend to impart deep color to fruits and vegetables: red peppers, beets, eggplant, purple grapes, blackberries, and yams have abundant anthocyanins, as does dark chocolate. Hawthorn berries (*Crataegus oxycantha*) also are rich in anthocyanins. These compounds strengthen the heart, protect circulation, and benefit the eyes.

Saponins: Toxic compounds that make soaplike foam when shaken with water. Saponins are chemically similar to many of the body's hormones; they tend to be very active and often exhibit hormonal activity. They thus have a stimulant nature and support recovery from illness. Wild yam (*Dioscorea villosa*) and licorice (*Glycyrrhiza glabra*) are known for their saponin levels.

Tannins: Harsh astringents that tend to tighten and contract tissues, stop bleeding, and/or dry up excessive watery secretions. Think of substances that make you pucker, like dry red wine or strong black tea. Oak bark and acorns (*Quercus rubra*) are high in tannins, as are purple grape skins and black teas (*Camillia sinensis*).

Vitamins: These substances support cellular activities, tissue and skin health, metabolic processes, and all sorts of healing and reparative processes in the body. Many herbs contain significant

levels of one or more vitamins: for example, consider rose hips (*Rosa sp.*) and watercress (*Nasturtium officinale*), potent sources of vitamins C and B1, respectively.

Volatile oils: Essential oils that provide a strong scent and diffuse or evaporate quickly. These are some of the most widely used herbal constituents. Tea tree oil (*Melaleuca alternifolia*) is an excellent example of a volatile oil with antiseptic and fungicidal qualities.

When working with constituents, you'll probably come across many unfamiliar terms. Be sure to look each of these up. For example, look back at the definition of mucilage, which includes the words *polysaccharide, viscous*, and *gelatinous*. To understand what a mucilage is, you also need to understand what these words mean:

- Polysaccharide: a complex sugar (carbohydrate)
- Viscous substance: a thick, sticky liquid
- Gelatinous: acts like a gelatin, i.e., a liquid that becomes semi-solid or jelly-like under certain circumstances.

Exploring each of these terms helps visualize how a mucilaginous herb treats diarrhea: the sugars provide easily absorbable nourishment, while the viscous, gelatinous mucilage helps solidify the liquid stool. Understanding a plant's constituent nature thus helps you understand what the herb will do, which is important in deciding how to use it.

When working with herbs, always work with reputable sources, meaning sources created by trained herbalists. This is *not* the time to use Wikipedia, where herbal entries are likely created by lay writers with no herbal experience. Find yourself one or two good herbal reference guides and rely on those. I've listed three excellent resources below.

Practice safely—and practice smart!

For Further Study

Bremness, Lesley. *Herbs. The Visual Guide to More Than 700 Herb Species from Around the World*. London: Dorling Kindersley/Eyewitness Books, 1994.

Chevallier, Andrew. *Encyclopedia of Herbal Medicine. The Definitive Reference to 550 Herbs and Remedies for Common Ailments*. London: Dorling Kindersley/Eyewitness Books, 2000.

Ody, Penelope. *The Complete Medicinal Herbal*. London: Dorling Kindersley/Eyewitness Books, 1993.

Apartment Gardens with a Magickal Twist

by Blake Octavian Blair

Most magickal people feel an innate connection with the natural world. Tending a garden is one of the most popular ways to nurture that connection. Having your own magickal garden provides an outlet through your kinship with the natural world for you to grow plants, herbs, and flowers for protection, spellwork, cooking, and many other purposes. However, Pagan apartment dwellers (such as myself) often feel discouraged by lack of space, limited natural light, and other logistical obstacles. Fear not, my fellow tenants! Although it can require extra planning, careful plant selection, creative space management, and a bit of trial and error, you can have your own wonderfully satisfying magickal apartment garden.

One of the first considerations you will need to address is location. Where in your apartment would you like to place your garden? Are you in a basement with very little light? Is your unit on the ground floor with a private patio? Are you on the fourth floor of a multistory building with only a tiny terrace or perhaps no outdoor space at all? These are all very viable scenarios for an apartment garden. Small or narrow terraces and windowsills provide a great opportunity for a window box planter, perhaps full of magickal and culinary herbs or a row of protective cacti! A patio can allow for space to include sculptures and to sit among your plants and meditate amid nature. A bathroom with a window provides a dash of occasional humidity that is perfect for a potted fern or two. The fairies will love you!

Once you have prospective locations in mind for your garden, it is time to consider their exposure. Almost any possible exposure scenario is capable of supporting some type of apartment garden with a little bit of creative design and plant selection. Most apartments only have exposure in two directions—the front and rear of the unit. If you live in an end unit, you may be lucky enough to have three directions of exposure. Furthermore, only one of those directions might be viable garden space. A southern or western exposure will give you the most direct sunlight. If you have a balcony, terrace, or patio of any size, consider yourself lucky to have the bonus outdoor real estate to work with. This may allow you to grow some produce. I have found fruits and vegetables stand the best chance of thriving in outdoor spaces because they generally require high levels of sunlight. Consider giving tomato plants a shot. With favorable growing conditions, they are fairly easy for the beginning gardener, as several varieties grow well in pots and can flourish in partial to direct sunlight. My husband and I went to our local farmers' market to purchase our tomato plants. Not only did we get a great deal, the grower helped us pick the variety best suited to our exposure conditions. We have also found that plastic five-gallon buckets work great for tomato plant pots! It can be a very spiritually satisfying experience to serve a salad with tomatoes you lovingly grew yourself!

If you think you would enjoy having a few colorful flowers around, a great magickally functional choice to add a splash of color are marigolds (*Calendula officinalis*). Not only are they cheery in appearance and bring blessings for a healthy home, but it is also said that putting a pot near your home's entryway helps keep unwanted visitors away. That is one handy flower!

Plants that thrive and grow best in direct sunlight are bountiful and quite easy to find. So rather than detailing those varieties, I'd like to spend some time on a few plants that will grow in partial- to low-light conditions, as this is

fairly common in apartment living. I myself have lived in several apartments that had only northern and southern exposures, with the only feasible growing area being the north. A southern exposure can be too strong for some herbs and more delicate plants. If your porch has a low light exposure, or you live in a basement with tiny windows, here are a few tips for successful plant selection. You will want to stick with foliage plants whose leaves are thick and have a leathery or waxy texture. Additionally, the darker green the foliage, the better. These are the signature signs of plants that will tolerate low-light conditions.

There are a few commonly available houseplants that are old standbys that will survive in conditions varying from a dim basement to a sunny patio. One of them is the pothos (*Epipremnum aurem*), a hardy vining plant that will tolerate both low-light conditions and infrequent watering schedules. A well-cared-for pothos grows rapidly and fills a space with its vibrant energy of growth in no time flat. Another great functional reason to grow pothos is that it filters toxins from the air! In a basement apartment, pothos can add a striking green splash of life when planted in a window box and set on a basement windowsill. In a very short time, its vines will begin to spill over the edges and begin to trail enchantingly through the space. Mother-in-law's tongue (*Sansevieria trifasciata*) is another good low-light choice. Its long pointed tongue-like leaves give it a very protective feel, even if the allusion of the plant's common name isn't very kind to your extended family! Mother-in-law's tongue is virtually indestructible and has survived even the neglect that comes from being under the care of a college dorm resident. Aloe vera (*Aloe barbadensis*) is another pointy plant with protective energy. Also dubbed the "medicine plant," it has wonderful healing properties in both the physical and metaphysical realms. Aloe is a perfect plant for both the kitchen and entryways. I have two large pots of aloe on my apartment's front porch guarding the entry. Should you burn yourself in the kitchen, simply break off one of the stalks and rub the gel on the afflicted area—first aid courtesy of Mother Nature! Also, any of the plant selections I just mentioned will survive just fine indoors or out in low to moderate light. However, if you keep your green beauties outside, depending on your climate, you may have to overwinter them indoors.

Apartment dwellers are rarely able to plant things into the ground itself and will need to utilize methods of container gardening. Don't worry, the many creative and enchanting options for containers are limited only by your imagination! However, there are some practical considerations. Most importantly, you need to consider both the material and drainage of the container and its appropriateness to the plant you will choose. Terra cotta, ceramic, and plastic pots are the three most popular commercially available containers. Terra cotta pots are earthy with wonderful natural appeal and are available in a wide variety of shapes, sizes, and styles. They are also lend themselves to easy decoration for spellwork (more on that later). However, terra cotta will absorb moisture, which means you will have to keep a closer eye on moisture levels and watering frequency. Glazed ceramic is a nice, natural material that will not soak in moisture. Plastic is also very popular and although less natural, it provides a durable lighter-weight pot than terra cotta or ceramic, and it also will not absorb moisture from the soil. However, a fun and affordable way to obtain containers is to create your own through finding and repurposing unused containers from thrift stores, yard sales, and around the house. Repurposing and reusing existing objects is also a more eco-friendly route. Teacups, teapots, casserole dishes, baskets, and even old shoes can make creative plant containers! Be sure to do a little research on how to prepare your found container to withstand soil and moisture and to provide appropriate drainage.

When being creative with the space available to you, do not forget to work in all directions—this means utilizing vertical space as well as horizontal space. Vertical gardens have become increasingly more popular in recent years, especially among urban dwellers. This can be achieved in many ways, including hanging planters on the wall in similar style to a sconce. A more portable option for apartment dwellers is to measure the space you have and draw up a simple plan to build a set of leaning shelves that resembles a stepladder. This will effectively increase the amount of space you have to arrange your pots.

As mentioned earlier, a magickal apartment garden is often multipurpose. Growing culinary herbs is an attractive prospect to most Pagans, and the connection of lending your own energy to the growing process of the spell ingredients you use gives an extra energetic zest to your magick! Remember that most herbs will need a fairly sunny growing space. The magickal uses for your harvested herbs are endless. You can hang a sprig of dried rosemary (*Rosemarinus officinalis*) in your home for healing or protection. Perhaps add a bit of thyme (*Thymus vulgaris*) to promote restful slumber in a dream pillow. Various members of the mint (*Mentha*) family also grow fairly well in an indoor herb garden. Imagine whipping up a dessert enhanced with prosperous vibes from homegrown mint!

Also, the simple presence of a plant can lend its energetic properties to the environment. One example is putting protective plants by your entryways. Many magickal folk place small potted cacti in their windowsills because the spiny plant's spirits provide protection. Creeping vines on a small trellis provide a feeling of privacy and security. Being in the presence of lavender can bring a sense of energetic calmness. There is even a bit of old lore involving red geraniums hanging on a home's front porch being a sign of the resident's witchy status. The possibilities are endless!

Before moving on, I would like to include a quick mention in regard to pets, small children, and apartment gardens. If you are a parent or pet owner, please research the toxicity of your potential plant choices to see if they pose a threat to your human or animal children. Your garden should bring you joy and satisfaction, so the last thing we want is for your child or Fido to take a bite of a poisonous herb like foxglove and cause a medical emergency.

The act of growing and caring for a plant can be a form of spellcasting in itself. Growing a plant consecrated for a specific purpose with intent can be a powerful form of manifestation. For example, you could obtain a small potted jade plant (*Crassula argentea*), which is known for

prosperous energy. Create sacred ritual space and plant the jade in a nice earthy terra cotta pot for the wealth aspect of the element of earth. Furthermore, you could then use green or gold paint to inscribe a sigil or rune for prosperity such as Fehu (ᚠ). You can also set a prosperity crystal such as citrine or jade on the soil inside the pot. Top it off with a simple incantation such as "May my prosperity grow abundant and strong, just as this plant of jade its whole life long. For the highest good of all, so mote it be." Now your apartment garden also has a plant that is working active magick! Of course, you will want to make double sure to take good care of the plant, because letting it wither and die of neglect would be very counterproductive to your goals, to say the least.

As in the spell just mentioned, decorating your plants' pots with magickal symbolism is a great way to lend a mystical touch to your apartment-gardening efforts. If you are lucky to be skilled at pottery, you can make beautiful custom pots for your garden. Terra cotta pots are paintable, and for the less artistically inclined, there are many wonderful stencils available at craft stores. I picked up a stencil set a few years back with a celestial theme that was wonderfully witchy. Acrylic paints are affordable, come in many colors, are readily available, and easily adhere to the terra cotta. I've also seen industriously artistic people mosaic their terra cotta pots with tiles and seashells!

Even the most inconspicuous potted plant can be a vehicle for a spell. You can create a Witch bottle protection charm by placing nails, shards of glass, protective herbs, crystals, and other curios into an empty glass jar and sealing it shut using either duct tape or wax. You can then bury the bottle in a deep pot and plant your flowers or plant on top of it. Place it by an exterior door and let it quietly work its undercover magick!

A touch that I always like to include in among my plants is bits of spiritual statuary. It seems clear to me that the plethora of gnomes, fairies, Green Men, and deity garden statuary are eagerly awaiting a home filled with magick. Also, just because a statue was designed for outdoor gardens does not mean it cannot be used indoors. Because a large portion of your garden will likely be indoors and not exposed to the weather, you can work with any other statuary you may already have as well. In my own apartment, I have a series of potted houseplants on stands of various heights in front of part of my glass patio door. They are positioned around a Buddha statue that meditates peacefully while holding a large amethyst crystal. I truly feel the Buddha enjoys being among the plants and the plants also visibly thrive near the Buddha! Behind the arrangement on the glass door itself are a few stained glass sun catchers—a Green Man, an Om, and the form of a man meditating showing the seven chakras. Through the door you can see the tomato plants, our star and moon wind chime, as well as the trees from our second floor patio. It has wonderful feel of melding the indoors with the outside world. Being an apartment dweller does not mean you have to forgo a connection with nature.

Whether you live in a dark basement apartment, in the middle of a high-rise, or in a suburban townhouse, it is still possible to have your own garden. I sincerely hope you have been inspired to use both your creativity and your resources to work your own bit of natural magick within your living space!

For Further Study

Bradley, Valerie. *The Complete Guide to Houseplants: The Easy Way to Choose and Grow Happy, Healthy Houseplants*. Pleasantville, NY: Readers Digest, 2006.

Beckett, Kenneth. *The Contained Garden*. New York: Penguin, 1993.

Cunningham, Scott. *Cunningham's Encyclopedia of Magical Herbs*. St. Paul, MN: Llewellyn Publications, 1985.

Donaldson, Stephanie, and Peter McHoy. *Small & Container Gardening*. London: Hermes House, 2001.

Dugan, Ellen. *Garden Witch's Herbal: Green Magick, Herbalism & Spirituality*. Woodbury, MN: Llewellyn Publications, 2009.

Jerome, Kate. *Ortho's All About Houseplants*. Des Moines, IA: Meredith Books, 1999.

Foxglove: A Most Magical Plant
by Ellen Dugan

Some folks are wise and some are otherwise.
–Tobias G. Smollett

Of approximately twenty species of herbaceous perennials that are known by the common name of foxglove, *Digitalis purpurea* is the best-known variety. This plant is steeped in folklore, especially in connection with witches and the faeries. It is aligned with the planet Venus and the element of water. Its blossoms can be incorporated into spells for protection and for faery magic.

The common foxglove is technically a biennial—a plant that grows vegetatively the first year and then is fruiting/blooming or dormant the second year. The average life of the foxglove plant is two seasons. However, occasionally the roots survive the winter and the plant survives and produces flowers for several seasons. *Digitalis* thrives in well-drained loose soils in partial sunlight to deep shade.

The common foxglove is grown as an ornamental plant and is popular with gardeners both magical and mundane, for its faery tale qualities and its vivid flowers. The bell-shaped blossoms of the common foxglove range in color from shades of purple, pink, and white with purple mottling—or even occasionally a pure white. The flowers are described as: bell-shaped and tubular, 1½ to 2½ inches long, flattened above, and inflated beneath. The lower lip is furnished with long hairs inside and marked with numerous dark spots, each surrounded with a white border. The shade of the flowers varies much, especially under cultivation, and sometimes the corollas will turn out to be perfectly white.

As a biennial plant, during the first growing year there is a rosette of leaves with no stem. In the second year, one or more flowering stems spear up, and these will bear long spikes of drooping flowers that bloom in early summer—typically by late May or early June (and into July in colder climates, as the bloom time of foxgloves vary greatly by region.) Foxgloves bloom from the bottom of the flower stalk up to the top. These flowering stalks can be top-heavy, so for best results in your garden, plan on staking and tying the flowering stems to keep them looking their best.

Foxglove is native to Europe, Asia, and Africa, but it grows throughout Europe and North America and as a wildflower in temperate climates all over the world. Foxglove can and will reseed itself in woods and hedgerows and shady gardens. Its scientific name *Digitalis* means "fingerlike," a nod to the way the blossoms of *Digitalis purpurea* slip over the fingers.

The common name of foxglove is an ancient one that has many ties to the faeries. The faeries were often refered to as the Good Folk, and foxglove may be a corruption of the old name for this flower, which was "folk's gloves."

The foxglove derives its common name from the shape of the flowers that resemble the fingers of a glove. The flower was literally the glove of the "Good Folk" or fairies, whose favorite places

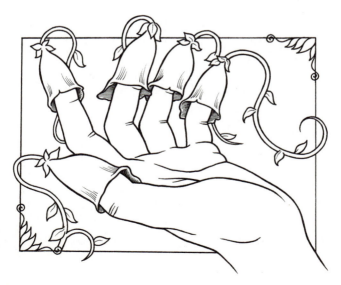

were thought to be in the deep hollows and woodlands, where the foxglove happily grows. "Folk's glove" is one of its oldest of this plant's common names, and is mentioned in a list of plants from the time of Edward III.

This may explain why Welsh folklore speaks of foxglove bells being the preferred hiding place for the fairies. In Scotland, this beautiful flower has the gothic names of "bloody fingers" and "deadman's bells."

In Wales, foxglove was called "fairy-folks-fingers" or "lambs-tongue-leaves," and "goblin's gloves." This bewitching blossom was thought to attract the hobgoblins who wore the long bells on their fingers. Those foxglove gloves imparted magical powers to the goblins.

What I find intriguing is that the earliest known form of the word is the Anglo-Saxon *foxes glofa* (meaning "the glove of the fox). Interestingly, in Norway the flowering plant was called *Rev-*

bielde, meaning "Fox-bell." It is rumored that the fairies gave these beautiful mottled blossoms to the fox. That way he could slip them on his paws to soften the sound of his steps. This was to help save the foxes from being hunted to extinction. It is also rumored that the faeries taught the foxes the secret way to ring the foxglove bells to warn other foxes of nearby hunters. Other colorful folk names include Witches' Gloves, Fairy's Glove, Gloves of Our Lady, Virgin's Glove, Fairy Caps, and Fairy Thimbles.

The mottling of the foxglove blossoms has its own folklore. These spots have been compared to the marking on a butterfly wings and the tails of peacocks and pheasants. These were all said to denote where the elves had placed their fingers. Another legend about this plant is a bit darker and claims that the marks on the foxglove were a warning of the plant's poisonous and deadly nature.

Foxgloves are poisonous and while beautiful and enchanting in the Witch's garden, no part of the plant should ever be consumed. The entire plant is toxic. This includes the roots and the seeds. If you have small children, I recommend waiting for them to grow older before adding this plant to your garden. Foxgloves do attract honeybees, hummingbirds, and other pollinating insects to the garden. Companion shady garden plants include hellebores, astilbe, coral bells (*heuchera*), and hostas.

For something different, try a perennial form of foxglove in the shady garden. That way you will be sure to enjoy it for many years. The yellow foxglove, while smaller in stature than its biennial cousin, is a true perennial. *Digitalis grandiflora* has butter yellow blossoms and blooms in partial shade in the early summer. I am always happy to see this yellow variety of foxglove come back in my gardens every year. It's like a little shot of sunshine in the shade.

Foxgloves in the Garden: What You Need to Know

Common foxgloves (*Digitalis purpurea*) are biennials: They may survive beyond two years. The first year the plant will be vegetative, the second year it will bloom. If it reseeds or you get lucky, it may survive and come back for a third or fourth year.

Cold Hardiness Zones: Foxgloves are hardy in zones 4 to 9.

Sun and Shade Requirements: Foxgloves perform best in partial to deep shade. They don't like direct hot summer sun.

Bloom Time and Color: Summer. Late May through July. Color can range from purple to pink to white. There are many new varieties of foxgloves. They can have purple, white, yellow, or pink flowers on 4- to 6-foot stalks. Blooms start at the bottom first and roll up to the top.

Foliage: Foxglove leaves grow in large rosette clumps close to the ground above which the flower stalks are held.

Growth Habit: Foxglove plants are upright and vertical accents in the garden.

Height: Foxgloves may grow anywhere from 6 inches in height up to 5 feet tall, depending on the variety.

Preferred Conditions: Foxgloves prefer partial to deep shade and humus-rich soil.

Maintenance: For best results, plan on staking and tying the foxgloves so the blooming stems stay upright. (The blooming stems are top-heavy and can bend or break.) Cutting spent foxglove blooms will encourage repeat blooming. Some gardeners choose to leave the last flower stalks of the season, because foxgloves will self-sow in the garden.

Toxicity: All parts of the foxglove are poisonous. However, they are deer resistant.

A Summertime Foxglove Spell

Bless your foxgloves in the garden with this simple Garden Witch's charm. Hold your hands out over the blossoms and repeat the chant. Water and care for your foxgloves and enjoy the magic they bring to your garden.

> *If you listen close some eve you may hear them ring,*
> *Protection and beauty they do naturally bring.*
> *May the spirit of the foxglove now bestow upon me,*
> *Protection and happiness, as I will so must it be.*
> *By the powers of the Witch's garden this spell is sung,*
> *For the good of all, this gentle magic brings harm to none.*

Working with Animal Allies in the Celtic Tradition

by Sharynne MacLeod NicMhacha

Thousands of years ago, our Pagan ancestors throughout ancient Europe venerated many gods and goddesses, as well as aspects of the natural world. These included trees, hills, springs, rivers and lakes, and of course, the sacred animals who inhabited that world. Some of the earliest Celtic artwork depicts animals, birds, and fish in a remarkably unique way. Rather than attempting to portray these creatures in a fully realistic fashion like the Romans or other ancient cultures, the Celtic artists seem to depict each creature as if to portray its character, essence, or inner power. This artwork also displayed some of the artist's own personality and perhaps his or her own perceptions about—or even connections with—those sacred animals.

In addition to swirling geometric designs (perhaps representing spiritual energy or the interconnection of living things) and interlacing patterns that appear to be derived from the world of plants, animals and birds are among the most commonly occurring designs in early Celtic artwork. Commonly depicted animals were the deer, horse, boar, and bull, as well as birds (especially swans, geese, ravens, and cranes). The Picts—a Celtic-speaking people who lived in what is now Scotland prior to the arrival of Gaelic-speaking Celts from Ireland—were known for their unique representations of native creatures, including the horse, stag, wolf, bull, boar, eagle, seal, serpent, eel, dolphin, and fish (salmon or trout). These animal symbols appeared carved on rocks or engraved on silver jewelry, and seem to have served as a sort of "totem" animal for certain families, clans, or tribes.

Animals are also omnipresent throughout the Celtic mythological tradition, and appear frequently in the tales—especially horses, deer, cattle, and birds. Many deities were deeply connected with particular animals or connected with animal imagery. Sometimes the appearance or arrival of an animal signifies that a significant personal or spiritual event was going to take place. For example, some animals were actually spirit beings who enticed or guided people into an otherworld encounter, luring them away from the known world (the village or settlement, the area inhabited by the tribe) and into the wilderness where they would come in contact with a deity or spiritual teacher. Often these beings tested the person to see if they were worthy of receiving their blessings. There are also stories of people who were born at the same time as a particular animal. In many cases, the connection they shared with that creature lasted a lifetime.

Many Pagans feel a strong connection with certain animals or animal imagery. They are drawn to photographs or artistic representations of particular creatures, feeling as though the animal were connected with them or had something to communicate to them or teach them. This is a very ancient aspect of spiritual work in many Pagan traditions—and is not "just one's imagination." In shamanic traditions, we understand that every person has spiritual teachers or allies, which in many cases appear in animal form. If we work to develop and maintain our relationship with these creatures, they will in fact guide and assist us (as long as respect and reciprocity are maintained).

Working with Animal Allies

In the Celtic spiritual tradition, there are several ways we can work with animal allies in our personal practice. The first step is to be aware of our inner knowing and connection with certain animals, birds, or amphibians. Paying

attention to our feelings and intuition is important in this regard, so that we can make a distinction between animals we respect and find interesting and those that are our allies. It should be said, of course, that as we all live together in the web of life, all animals should be honored, whether or not we feel a special affinity or personal connection with them.

If you are receiving a strong feeling toward a particular animal, there are several ways to determine if it is your spiritual ally. Many people feel it is important to place pictures or images of the animal on your altar to show your respect and signal that you wish to know more about them. You can place offerings in front of them—perhaps food that they would enjoy or another appropriate offering. If you tend to work in a more ritualistic and meditative way, light a candle and darken the room. Let yourself sink into a relaxed state of mind, and focus on your breath. Let yourself drop deeply into a meditative state with the picture or image of the animal in front of you.

You may wish to open your eyes briefly from time to time to strengthen the animal's image in your mind's eye. Begin to speak a silent inner prayer to the animal. Let it know that you have been feeling a connection for some time, and wish to know if it would like to work with you as well. Open yourself fully to its energies, for animal allies are compassionate and beneficent beings. If the animal remains distant, it may not be time, or perhaps it is a helping spirit that can step in from time to time, but not one that will work with you on a daily basis. If you sense the animal approaching you, filling you, touching you, surrounding you with its energy, this may signal that it wishes to work with you.

If you work in a more shamanic path, journey with a known spiritual ally and ask them to take you to the Upper or Lower World to meet the animal in question. When brought into its presence, you may ask it directly if it is a spirit ally. Traditionally, if the answer is yes, the animal will present itself before you three times—usually in three different poses or postures. This means that it is "showing itself" to you and responding to what you have said. If the animal does not move or change position, or stays distant, the answer may be no or "not yet." If it does show itself to you, thank it and state your intention to learn more about it (both in ordinary and nonordinary reality). Let it know you are excited and honored to begin forming a long-term relationship and learning what this spirit has to teach you.

Animal allies can be active in our spiritual practices in many ways. They will often show up in dreams, meditations, rituals, or journeys. We may sense them near us, guiding us, warning us, or simply "getting our attention" in certain situations. Remember that all animals—from the very smallest mouse to the most enormous whale—possess a huge amount of spiritual knowledge and power. It is important not to have any preconceptions about animal allies and to be open to the vast amount of information and abilities they possess. In a good relationship, the animal will be friend, guide, and teacher; protect us from dangerous situations; bring in healing energies; and provide guidance and assistance in numerous aspects of our lives.

In order to maintain our relationship with them, we must never forget our spirit allies. Some people wear jewelry with their animal ally's image to carry it with them at all times and to show proudly (but not boastfully) their connection with this sacred creature. Other people get a tattoo of long-term and deeply connected animal allies (although it may be a good idea to wait a few years to do this, as some animals work with us for only a short time). We can honor them by giving offerings in ritual or by allowing them to enter our physical bodies during a trance state and letting them run, dance, or express themselves in physical reality through us. We can also donate money or time to wildlife charities to help protect these animals in the mundane world.

Sacred Creatures

Here is a list of some of the most sacred creatures in the Celtic spiritual tradition, along with some of their ancient powers and attributes. Of course, your own animal allies will show you over time their own powers and attributes, which may likely be even more comprehensive and varied than those given below. However, utilizing the wisdom of the ancestors and their experience and knowledge of these creatures is a good starting point for understanding them, honoring them, interpreting their symbolism, and working respectfully with their many powers.

Stag/Deer: Deer often guide or entice people into an otherworld encounter, bringing them away from that which is known and into contact with the supernatural realms. The ancient and widespread antlered god seems to have been connected with deer, as was the Irish goddess Flidais, who rode in a chariot drawn by deer. There are even a few depictions of an antlered goddess as well!

Horse/Mare: While the deer entices people toward the otherworld, the horse seems to actually carry them there. It symbolized speed, beauty, power, journeys, fertility, and sexuality. The horse was associated with the Sovereignty goddess, who appeared as Macha in Ireland, Rhiannon in Wales, and Epona in Britain and Gaul. Otherworld horses could be any color, but sacred horses were often white, gray, red/chestnut, or black.

Bull/Cow: Cattle symbolized wealth for the ancient Celts, and were greatly valued. The bull was associated with power and fertility, while the cow signified abundance and nourishment. There are many descriptions of otherworld cattle, which were white with red ears. The Irish goddess Boand ("White/Bright/Blessed Cow" was the tutelary deity of the river Boyne.

Boar/Sow: Like the deer, the boar hunt sometimes served to lure people into a powerful and even dangerous otherworld encounter. The boar was a very determined and tenacious creature, and especially enjoyed its food— the nuts of the sacred oak tree. Pigs were believed to have their origins in the otherworld, and the boar was also associated with the feasting at Samhain.

Hound/Wolf: Dogs were highly prized by the Celts for their bravery and loyalty. They were also associated with healing, due to the healing properties of their saliva. The wolf was somewhat more feared, and its name was in some cases taboo. For example, in Scottish Gaelic, it was called *Mac Tíre* ("Son of the Land"). The legendary Irish king Cormac mac Art was said to have been raised by wolves.

Bear: Bears were associated with a number of ancient Celtic deities, including the goddess Artio, who was depicted seated in front of a bear and feeding it from a plate. She may have been a protectress of bears as well as a goddess of hunters. The root word *art,* which appears in her name, means "bear" and is also seen in the names of King Arthur and Cormac mac Art.

Fish: The salmon and the trout were the most highly venerated fish in Celtic tradition. Both were said to live in sacred wells, which were protected even into the twentieth century. The famous Salmon of Wisdom lived at the Underworld Well of Wisdom, where it cracked open the divine hazelnuts of knowledge and consumed their inner essence.

Serpent: The antlered god was often depicted holding a ram-headed serpent, which seems to represent the power of the underworld. Snakes were associated with wisdom, healing, and transformation. In Scotland, a charm was recited at Imbolc at the den of the hibernating adder as a form of weather divination in preparation for spring.

Raven: The raven is one of the most commonly depicted birds in Celtic tradition and has many powerful attributes, including wisdom and prophesy. The goddesses Macha, Morrigan, and Nemain were called *Badb* ("Scald-crow"), while the god Midir owned two white ravens which protected his *síd* or "fairy" mound. The ancient Gauls were

known to perform divination by the flight of two crows with white wings.

Swan: Swans are depicted in some of the earliest Celtic artwork and were associated with beauty, healing, and the beneficial properties of water and sun. In the myths, deities may appear in swan form, sometimes connected by chains of silver or gold. This may reflect the fact that swans mate for life. Otherworldly women were often associated with the appearance of the swan.

Crane: In early times, the crane was associated with divination, prophecy, and powerful magical women. The deity Manannán mac Lir had a sacred object known as a "crane bag," a sacred container made from the skin of a crane that had been a woman transformed into crane form. It contained many powerful talismans. In later times, the Church appeared to disapprove of cranes and their association with magic and women.

Eagle: The eagle was often associated with images associated with the sky realm, as it is the bird that flies the highest in the air. It was connected with wisdom and the power of gods and spirits who reside in the Upper World. In many ancient European cultures, the eagle was also associated with the sun and the oak tree.

~

By reading the authentic Celtic myths, legends, and folk traditions, we can begin to learn more about all of these sacred creatures, and how the ancients perceived and interpreted their powers, attributes, and symbolism. Working with animal allies is a lifelong pursuit and experience, and will surprise even the most experienced of practitioners with the deep levels of wisdom and ability that every sacred creature possesses.

Doing Life & Creating Life: An Introduction to the Birthing Mystery through Tantra

by Chandra Alexandre

Whether it is an art project or the birth of a child, the creation process is mysterious. We all know the magic involved in bringing something to fruition, whether we've nurtured life within our wombs or gestated a project. Either way, we know the struggles of the journey and what it takes to hold true to our virtue and soulful purpose amidst others' opinions and our own doubts.

Creation, according to the philosophy of Tantra, is called *srishti* in Sanskrit. It involves fifty-one distinct components. This article deals with a subset of these components in order to provide insight regarding the creative process and the way in which Shakti (the primordial feminine/female principle) enlivens our engagement. Shakti is energy, the divine spark we call Goddess.

Ten phases are involved in Shakti's descent into this world of space-time, a descent known as *pavritti*. The phases of Shakti's involution are analogous in number to the lunar cycles from conception to childbirth. However, depending upon your individual creative process, each can last weeks, days, hours, minutes, months, or years. (The time spent on each phase is relative. For example, if your creative process takes about thirty days, you would devote one day to phase one, four days to phase two, and so forth.) The sections below contain a description of one of the ten *tattvas* (principles or elements) based on the Tantric practice of Tattva Shuddhi in order to help guide your personal awakening on the journey.

Phase 1: Prana Shakti – Source (Duration 1)

In the first phase, we recognize alignment with Source. Prana Shakti is the flow of vital energy within us linking us to our origins and potentials. She is our first teacher and guide, the one who invites us to dive into spiritual practice so we can (re)discover the fundamental patterns and movements of energy that keep us alive. She reminds us that this is not the time for agendas or expectations. Instead, it is a time for heartfelt deepening into self and world, for it is from this place of relationship to everything and everyone that the specific components of our creative process will be revealed to us.

Reflection: What is it in me that gives rise to this potential, this awakening, this project, or this child (metaphoric or literal)? Can I remain free of expectations and agendas in order to serve and honor the end as one unto itself?

Ritual: Think of all you have done to get to this point of creating. Honor yourself and those who have helped you. Set a *sankalpa* (sacred intention) for the journey (this can be revised as you progress). You may wish to place a marker on your altar denoting the initiation of your process. Something that is personally meaningful and symbolic of your path is most likely to inspire you, whether in the most happy of moments or during the challenges and obstacles that you may face ahead. Make time to gaze at this object every day to reconnect and embolden your efforts.

Phase 2: Prakriti-Purusha (Duration 4)

In phase two, we rest in the dance (largely unconscious) of *prakriti* and *purusha*—the push and pull of energy and consciousness that create a dynamic tension from the divine spark—and we are offered clues about them through dreams and synchronicities. Prakriti activates our imagination and intuitive juices, and Purusha provides connection to soul. Together, they are partners who keep us focused and provide the impetus toward action, helping us avoid mindless pursuits that do not serve our purpose, essence, or the greater good.

By reflecting here, we gain the ability to see the potential of the sacred and of evil, of compassion and of violence; of all the ways in which harmony is achieved not by forceful resistance to the flows of the divine will, but by the application of holistic vision to all that life has to offer.

Reflection: Do I allow myself to trust intuition, that sacred balance of embodied knowing and spirit? Can my motives stay pure, as in reflective of a harmony between outer perception and inner experience? How do I reflect the dance of prakriti and purusha in and through my choices, actions, speech, and thought?

Ritual: Create a list of all the things that you desire for your creation to be born whole and perfect. Choose four to be the cornerstones of your birthing process and meditate on these, holding them in your mind and heart. You may wish to create a collage or work of art to represent this phase and use it as a mandala to help strengthen your resolve and commitment.

Phase 3: Mahat Tattva (Duration 5)

Mahat Tattva, the Great Principle, is the expression of higher mind (called *buddhi*) within us. It is the discriminating force of judgment that is unclouded by ego or emotion. Mahat Tattva is therefore what guides our motivation toward intention aligned with soul and then action.

In phase three, we connect to deeper contemplation, self-reflection, emerging wisdom, and continued release from things that may hinder our ability to make good decisions. As you consider this, know that in Mahat Tattva we must learn to trust in order to augment the previous work done. Our attitude must be one of soulful caring in which we trust our intuition and not our instinct.

Reflection: Where and in whom do I place my trust as a provider of information? Do I listen to others before I listen to myself? Can I release myself from the tangled strands of gossip and half-truths that surround me in all the spaces I inhabit (work, school, family, friends, etc.)?

Ritual: Meditate on a time in which you were emotionally charged by something or someone. Go through the instance or episode again briefly in mind and body. Return to heartfelt breath and bring in *sakshi*, or witness consciousness. This is the power cultivated through mahat tattva of nonjudgmental discernment. Now, replay the incident again and allow yourself to notice your reactions. See what you notice and what you learn.

Phase 4: Ahamkara (Duration 1)

Ahamkara in Sanskrit means "I-ness," often just called ego. Ahamkara is the birthplace of self-awareness. It is therefore a starting point for us as individuals to take full responsibility for ourselves and our actions. In phase four, you may wish to think of ahamkara as a point around which both freedom and fetters circle continuously.

We are limited here in that ego is what ties our soul to this reality. But we are also liberated through ahamkara because it provides a focus for our unique soul imprint (called *jivatman* in Sanskrit) on the backdrop of creation as a whole. In this way, the Divine may experience itself through us and we may in turn experience the Divine. As we increasingly realize this reflection as true, ahamkara is shattered and we are able to take in reality as Reality.

Reflection: Am I stuck in the grooves of past incarnations, of pleasures, addictions, worldly goods, or arrogance? How do I fall into the entrapments of ego? Am I willing to take on the full ramifications of my thoughts, words, and actions? What do I need to change or do to make it so?

Ritual: Do *sadhana*. That is, make a commitment to spiritual practice. Let it be fun and transformational, deepening and enlivening. Perhaps you will chant while doing laundry or memorize verses while running. Perhaps you will sit in silence or stare at a candle flame. No matter what you do, understand this dedication as a strengthening exercise, one that will make you ready for all it takes for a strong relationship to ahamkara, one with true humility and open-hearted presence, to emerge.

Phase 5: Akasha/Ether (Duration 2)

An important transition is occurring as we move into the realm of akasha. This is the void, space, and blackness, the final space in which the subtle body dominates our creative process. As akasha enters with phase five, we begin to sense the world of forms and can tune in to the most delicate of impressions. With this influence, we begin to listen to our spiritual impulses, and it is increasingly important to be mindful of all that impacts us.

Akasha is keenly tied to our sense of hearing, and it is here that the voices of those speaking from our clan wave and the realm of the ancestors become clear. Listen well to the promises of others, to the whispers of your imagination and for the sounds of falsehood.

Reflection: What is the substance of my psychic self and how can I cultivate a relationship with my subtle body? Am I willing to truly listen? Do I need to protect myself in any way for this creative process to unfold in alignment with soulful purpose so that inimical influences do not sway or hinder me?

Ritual: Give your creation a spirit name (even a temporary one). Tie a red, black, and white piece of cloth to a stick and place it on your altar like a flag. White represents our highest spiritual power, red our activity in the world, and black our latent potential. These forces, known as *gunas* (qualities of nature) arise with akasha and inform all of our elemental work. Imagine now connecting to the very first vibration of the cosmos, that from which all else arose. Let this inner sound reverberate. As you feel ready, pick up your flag, press it between your palms, and move it to the sounds and rhythms of this vibration, intoning the name you have chosen. You may wish to record any impressions or experiences you have as messages from akasha.

Phase 6: Vayu/Air (Duration 4)

Vayu arises from the void because of excitement. It is the current that powers the spiraling of the elements within nature even while it remains formless. Each part of manifest creation is made up of the elements in different proportions, and vayu provides the creative turning, fast or slow, that propels the combinations into actuality. Vayu is also simply the wind that caresses us gently, and it is the life-force energy that carries us more deeply into the body.

In phase six, we enter a time of heightened intuition, of flowing thoughts and ideas, of increased potential for success, of heartfelt connections, and of constant change. Because things may seem to be moving along quickly now and variance is a key part of the journey, it is a good time to reflect on the patterns we perpetuate. Stay present to the constancy of your commitment despite the challenges of flightiness that vayu can bring. As you sense the winds of change, allow tingles of vitality—vayu's reminder of purpose—to enliven your efforts.

Reflection: What is it that distracts me or makes me lose focus? Do I need help or assistance now to stay on track with my efforts, centered in myself, nourished, and feeling vital?

Ritual: Take time to pause and be present for the thrill of the moment. You are alive and the world is turning. The moon, sun, and stars are all waiting. Open yourself in a stance of gratitude and humbleness, awe and yearning, to the potentials that lay ahead. Allow *prana*—the vital energy carried on vayu—to fill you as you breathe. Send the breath from the tip of your toes to the crown of your head and back down again, relaxing into every cell of your being so that the vital airs that sustain you provide deep cleansing . As you perform this exercise, you may also wish to chant (silently or aloud) vayu's mantra, YAM (pronounced YUH-M). Use this seed syllable to get into those hard-to-reach places.

Phase 7: Agni/Fire (Duration 6)

Agni, or fire, is the awakening of light in this world, and it is a defining force. In phase seven, we welcome in a sense of wonder as well as a greater sense of self and other. The difference between us and the world seems to expand (if left unattended here, ego can take center stage).

Agni both consumes and radiates, all the while transforming, catalyzing, and sparking something new. A guide into the darkness of our personal shadow, agni offers an opportunity to move into and out of pain, sorrow, fear, hatred, jealousy, and rage. Allow the burning of agni to cleanse. Anoint yourself with the ashes. There is more than meets the eye to this phase of the journey.

Reflection: Who am I that gives rise to this creation? Am I the same person I was when I started? What has transformed, seen increase, or seen burning away?

Ritual: The yantra or sacred diagram associated with agni is a red downward-pointing triangle. In embodied purification practice, it is situated between the heart and navel. At each point of the triangle, there are *bhupura*, or gates. Either seated or lying down, visualize this yantra within your own body. Now, imagine the ingredients of your life that have been with you since the beginning of this voyage as grains of sand filling it. Just the filling completes, the yantra begins turning clockwise, gradually getting faster and faster. At the climax of the spinning, the bhupura open and grains are flung out, but not all. The ones that remain are the building blocks of your looking glass. Take time to see and reflect on whatever you put into the mix that lingers. Look deeply into that mirror and take in the gaze of the one who looks back.

Phase 8: Apas/Water (Duration 8)

With the arrival of *apas* we find a perfect balance of order and chaos, head and heart. Apas feels intimate. It is the stuff of our blood, our tears, our sex, our secretions. It is the fluid of life and in this way it is the magic of creation on Earth. Apas therefore tells us to soak—not bathe; to make ablutions—not wash. It reminds us to play in fountains and slurp down rainbows.

Apas in phase eight pervades everything, and consciously or unconsciously, we drink it in. A time of heightened creativity and imagination, apas opens us to potentials for laughter, love, delight, and healing. It invites us to listen to our intuition, for it may have meaningful messages. But at the same time that we feel a bounty of divine blessings, apas asks that we begin to feel the edges of practical concerns. This is the time to balance fluidity with a measure of confinement, such as the setting of goals and establishment of guidelines. Therefore, find the edges of your stream, and knowing the beauty of its source, seek to navigate safely toward its conclusion.

Reflection: Where do I flow and not resist? Where do I resist and wish to flow? Can I surrender as a stick upon a river to the currents of life while still surely placing footfalls on the path?

Ritual: Gather beads or make some of your own. Collect charms and amulets from broken bracelets and necklaces that have sat in boxes or drawers for years. Meditate on the gifts they brought you when actively worn, and on the ways they might serve you now. Gather these energies to you and consider a new piece of jewelry or altar adornment. String it together and let magic flow. Alternatively, make soup. Cut your favorite vegetables into chunks, add broth and seasoning, stir, simmer, and let sit for thirty minutes before eating. In other words, find a way to nourish yourself soon.

Phase 9: Prithvi/Earth (Duration 10)

The end is almost in sight, but patience is required because we remain under prithvi's spell for a while, this phase of the journey offering us a chance to assess our position. Fitting the solidity of Earth, we stand our ground in phase nine as prithvi weaves and knots the energy of apas into form, and we mark our journey noting what was, what will be, and what shall be

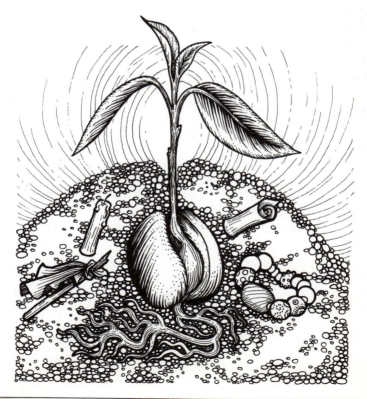

no more. Prithvi offers us a chance to feel the fullness of our belly and rest. In our repose, we are invited to sweeten the foundation of our work with fragrant memories.

Reflection: Now is a time for preparations, for readying, and for deciding how to honor this passage as it draws nigh. What ritual components will be fit for the coming occasion?

Ritual: Sprout a seed or bud from your next fridge foraging and plant it in your home or garden. Avocados, potatoes, onions, and fruits work well. As you do the planting, bury any ritual materials you have acquired during this whole manifestation time that you wish to return to Earth. Note the coming full circle and offer your gratitude to the dirt for all that this sacred substance contains.

Phase 10: Completion: The Birthing

An ending and a beautiful beginning, birth is violent, as matter is both created and destroyed. Perfect in every way, the process nonetheless leaves us whole and complete. Today, we reap the rewards of our journey and take in the awesome power of Shakti engaged and fulfilled. The magic of the moment brings us into heightened awareness of the world. If awe is not immediately apparent, we are at least given the potential to see through new eyes. Here, we awaken to the mystery. In this way our journey is soul-making. May you be thus inspired to willingly create again.

House Elves

by Magenta Griffith

Many peoples believe in some kind of elf or spirit, usually unseen, which helps the people who live in a particular house or dwelling. In the British Isles, they are called brownies, hobs, hobgoblins, urisks, or bwbachods, depending on region. In Scandinavia, tomte or nisse are found in households; in Slavic countries, domovoy. In German-speaking areas, house spirits are called kobolds or gnomes. Although there are different rules about how to get and keep the assistance of these supernatural workers, there are also many similarities.

Most of these house spirits like order and cleanliness, and they are angered by dirt and neglect. They will help, but the household has to do their part as well. They expect gifts, usually food, but only the best will serve. If the gift is called a payment, or is second-rate, they may leave—or even worse, cause mischief. Other less-desirable gifts, such as clothing, would cause them to leave as well.

In English folklore, brownies are said to stay in houses and aid in domestic tasks. They do not like to be seen and work at night, traditionally in exchange for small gifts or food. They especially enjoy porridge and honey. Brownies are called that because they tend to dress in ragged brown clothes and have brown faces and brown hair. Brownies make their homes in unused part of houses and seldom appear to, or speak with, humans.

Around the end of the harvest in Scotland, the urisk becomes more likely to help around farmyards, stables, and barns. He particularly enjoy milk and cream and tended to bother the milkmaids, who made regular offerings to prevent trouble. The urisk is usually seen only by those who have second sight, though there have been instances when he made himself visible to ordinary people as well. He is said to be a jolly character with a distinctive flair about him, distinguished by his flowing yellow hair, a broad blue bonnet, and fondness for carrying a long walking staff. Many large houses have their urisk, and a seat close by the fire in the kitchen is left empty for him.

In the north and midlands of England, the household spirit is called a hob. They could live inside the house or outdoors and helped with farmwork. If offended, they can become nuisances. The customary way to get a hob to go away is to give them a set of new clothing, which usually works. The worst hobs could be impossible to get rid of, however, and might stay and bother people.

Hobgoblins appear as hairy little men who, like brownies, are often found in houses, doing odd jobs around the house while the family is asleep. Such chores are typically small deeds like dusting and ironing. Often, the only compensation required in return for these was food. Again, attempts to give them clothing would often banish them forever, though it is not known whether they take offense at such gifts or are too proud to work in new clothes. While brownies are more placid creatures, hobgoblins like to play practical jokes. They also seem to be able to shape-shift. However, like all of these folk, hobgoblins are easily annoyed.

When teased or misused excessively, hobs, hobgoblins, and brownies become boggarts: creatures whose sole existence is to play tricks and cause trouble for people. They can be mischievous, frightening, and even dangerous, and they are very difficult to get rid of. There is a story that a family moved from Scotland to the New World, and the family boggart followed them by hiding in the butter churn.

The Welsh house spirit is called the bwbachod, pronounced "boob-a-chod." They had one noticeable difference from others of their kind—a dislike of teetotalers. Dobbs, or Master Dobbs, is a Sussex brownie, known to be especially kind to old men. Dobby is the common name for a brownie in Yorkshire. (Dobby is the name of one of the house elves in the Harry Potter books.)

In Scandinavia, tomte (Sweden) or nisse (Norway and Denmark) are believed to take care of a farmer's home and protect the children from harm, particularly at night. The Swedish name tomte is derived from the word for house: tomt. The tomte or nisse was usually seen as a small, elderly man, from a few inches high to about half the height of an adult man. He often had a full beard and was dressed in the everyday clothing of a farmer. (Modern ones are usually clean-shaven.) Since the nisse are thought to be skilled in illusions and sometimes able to make themselves invisible, one was unlikely to get more than brief glimpses of him. Norwegian folklore states that the nisse has four fingers and is hairy all over, sometimes has pointed ears and eyes that glow in the dark. The tomte has to be given specific gifts or harm would come to the household. If he isn't given his payment, he will leave the farm or house, or engage in mischief such as turning objects upside down and breaking things. One particular gift was porridge with a pat of butter on the top. In a popular story, a farmer put the butter underneath the porridge. When the tomte of his farmstead found that the butter was missing, he was angry and killed the cow in the barn. But when he became hungry, he went back to his porridge and ate it, and found the butter at the bottom of the bowl. Full of regret, he searched the neighborhood to find an identical cow, and replaced the dead cow.

A domovoy (literally, "he of the house") is a house spirit in Russian and Slavic folklore. The main purpose of a domovoy is to protect the household from "the evil eye" and to prevent harm to family members. A domovoy appears to be a small, old, bearded person, or sometimes is completely covered with hair. However some stories describe them as looking like the male head of the family, only smaller. Domovoys are often described as liking some members of the household and disliking others. Traditionally, every house is said to have its domovoy. It does not do mischief unless angered by a family's poor housekeeping, blasphemous language, or neglect. The domovoy sometimes helps with household chores. People leave gifts in the kitchen for them, like milk and biscuits, or bread and salt. To attract a domovoy, go outside of your house wearing your best clothing and say aloud, "Grandfather Dobrokhot, please come into my house and tend the flocks." When moving, make an offering to the domovoy and say, "Domovoy! Domovoy! Don't stay here but come with our family."

In German-speaking areas, house spirits are called kobolds or gnomes. At night, kobolds do chores that people couldn't finish before bedtime, such as cleaning the stables, feeding and grooming the cattle and horses, scrubbing the dishes and pots, and sweeping the kitchen. In return, the family must leave a portion of their supper for them and must treat the kobold with respect, never mocking or laughing at them; they play malicious tricks if insulted or neglected. They sometimes have particular names in certain regions or cities. For example, Heinzelmännchen are house gnomes said to have done all the work of the residents of Cologne, Germany, during the night, so that they became very lazy. According to the legend, this went on until a tailor's wife got so curious to see the gnomes that she scattered peas onto the floor of the workshop to make the gnomes slip and fall. The gnomes, angered by this, disappeared and never returned. From that time on, the people of Cologne had to do all their work by themselves.

~

These house spirits are usually invisible, but they make their presence known. They want to be recognized for their help, but in specific ways. Treat house elves well, and if you want to keep them, don't give them clothes (but you knew that, didn't you?).

For Further Study
Briggs, Katharine. *An Encyclopedia of Fairies, Hobgoblins, Brownies, Bogies, and Other Supernatural Creatures*. New York: Pantheon, 1976.

Air Magic

Tibetan Buddhism and Its Ritual Tools

by Raven Digitalis

It's both interesting and reassuring to me that so many magicians, Witches, and Western-tradition occultists are drawn to Eastern mysticism. From the Eastern esoteric callings of Theosophy's Madame Blavatsky to Thelema's Uncle Al (Mr. Crowley, that is) and numerous other historical magicians and philosophers, a deeply spiritual vein undeniably flows between what is termed the "east" and the "west."

Buddhism is practiced in many forms worldwide, but Tibetan Buddhism is one of the most well-known

branches—it's certainly one of the most visible. It's from Tibet that we get numerous highly recognizable symbols, deities, paintings, altar décor, prayer flags, saffron robes, gorgeous monastic yellow and red hats, intricate texts (including the Tibetan Book of the Dead), and identifiable Tibetan written script including the famous and simple-yet-complex mantra "Om mani padme hum." The rich history of fourteenth Dalai Lama of Tibet is equally fascinating; his activism and educational outreach have served to put Tibetan Buddhism in the public eye.

Personally, I developed an interest in Buddhism shortly after developing an interest in witchcraft, magic, and occult spirituality. While my coven and I have an uncanny connection to the spirituality of India—and indeed actively observe, fast, and perform Sanskrit ceremonies for Hindu holidays—I still feel a unique connection to Buddhism, which springs from Hinduism.

I had the pleasure of grading essays for a university course, Intro to Buddhism, for three years. With each captivating year, I learned more and more about the religion (or, more accurately, the lifestyle) and other people's perception of it while simultaneously absorbing a number of Buddhist principles and assimilating them with both my personal Craft and everyday ethics.

Buddhism was born in India: the ancient land of Hinduism. The common story for the beginnings of Buddhism is as follows: Siddhartha Gautama was born to a Brahman (upper-class) family in 550 BCE in Kapilavastu (presently a border between India and Nepal). Upon witnessing an old man, a sick man, and a corpse, Gautama's insular views of life as a painless process became instantly shattered. Leaving his wife and child behind at the palace, he went on a journey of self-discovery. For six years, he practiced the opposite of what he was accustomed to: self-mortification and the renunciation of all things material (including food) alongside a group of Saddhus—India's wandering holy men (many of whom are yogis and shamanic devotees of Lord Shiva). Feeling unsuccessful in this perhaps overly reactionary lifestyle, Gautama took refuge beneath a tree and meditated for days on end. Upon attaining enlightenment, he became known as a Buddha (Sanskrit title meaning "Awakened One" or "Enlightened One") and began professing the wisdom of the Middle Path: a path that exists balanced between extremes.

Much like witchcraft and other magical systems, Buddhism has a number of developmental branches. Though there are innumerable Buddhist groups in the world, both scholars and Buddhists recognize three primary paths in the development of Buddhism as a religion.

Theravada Buddhism is the oldest school of Buddhist thought and is the "path of the Elders." Theravada is highly focused on the words of the Buddha and can be considered a rigid or strict school of ancient Buddhist thought and practice.

Vajrayana Buddhism is said to be the fastest method of attaining enlightenment. This "diamond vehicle" makes use of tantric texts and an emphasis on ritual as opposed to meditation alone.

Mahayana Buddhism, the third main "path to enlightenment," is focused on the Bodhisattva Virtues, and believes that the path toward enlightenment is possible with the practice of utmost compassion toward one's fellow beings. Mahayana Buddhism includes schools of practice such as Zen (Chan) Buddhism, Pure Land Buddhism, and Yogacara.

Tibetan Buddhism, uniquely, often prides itself on being a conglomeration of principles and practices seen in Theravada, Mahayana, and Vajrayana Buddhism, allowing the possibility for a fourth phase of Buddhism to emerge in modern times. Before exploring the tools of Tibetan Buddhism, allow me to briefly summarize a few of the principles observed within Tibetan Buddhism and other schools.

The Buddha Dharma can be roughly translated as "life teachings of the Enlightened One," and is observed by all types of Buddhists (though interpretations may differ) and generally includes the following concepts:

The Cycle of Samsara: All beings incarnate experience some sort of suffering, called *samsara*, and are subject to repeating the twelve-link cyclical wheel that the Buddha laid out. Each human experience gives rise to the next. A rough translation of these links, minus appropriate descriptions, are: ignorance, mental formations, consciousness, name and form, the six senses, contact, feeling (experiencing), craving (desire), attachment, becoming, (re)birth, and death.

The Four Noble Truths: These truths of reality assert the following: suffering exists in life, suffering arises from craving or desire, suffering can be alleviated with the cessation of craving, and the freedom from human suffering exists within the Noble Eightfold Path.

The Eightfold Path: A "weak link" is said to exist on the cycle of samsara, existing between feeling (experiencing) and craving (desire). If a person breaks this chain in their own life, it leads to the Eightfold Path toward enlightenment, whose foundation is wisdom, ethics, and meditation, and whose arising manifestation is right understanding, right intention, right speech, right action, right livelihood, right effort, right mindfulness, and right meditation.

The Three Jewels: These metaphorical treasures of Buddhism, which are revered and "taken refuge in," are the *Buddha* (Awakened One), the *Dharma* (the teachings), and the *Sangha* (the spiritual or monastic community).

The Three Marks of Existence: The first, *anicca* (impermanence), asserts that all things in reality are subject to change and that nothing in reality—whether physical, mental, or emotional—is truly fixed. The second, *dukkha* (unsatisfactoriness or disquietude), asserts that discomfort exists in reality and can be explored through the observation of the Four Noble Truths. The third, *anatman* (the absence of self), asserts that nothing exists on its own accord or has its own independent "beingness." Everything that exists is a culmination of previously existing forces, which, themselves, arose from other previously existing forces.

With strong threads of unity and connectivity, it's easy to see how Tibetan Buddhism absorbs and integrates other principles and practices, and vice versa. For example, Tantra, while not a definitive school of Buddhism, is a spiritual way of life, similar to Gnosticism within Western mysticism. Tantra refers to practices and meditations that have a direct emphasis on the experience of gaining enlightenment. The foundations of Tantra arise from esoteric texts or scriptures that highlight certain rituals, meditations, visualizations, images, and philosophies that have this goal of universal union in mind. Some of these texts, which are called *tantras*, also refer to themselves as *sutras*, including the renowned Kama Sutra. However, contrary to popular belief, sexual magic is only one of many mystical methods recognized within tantric belief. The origin of tantra is ambiguous, as all the various branches have their individual origin myths.

When it comes to Tibet, it's interesting to note that the country has a minimal historical record. Much of what's documented is said to be "in preparation" for Buddhism's rise in Tibet, which occurred around AD 800 to 900. Tibetans have long felt a deep, and understandably inherited, connection to Buddhism as their people's spiritual expression.

A highly important emphasis of the path is that only highly compassionate and intelligent who help other sentient beings find relief from *samsara* (suffering) are eligible to truly become tantrikas. This idea seamlessly melds with the Tibetan Buddhist view of the *Bodhisattva path*. Even His Holiness the Dalai Lama has referred to Tibetan Buddhism as a practice of *Tantrayana*.

In short, Tibetan Buddhism is concerned with combining various developmental schools of Buddhist thought and practice, with the primary goal of attaining *Buddhahood*, in order to help alleviate the suffering of others. The idea of cultivating and arising *bodhicitta* (limitless compassion and wisdom) within oneself is the primary goal for those wishing to become Bodhisattvas. They are those who have reached an extreme state of wisdom, yet who put off their own enlightenment, *nirvana*, or Buddhahood (ideas that believe in no more earthly rebirths upon attainment) in an act of compassion so that they may better help everyone else around them attain awareness.

Old Tools, New Uses

To close this article, allow me to route my focus to a few of the fascinating ritualistic tools of Tibetan Buddhism. Since melding principles into practice is a key concept, it's my hope that you recognize and understand some of the latent symbolism these tools possess for the next time you're in a metaphysical store or Buddhist sangha; or, perhaps, to discerningly integrate them alongside your own Neopagan or occult practices.

Mandala: Numerous people across the world can easily recognize a Buddhist mandala. *Mandala*, which in Sanskrit means "circle" (whereas *chakra* means "wheel"), refers to a circular diagram depicting various deities, symbols, and images associated with Buddhist mythology, enlightenment, and the various realms of existence. Mandalas are two-dimensional forms of three-dimensional structures (such as a temple or a celestial realm) viewed from above, much like a spiritual architectural floor plan. Mandalas may be drawn, painted, or meticulously formed with colored sand. Sand mandalas are a Tibetan Buddhist practice, and each piece of sacred art is ritually offered to the elements to represent impermanence. These images generally depict concentric circles and squares with entrances in each cardinal direction. Mandalas may also serve as tools of focus during meditation, priming the practitioner to have a more focused shot at removing obstructions and distractions that may arise during the act of meditating, thus bringing the practitioner closer to Buddhahood.

Prayer Wheel: An easily recognizable Tibetan Buddhist symbol is the handheld, spinning prayer wheel. These ritual objects are representations of the power of intention. Prayer wheels consist of a wooden or metal base with a hollow metal structure (and weight for spinning) at the top, which contains a long, rolled sheet of paper containing prayers and scriptures. With simple flicks of the wrist, the practitioner sets the wheel in motion, releasing the condensed energy of the prayer paper. This is said to scatter the Dharma, and the practitioner's prayers, to the four directions instantaneously.

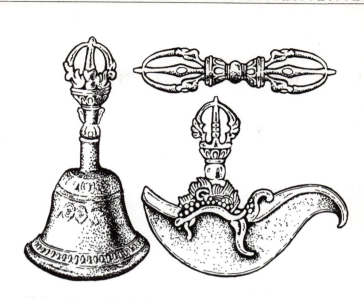

Vajra: Also called a *dorje*, this primary symbol of tantra and Vajrayana is the "thunderbolt" or "diamond" that represents the acutely and unwaveringly enlightened mind. This beautiful metal tool has prongs at both ends and is meant to empower the practitioner in the unshakable, penetrating force that is spiritual awareness. I personally draw a parallel between the symbolism of the vajra with the Hermetic "as above, so below" principle, as well as the Kabalistic notion of instantaneous creation—the Big Bang.

Ghanta: When the half-vajra is placed at the end of a bell, called a *ghanta*, the symbolism speaks of the active means of penetrating awareness (method) coupled with the perfection of awareness (wisdom). The bell itself creates sound because it's an empty vessel: a representation of the emptiness doctrine previously mentioned. This combination is also indicative of the combination of masculine and feminine forces, much like the ancient Egyptian ankh.

Kapala: These gorgeous bowls are literally the cap of a human skull. Often intricately carved and bejeweled, these half-skulls serve their purpose as ritualistic offering bowls. These are often used during ascetic rites and are to be used only by people who understand the impermanent, transitory nature of existence. Some believe the kapala is a nod to more ancient traditions of human sacrifice, while others cite its sacred role in providing a more carnal ritual implement that can successfully appease both wrathful and protective spirits.

Phurbu: This ritualistic metal dagger is typically shaped like a long pyramid with a vajra at the handle. Originally an ordinary nail, this evolved tool is used to keep away illness and to control (or battle against) negative spiritual forces. Three faces that represent the three mental poisons recognized in Buddhism (greed, hatred, and delusion) are situated at the top of the handle, each looking a different direction. This represents, among other things, the transformation of one mental state to another.

Kartika: Also called the *trigug*, this swooping blade usually has a vajra for a handle and represents severing the bonds of ignorance and material attachment. Nothing that can potentially hinder the practitioner's journey to enlightenment stands a chance when the kartika is used. The swooped or hooked formation of the knife is a representation of compassion: the highest force which with to sever these worldly hindrances. Similarly to the vajra being commonly paired with the ghanta, the kartika is generally paired with the phurbu in Tibetan Buddhist ritual practice.

Mechomancy: Steampunk Sensibilities in Pagan Traditions

by Sybil Fogg

For some people, "steampunk" is an aesthetic, a guiding principle that they use to govern their choice of dress, music, or home décor. For others, it is a means of escape via literature or film, or by visiting a costume play (cosplay) convention and donning Victorianesque clothing tricked out with gears and clocks to rub elbows with others of a similar mindset. To some, steampunk is a way of life, and they find ways to filter the steampunk sensibility through their everyday life. And for some, steampunk includes magic.

The best way I have heard steampunk described is "Victorian Science Fiction." This sums up the counterculture's fascination with a specific time period and the conceptual consideration of a "steampowered" fantasy world as imagined by such writers as Jules Verne and H. G. Wells. Modern steampunk literature often incorporates a future similar to what may have been envisioned by Victorians: a reliance on steam as a means of power. Examples of newer authors include Richard Harland, Wayne Reinagel, G. D. Falksen, and Leanna Renee Hieber. Much of their work would fall very close to the realm of science fiction, where steampunk resides.

The costuming choices of this subculture's membership run the gamut from Victorian/Edwardian to Wild West to a future dystopia powered by steam. Building a steampunk outfit calls for certain considerations. These can be broken down into three categories: time period, locality, and/or fictional character. Some steampunks choose to build an outfit with historical authenticity. The most common time period seems to be Victorian/Edwardian, but some steampunks look even further into the past or to the future to create costumes that are otherworldly. Because there is a multicultural movement within the steampunk community, many choose to weave fashion from across the world together. Others look past our Earth and even our solar system for inspiration. There is also a strong draw on literature and film for ideas. Some steampunks will take a favorite character, such as Boba Fett, Alice, Dorothy, Professor Snape, or Sherlock Holmes, and "steampunk" him or her out by adding elements of leather (or faux leather), gears, clock parts, electricity, motors, and so on.

The outfits spied at any steampunk gathering will be an eclectic array of the past fused with the present or future. Victorian-tailored vests, shirt collars, trousers, gowns, bustles, petticoats, bloomers, kimonos, saris, pith helmets, and the ever-popular corset are often tricked out with gears, timepieces, motors, and rehabbed mechanized metal parts in an almost definitive nod to *Star Trek*'s Borg race. These are accessorized with gas masks, parasols, braces, pocket watches, weapons, battery packs, clockworks, and/or anything one can think of.

And the style is evolving. At one point, the color choices trended toward muted browns, blacks, and tea-dyed whites, but even that signature style has been challenged. Reds have become prominent and even such bright colors as turquoise have been spotted. Probably the only real fashion trend that threads steampunk together is the ever-present pair of goggles, but even those are not always necessary. Steampunk fashion brings out the creativity of those who gravitate to it, as much of the costuming is one-of-a-kind created by the wearer. This is what makes being an observer extraordinary.

Steampunk music is almost impossible to define. What constitutes a "steampunk band?" Do artists put themselves in this category intentionally, or are they brought in because steampunks are drawn to their music? Is it instrument choice, musical technique, costuming, lyrics, or story? A genre, defined by Merriam-Webster's Dictionary is a "category of artistic, musical, or literary composition characterized by a particular style, form, or content." But for steampunk, this doesn't fit. Some of the more well-known steampunk bands—such as Abney Park, Professor Elemental, Eli August, Sunday Driver, The Cog Is Dead, Diablos in Musica, Petal Blight, Emperor Norton's Stationary Marching Band, Rasputina, Voltaire, Steam Powered Giraffe, This Way to the Egress, and The Clockwork Dolls—have little in common musically. What these bands do all incorporate is a community to which they belong.

Some have embraced the steampunk movement and adapted their fashion and art to emphasize their interest. This can range from playing music from a certain era with historically accurate instruments to looking ahead to put together what they have decided would be authentic instruments in a future powered by steam. Artists such as Abney Park and Professor Elemental have written songs that tell stories of their exploits. Others draw on universal abstract concepts of love and loss, such as Eli August. The movement also includes writers who employ a steampunk slant within their primary genre. In fact, some people who identify with the steampunk mindset have incorporated this interest into their everyday life in the form of clothing, home décor, and more.

So why not magic for those with Pagan tendencies?

How one weaves steampunk into their magical life is wholly dependent on the individual. Perhaps outfitting certain magical tools would be sufficient for one person, while another would want a sacred space complete with Victorian furnishings. Another might choose to work the aesthetic through a ritual wardrobe.

Mechomancy is a term that I ran across in Stephen Hunt's novel *The Court of the Air* back in 2008. Since then, the term has appeared elsewhere, from role-playing games to common speech amongst steampunks. Mechomancy is infusing magic into machines, essentially filling them with *aether*, a kind of "fifth element," or energy drawn from the magical realm. Since steampunk prides itself on machinery, from dirigibles to submersibles and blunderbusses to light sabers, it seems mechomancy is a good place to begin incorporating a bit of steampunk into one's magic.

The following ritual will charge any tool for magical workings, but it is designed to bring the magic out of steampunk items.

Time: May 23 or August 23
Gods: Vulcan/Hephaestus/Thor
Tools Needed: Any tools that need to be charged within the spiritual fire of Vulcan. These would include but are certainly not limited to an athame, wand, pocket watch, goggles, pipes, glasses, walking sticks/canes, and clothing (I charge corsets because of the metal boning, but it's your choice).

Besides the tools you charge, you'll also need these items: a blanket to sit on, a metal or wooden altar, a metal pentacle to charge the items on, metallic bronze taper candles with holders, and a bowl holding a bit of soil.

Incense: Sun, fire, cinnamon, cedar, cloves, frankincense, myrrh

Metal chalice filled with charged water. I generally charge water under a full moon when I know that I have spellworking coming up. Alternatively, time can be set aside to charge the water during the ritual.

Quarter candles: Copper for the south, silver for the west, brown for the north, bronze for the east

Music: Whatever helps keep focus

Prepare your space. I like to do this before I prepare myself. That way everything is in place when I am ready to begin the ritual. Set out your blanket and your quarter candles. Place the altar in the center of the blanket and lay out your tools around the pentacle. Be sure to put the chalice on

the left (for the Goddess) and the candle on the right (for the God). Set out the dish of soil and set up the incense.

Usually, I set up the music to play while I take a ritual bath. That way, I am engaged in the task at hand as I relax. When I am finished, I will dress in whatever clothing I plan on charging and then return to the ritual area.

Cast the circle and call the quarters in your usual manner or if the mood suits you, change things up a bit by adding a touch of steampunk to your ritual casting.

Light the candles and incense. Choose one of the ritual items collected and place it on the pentacle. Spend some time meditating on what kind of power you wish to infuse into the piece. This is important. Are you planning on using these items for spellcasting? Or are you working to attract the past to you through their proximity? Maybe you are charging them to give you strength when you are out and about in the world. Take some time here to really understand your intent.

Once you have determined your purpose, sprinkle some water over the item, followed by soil, then pass the object through the incense, and finish with the flame. Your item is charged. Thank the God and Goddess. Repeat with each item you have collected. Give thanks and close the circle. Now you have infused your magic with a little bit of steampunk sensibility.

When the Goddess Calls ...

by Barbara Ardinger

... be sure to answer. Politely.

If you're reading this, you have presumably already taken one of the Goddess's calls. "Come home to me," she probably said to you. "Worship me and worship the ground you walk on. Find pleasure in my rituals. Find beauty and strength, power and compassion, honor and humility, and mirth and reverence."[1] I bet that's more or less how you became a Neopagan.

As we're traveling along the labyrinths of our lives, we often receive calls from the Goddess. But when I had lunch with my friend Ariadne a few days ago and told her I'm writing this article, the first thing she said was, "How do you know it's the Goddess calling? Does she have caller ID?" Good questions. Let's play with this telephone metaphor and see how far we can stretch it.

What's on her caller ID? It might be a name. Isis. Hera. Freya. Sarasvati. Is this a goddess you usually hear from? Why is she calling? In reply to your prayer or call for help? To help you work on some of your issues? To ask you to take action and do something useful for her or the planet or her other children? To say, "Straighten up and fly right"? Like most mothers, when she calls, she's usually checking in to see how we're doing, so it seems to me that the primary reasons she calls us are to (1) help us learn more about ourselves and live better-examined lives, (2) lead us to a teacher or a tradition that will help us grow, (3) tell us to take action to help our Mother Earth survive what humankind has been doing to our beautiful planet, and (4) yes, admonish us to behave ourselves.

---

1. This is of course from Starhawk's poetic version of The Charge of the Goddess.

Pay attention to what's going on around you. The world is not just a dial tone. Things we hear "accidentally" may be echoes of divine phone calls.

OMGss. ive bn calln u! Where r u? Wheres ur hed?

Maybe she's sending text messages. In the past, her messages came mostly in dreams and visions, but if process philosophy is valid (and I think it is), then goddesses and gods are evolving just like we are. That's why I'm willing to allow for a goddess who is sitting in her technotemple somewhere with a smartphone in her divine hands. She'll do whatever she has to do to get our attention.

The Goddess has apps, too. We call them the psychic sciences. Maybe she calls and tells you to get a natal chart so you can learn how the planets and asteroids are affecting you. Maybe she calls to advise you to learn numerology or the tarot so you finally get some insight into what you're doing and where it might be taking you. Consider her astrology app. I don't speak astrologese and am a total nincompoop where charts are concerned, but the Goddess has called me in the voices of some of my friends who are very talented astrologers. I've been shown why I do some of the dumb things I do, and I've also been shown how to stop doing them and do better things. Has this happened to you yet?

If we're using her tarot app, I think the Goddess may be helping us shuffle and lay out the cards. (It's called divine psychokinesis.) What we see are patterns of possibility in our lives. My friend Mary Greer has a deep knowledge of tarot. When I asked her what the Goddess might be telling us via the cards, she sent me an e-mail that I saw as a little poem:

Come play with me.
It's not who wins but how you play the game.
We're all One.

Reflect on this.[2]

---

2. Personal e-mail, July 6, 2011. Mary didn't intend it to be a poem, she said when I wrote to thank her, but I think her reply works that way. From Shakespeare to Bob Dylan, some of the world's niftiest wisdom has come through poets and poetry.

If you think the Goddess may be using an app on you, try this combination of tarot and numerology. Calculate your life path and other significant numbers, then reduce them to numbers between 1 and 21. Get out all your decks and look carefully at the major arcana cards that correspond to your life path and other numbers. Reflect on what you see.

Her other apps, of course, include all the ways we do divination. She doesn't always make direct calls, so pay attention to the apps and see what she's trying to tell you in a reading.

Where r u goin? How r u gnna gt there?

Back in the early 1990s, I was teaching a weekly class called Practicing the Presence of the Goddess (which became the title of one of my books). This class was an introduction to Goddess scholarship at a time when there wasn't much except the works of authors like Merlin Stone, Starhawk, and Marija Gimbutas. What practicing the presence of the Goddess really means, of course, is living mindfully, being aware of what's going on in our minds. Practicing her presence is steering our thoughts away from gossip, insults, bigotry, and other types of stupidity. One way to fill the mind is to adopt a mantra or learn some of the better known chants, like Deena Metzger's Goddess Chant, *"Isis, Astarte, Diana, Hecate, Demeter, Kali, Inanna."* But just reciting names, while it does push the monkey chatter out of our heads, is only half the lesson. I brought in little statues of the goddesses and taught their myths. The point is to understand what these goddesses can mean to us today. Understand which goddess calls you and when she calls. And why she calls.

B wht u cn b, but b bettr at it. U nd to lrn ths lssn. U nd a gd techr. Follo ths path & play nice tgethr.

Sometimes when the Goddess calls, it may be to send us to a pantheon, a tradition, a coven, a priestess or priest, or a teacher. Wherever you go, be sure to use her text message as your touchstone. *Play nice tgethr. B kind 2 each othr.* If you visit a coven where you're required to use drugs or alcohol, where you feel jealousy seething among the members or hear little hissy fits buzzing around the circle, where gossip and sexual intrigues pass for teaching ... immediately take out your divine smartphone and read her text messages again. This is a lesson you can learn real fast. Are these people playing nice? Are they being kind? If they're not, go away. Now.

Any group that does not promote courtesy among its members and with people who are not members is not devoted to the Goddess. If you think the Goddess called you to such a group, think again. Think, in fact, what your mother would say if she found you hanging out with mean and nasty kids. Would your mother approve? Would our Mother approve?

Sometimes she does something to really get our attention. *Yo! Lsn to me!* Twenty-five years ago, I was introduced to a very wise Wiccan priest in Los Angeles who said that if we're looking for new ways to work on spiritual issues in our lives, then it's useful to develop a relationship with a deity who lives on the other side of the planet. That made sense to me. Who says the only good goddesses are the Western ones? One day soon after that conversation, I was standing in the Bodhi Tree Bookstore. A flyer actually flew off the bulletin board. Right in front of me! It was a notice for a class to be taught by Dagmola Jamyang Sakya. Now when a flyer flies off a bulletin board and lands on you, that's a pretty clear message. I went to the class, where I was the only Pagan in a room full of Buddhists. No one cared! What was important was that I was there for the Goddess. I took refuge with Dagmola and learned the Tara mantra. Over the years, I have learned some significant lessons about living mindfully, and to this day, I am as devoted to Tara as to any Western goddess. Has something like this happened to you yet?

It's not, of course, just the Goddess who calls. Gods call, too. The myths in which gods romp across the countryside, raping girls, bullying other gods, and taking sides in wars, may be fun to read, but do we have to emulate them? I asked my friend Galina Krasskova, who has been devoted to Odin and Loki for twenty years, about dealing with gods who are known to be challenging. "I am pushed," Galina told me, "to become better as a priest, a shaman, a devotee, and most importantly a human being. ... I have never, ever had any of the Norse Gods suggest or push me to be less than the best and most exemplary person I could be.[3]

To repeat: if you think a god or goddess is telling you that you're better than anyone else, that you have permission to use drugs of do anything dishonest or trash other people's religions and holy books, that you have permission to be a Pagan bully ... then I'm sure you're hallucinating.

Cln ur room! Tke care of ur cusins. Ths is ur Mother spking.

I also can't help but wonder if some of the e-mails and telephone appeals we get might be disguised calls from the Goddess. Not the partisan political appeals (well, let me confess that I think the Goddess is progressive, but that's only my opinion), but the notices about endangered forests and animals, the appeals to help the hungry and the homeless. We decide for ourselves what our causes are and how we support them—from going to demonstrations to sending $25 on the first of every month—but

---

3 Personal e-mail, July 5, 2011.

when we hear the voice of the Goddess in some of these calls, that's another way we can help the whole planet.

Play nice 2gethr. B kind 2 each othr. Ths is ur Mother spking.

This, I believe, is the primary reason why the Goddess calls us. This is the message she sends to all her children, whether they believe in her or not, no matter where they live, no matter what they're doing in their muggle lives. If everyone played nice and we were kind to each other, I'm sure the world would be a better place. I like to think we who reply to the Goddess and try to live more mindfully, more courteously, more ethically are building up to a critical mass. Maybe I'm an idealist, but I believe that the Goddess calls us Neopagans to be examples of peace and courtesy in the world. Even if just one of us responds, even if it's just one person playing nice, that's one drop of courtesy in a parched world. We need oceans of courtesy, but if we start

listening to our Mother now, maybe we can build up to streams of courtesy that flow into rivers that flow into oceans.

And sometimes the Goddess calls in unexpected voices. I believe she spoke through Hildegard of Bingen, the twelfth-century abbess, author, and composer who taught the concept of *veriditas*. "The heavens were opened," Hildegard wrote, "and a blinding light of exceptional brilliance flowed through my entire brain ... and it kindled my whole heart and breast like a flame." Perhaps the Goddess was also speaking when Dame Julian of Norwich, a fourteenth-century anchorite and mystic, wrote, "All shall be well, and all shall be well, and all manner of things shall be well." If you're having a bad day, pull the flames of veriditas into your body, mind, and soul. Remind yourself that "all manner of things shall be well." But please don't think Hildegard and Dame Julian were Pagans. They were Christian mystics whose messages are, to this day, universal.

～

The Goddess calls us all the time. It is possible—with persistent practice—to engage in conversations with her. It's possible to learn to live more mindfully and to play nice with other people.

B wht u cn b, but b bettr at it. Play nice 2geth. B kind 2 each othr. Ths is ur Mother spking.

When the Goddess calls ... answer the phone. Don't hang up!

Ribbon Magic

by Ember Grant

Ribbons can add color and texture to spells and be used for magic alone or with other items. Binding, bonding, and bundling are among the many ways to weave spells with ribbons. And while you can use string, twine, leather, or hemp for similar types of spells, the focus here is on fabric ribbons.

Ribbons are one of the easiest spell tools to find. Fabric and craft stores have nearly every type and color you can imagine. Look for sales and stock up on discounted and seasonal ribbon so you'll always have a variety on hand. Another good way to diversify your collection is by saving the ribbon from gifts you receive. In addition, ribbon you purchase will most likely be on a spool, but sometimes you can find remnants for sale that have been cut. Use a box or bag to store spools and scraps of ribbon. I like to use large clear zipper-style bags for my remnants. You may want to secure scraps so they don't become tangled. You can wind them around old spools or secure them with a twist tie from a bread bag.

Binding

Binding magic, done traditionally by wrapping or tying knots, is often performed to stop someone or something from doing harm. However, you can also use binding magic on yourself in order to break a bad habit. Find a symbol of the habit you wish to break or simply write it on a piece of paper. For example, if you're trying to quit smoking, you may wish to use a cigarette or a cigarette package. Wrap a black ribbon around and around the item, visualizing the bad habit being bound and trapped. Leave room on the ends so you can tie the ribbon, and secure it using three knots. Chant as you wrap:

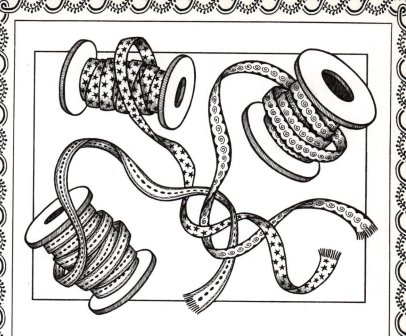

I'd stop this habit if I could,
This is for my highest good.
Cease behavior causing harm,
With this bond I cast a charm.
Help me heal and make it last,
Guide me in this worthy task.

Braiding

Braiding is another easy way to use ribbons that also allows you to weave several elements of a spell together to create unity. For example, in a spell for prosperity, you could use three ribbons to represent success, prosperity, and good fortune (yellow or gold, green, and purple). Typically, this is done with three ribbons, but if you're skilled in braiding, you can use more. Another use for a braid is to create a bond between people. Something like this could be used in a handfasting ceremony. Use two white ribbons, one for each person, and a pink or red ribbon to represent love. Create a braid like this with your partner to strengthen your bonds of love or friendship. (Of course, remember to avoid forcing a bond.)

Here's a chant to use as you create the love braid:

Over, under, through and through,
You for me and me for you.
Let us keep a bond that's true
Love and peace between us two.

Breaking Unwanted Bonds

Breaking an unwanted bond or establishing a new beginning can be accomplished by cutting ribbon. Ribbon-cutting ceremonies are often used for dedications and new beginnings, groundbreakings, and so on. A symbolic cutting is a good way to use magic to free yourself from difficult circumstances.

First, make a symbolic bond that represents the situation. You can do this by simply tying the ends of a ribbon together. Visualize the bond as you do this; feel the discomfort it's causing. For the spell you will simply cut the ribbon, visualizing the bond being severed.

Here's a spell for breaking bonds that you can adapt to suit your needs:

Perform this spell on a day that corresponds to your need, when the moon is waning. Select an appropriate moon sign if you desire. This is a spell for release. You may desire freedom from a particular attachment, a broken heart or bad relationship, financial burdens, a job, or even a bad habit. You will need a piece of ribbon in a color appropriate for your need, scissors, and a black candle.

Tie the ends of the ribbon together to form a circle. As you tie the knot, visualize this bond as the controlling force from which you wish to break free. Name the bond aloud by saying, "This ribbon represents _____."

Next, pick up the scissors. Imagine them as a sword you carry into battle. Pass them through the candle flame, envision the fire as your passion to be free, empowering the blades. Say the following:

As the moon wanes,
Release this bond.
As the candle expires,
Release this bond.
As I sever the tie,
Release this bond.
I am free.

As you cut the ribbon into pieces, clearly visualize circumstances unfolding to set you free. See yourself being rid of this force outside your control. After you cut the ribbon, bury the pieces in separate places; the Earth will absorb and neutralize the unwanted energy. Alternatively, you could burn the pieces of ribbon. Allow the candle to burn completely.

Bundling

Another simple way to use ribbons is to make a bundle or sachet and tie the ends together. These bundles can contain herbs, stones, or other objects and are often used as talismans and amulets. Use the appropriate color of fabric and ribbon, chanting as you wrap and tie with several knots:

Ribbon wind, tightly bind,
Wrap this spell that I design.

～

There are many other ways to be creative with ribbons in your magical practice. Naturally, you can decorate with them by using them to tie bundles of flowers, herbs, or branches; tying them around vases; or using them on wreaths. Use a ribbon to string a special pendant to wear or display, or wear them in your hair. Ribbons have become a tradition as symbols for various causes and are popularly displayed or worn to show support for a cause. Beyond the list of magical color correspondences, or seasonal colors, some colors have come to stand for the fight against different types of cancer, or to promote peace, pride, and other issues. Feel free to incorporate these colors into your magic as well, or magically charge a ribbon to wear for a cause you believe in. Remember, use colors that have symbolic meaning for you. Happy spell-weaving!

List of Ribbon Color Correspondences

White: neutral, all-purpose, full moon energy, protection, purity, meditation

Black: banishment, breaking bad habits, binding, new moon energy

Red: protection, passion, energy, courage, strength, sexuality, will

Pink: romance, love, friendship, harmony, emotions

Orange: success, commerce, motivation, courage, legal problems

Yellow: mental skills, communication, self-confidence, charm, travel, health, success

Green: money, fertility, growth, abundance, health

Dark Blue: dream magic, transformation, instinct, psychic awareness

Light Blue: beginnings, endurance, awareness, joy

Pale Violet: inspiration, divination

Dark Purple: authority, good fortune, spirituality

Gray: neutrality, mystery, dimness, concealment, secrets

Brown: home, domestic issues, animals, grounding

The Art of Physiognomy

by Autumn Damiana

Most of us are familiar with at least a few different types of divination. Some of the most well-known methods include tarot, astrology, numerology, scrying, and palmistry. However, few people know the term "physiognomy," even though it is also one of the divinatory arts. Throughout its long and sometimes controversial history, the popularity of physiognomy has varied, and it is just now being rediscovered in modern scientific circles. But what is physiognomy? A good way to describe the practice is to say that it is to the face what palm reading is to the hand. From the analysis of the size, shape, and relative placement of facial features such as eyes, mouth, nose, and chin, physiognomy can give a reading of one's personality, fortune, and fate.

The word *physiognomy* is derived from Greek, and roughly means "natural (or physical) indicator." Although there is evidence that ancient Greek philosophers developed a system of physiognomy and physiognomic theory, the art is believed to have originated in ancient China, where complex, formal systems of "face reading" were widespread—and still exist to this day. Physiognomy was also prevalent throughout Europe in the Middle Ages and had become a kind of folk wisdom and superstition among the common people, as evidenced by literature of the time, notably Chaucer's collection *The Canterbury Tales*. The more concrete and methodical principles of physiognomy in use by the

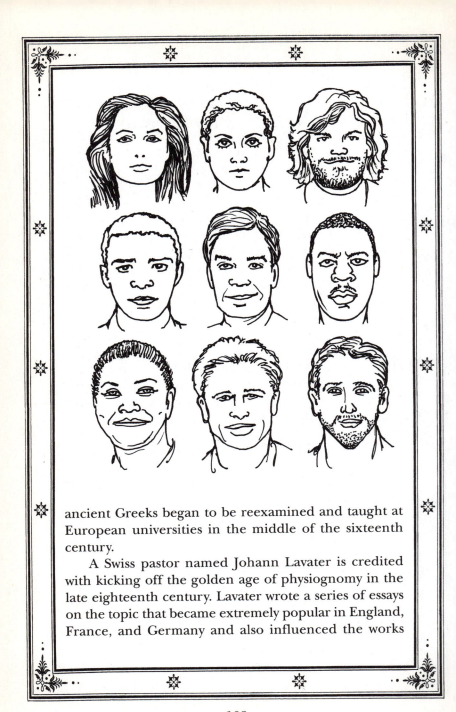

ancient Greeks began to be reexamined and taught at European universities in the middle of the sixteenth century.

A Swiss pastor named Johann Lavater is credited with kicking off the golden age of physiognomy in the late eighteenth century. Lavater wrote a series of essays on the topic that became extremely popular in England, France, and Germany and also influenced the works of such writers as Charlotte Brontë, Charles Dickens, Edgar Allan Poe, and Oscar Wilde. In the late nineteenth and early twentieth centuries, Holmes W. Merton used the principles of physiognomy to invent the Merton Method, which theoretically could match a person to his or her ideal job and was used widely by employers at large corporations. Law enforcement has historically also been linked to the practice of physiognomy, believing that it could be used as a tool to glean hidden information about suspects, witnesses, and potential jurors. The rise in popularity of physiognomy caused other related "sciences," such as anthroposcopy, phrenology, and personology to become popular as well.

Physiognomy differs from these three disciplines in several ways, even though the words are often used interchangeably. The methods of anthroposcopy are used by forensic anthropologists to determine the visage of an individual, including skin, hair, and eye color. Phrenology is the analysis of markings, measurements, and features (such as bumps) on the cranium to determine personality traits. Personology, while closely related to physiognomy, is also concerned with facial lines and other marks, and how the features of the face express emotion and other mannerisms. Physiognomy is typically limited to the analysis of more permanent and unchanging facial features that are determined by the bone structure of the face, such as nose size or the shape of the forehead.

So how accurate is the art of physiognomy? Now is your chance to grab a mirror or get together with a friend and find out for yourself! Here is a list of some basic facial characteristics and their corresponding meanings using physiognomy:

Eyes

Shallow-set (bulging): energetic, outgoing, sometimes easily influenced. *Deep-set*: introverted, reserved, analytical, can be suspicious.

Slant upward: optimistic, clever, an opportunist. *Slant downward*: pessimistic, kind, can be taken advantage of for being too gentle.

Wide-set: tolerant, open-minded, disdains authority. *Narrow-set*: conservative, more judgmental, sometimes more dependent on others.

Eyebrows

Long: can deal with many personality types, probably has a lot of friends. *Short*: less involved in other people's lives, more likely to keep to one's self.

Curved (arched): friendly, a go-getter, eager to please others. *Straight (little or no arch)*: logical, skeptical, will think things through before acting.

Wide space between: sociable, a team player, likes to be where the action is. *Narrow space between*: independent, cautious, prefers to be alone more often.

Ears

Large: intellectual, a good listener, more prone to taking risks. *Small*: cautious, acts on instinct, can become easily overwhelmed.

Set close to head: frugal, likes to plan ahead, listens to what others have to say. *Sticking out*: idealist, nonconformist, can be stubborn and opinionated.

Earlobes connected to head: strong attachment to family (sometimes too reliant). *Earlobes detached from head*: can separate oneself from family, cares more about friends.

Long earlobes: Looks ahead to the future, makes plans for later on. *Short earlobes*: Easygoing, lives life in the present.

Nose

Large: ambitious, pioneering, confident, can be arrogant or selfish. *Small*: more easily contented, noncompetitive, sometimes reserved or shy.

Pointed tip: curious, detail-oriented, may be distrustful of others. *Round (full) tip*: enjoys luxury, can be materialistic.

Turned up: sentimental, trusting, generous. *Pointed down*: prudent, sensible, clever.

Curved (aquiline): assertive, fearless, a natural leader. *Straight*: sensible, methodical, idealistic, not very interested in material things.

Mouth

Large: generous, cares about relationships (both personal and professional). *Small*: has fewer long-term relationships, can be restless and change often.

Corners turned up: cheerful, upbeat, encouraging, may be a little naive. *Corners turned down*: shrewd, discontent, may have a negative outlook.

Full lips: intense, enthusiastic, prone to overindulgence. *Thin lips*: impatient, less emotional, keeps secrets well.

Chin

Pointed: emotional, has a flexible personality, may be moody.

Square: practical, tough, enjoys a challenge, has strong convictions.

Rounded: kind, tactful, friendly, easy to approach.

Prominent (large): willful, determined, tenacious, stubborn. *Receding (small)*: sensitive, timid, may be passive or give up easily.

Cleft/dimple: craves appreciation and recognition, can want to be the center of attention.

Other Features

Curved (rounded) forehead: creative, imaginative, intelligent. *Flat or broad forehead*: ingenious, practical, pragmatic, a problem-solver. *Forehead slants backward*: spontaneous, makes fast decisions, can think outside the box.

Indented temples: tendency toward compulsive behavior.

Prominent cheeks: commands authority and prosperity, can also be controlling or bossy. *Flatter cheeks*: laid back, thrifty, may need to work on being more communicative.

Protruding brow bone: dominant personality, likes to be in charge.

Strong jaw: courageous, resolute, can sometimes be harsh or overbearing. *Narrow jaw*: adaptable, easygoing, may be wishy-washy.

Pop-Culture Physiognomy Oracle

Here is another fun way to use physiognomy as a tool for divining. All that is needed is a fashion or entertainment magazine that features numerous photos of people's faces, and the list of facial correspondences above.

Holding the magazine on your lap, close your eyes, and take a few deep breaths.

As you exhale, empty your mind and allow your body to relax until you feel calm, centered, and ready to tap into your psychic abilities. When this is the case, ask a question (either silently or out loud) that can be

answered using the properties of physiognomy, such as "what kind of person has had the most influence on me lately?" or "what trait that I have been exhibiting is having the most impact on my life?" Without looking, flip through the magazine until you feel an inner prompting that tells that you what page to stop on. Open your eyes, look at the page, and obtain your answer from the first facial feature that grabs your attention.

There are no set rules how to interpret your answer, so you will need to use your intuition. As an example, perhaps your eyes will fall on a curved, long, arched eyebrow. If your question concerns who is influencing you, in this case you can be sure that it is a sociable, outgoing person who has a lot of friends because he or she likes to please others. Also, it's possible that the shape of the eyebrow itself may instantly remind you of someone you know, and that person would then be the answer to who is influencing you. If your question was about how your life has been impacted based on a trait that you exhibit, then congratulations! It would seem that your open, friendly attitude is being noticed and having a positive effect, such as you making new friends. Just make sure not to work so hard making others happy that you forget about yourself. Experiment obtaining and interpreting your answers with the oracle, and see what comes up.

Sometimes you may follow the above directions only to find that you have opened the magazine to a page with no photos of faces. When this happens, simply close your eyes and try again or switch magazines if you wish. If you still haven't achieved the desired results after several attempts, then the universe is telling you to put the oracle aside for the time being and try again later. With time and practice, this method can become a tool of divination that you can use anywhere you have access to magazines. It's also fun to demonstrate at parties, and can be a great way to pass the time waiting for your doctor, dentist, or hairstylist!

∼

Many have criticized physiognomy throughout the years, including Leonardo da Vinci and other members of the scientific community. Although physiognomy began to fade into obscurity after the nineteenth century, it is undergoing a small twenty-first century revival. Thought to be accurate in predicting both a person's character and their future, Chinese face readers have gained popularity in the Western world and are asked to "read" fortunes, help understand clients, or size up potential love interests. Mass media will sometimes run stories (often with amusing "pop quizzes") concerning physiognomy and its perceived sway on our culture. Most interestingly, physiognomy is also tentatively being investigated in the field of psychology, as new evidence has shown that many different people will have the same "snap judgment" reactions when exposed to the same unfamiliar face, and that there may be an evolutionary reason for this phenomena, although this is still unclear. Research is also asking whether or not a person's visage really does shape his or her destiny, as studies show that people with certain types of faces and specific features gravitate to certain professions. Kind-looking or baby-faced individuals will often be nurses or social workers, men and women who look forceful or dominant are more likely to become executives, and politicians with attractive or aesthetically pleasing features will beat out their plain or homely opponents almost every time.

Whether you accept the theories behind physiognomy or believe it to be good for nothing more than entertainment is entirely up to you. With further research and exploration, physiognomy can become a serious course of study, or you can just have fun with it and use what you have learned to wow your family and friends. One thing seems to be certain—the idea that physiognomy, in some form or another, is here to stay. From its use in divination to its depictions in classic literature to its potential as a branch of accepted science, the art of physiognomy has fascinated humankind for centuries, and probably will continue to do so for many years to come.

The Digital Night Sky

by Susan Pesznecker

Most Pagans find that their practices intersect with the celestial sphere in some way, whether they garden by the moon's phase, worship the sun, track the astrological zodiac's planetary influences, or enjoy lunar rituals. Yet their actual knowledge base about the heavens often tends to be woefully sparse. It's interesting, because in past eras, no self-respecting Witch would have called herself such without having a sound understanding of the heavenly movements overhead. Indeed, training as Witch or shaman often required a set period of observation, during which the initiate marked the positions of sun, moon, stars, and planets, learning their essential natures as well as how they moved through the night sky.

Alas, while today's magick users may revere the heavily bodies processing overhead, it turns out most people know very little about what's really happening up there. There are some valid reasons for this. Some people simply don't feel a need to know. Others view astronomy as something that's complicated and far beyond their grasp. In truth, astronomy is a branch of both mathematics and physics, and taken to the level of astronomer or physicist, yes: it can be intense. But we don't have to go that far. The fact is, the position and movements of each of the heavenly bodies are both logical and predictable, and with only a little effort, it's reasonably easy to understand how the night sky "works." This is important, because an understanding of celestial movements can inspire and enrich just about anyone's magickal practice, whether

as part of spell craft, ritual, herbalism, or just about any approach. Besides, it's just plain cool.

Taking this a step further, let's consider the realities of today's digital revolution. For the first time in recorded human history, we're in the midst of a intellectual and cultural paradigm shift that we can actually *see* happening—versus the usual process of looking back a hundred years later and saying, "Oh, gee. The Enlightenment. That was a paradigm shift, wasn't it?" Our digital world reality changes almost from minute to minute, taking us with it. Hair-raising as it sometimes feels, it brings its own wonders along, and one of those is the "digitalization" of the celestial sphere.

Yes, if you own a laptop, smartphone, or tablet, a world of amateur astronomy, stargazing, and celestial magick awaits you. Some of these apps and software applications teach, while others tantalize and entice you to work magick. All have multiple layers to explore, starting simple but becoming as complex as you're willing to explore. These tools may be used to study or monitor heavenly movements, determine where heavenly bodies are in relation to planning or timing ritual or spellwork, cast astrological charts, and more. Settle back and let's explore some of my favorite celestial software and apps. And rest assured, even if the availability of these products changes between the time I'm writing this and the time you read it, it's certain that even more dazzling versions will have appeared.

Note: Unless otherwise specified, the reviews below are for products that work with the iPhone, iTouch, and iPad. Since I'm an i-user, my experience is decidedly i-centric. In doing the research for this piece, it quickly because apparent that a wonderfully similar array of apps is available for the Android system; in most cases, the Android/i-apps are more or less identical. However, since I am an i-user, I am confining my comments to those products with which I'm familiar. And yes: I've used every product mentioned below.

General Astronomy Apps and Software

Astronomy-modeling software creates a complete two-dimensional model of the night sky as seen from a designated place and time. The model can be used to explore or demonstrate heavenly movements or relationships and even can look forward or backward in time. You enter the date, time, and location, and the software will show you what is or was in the night sky at that moment.

One of the best examples of this is **Starry Night**, a fully featured software package available for both Mac and PC. Starry Night allows one to see the night sky anywhere in the solar system from any vantage—you could even for example, watch Earth rise from the planet Mars! This is complex, elegant software that is simple enough for anyone to use yet loaded enough to keep astronomers busy.

The iPad app, **Starmap**, provides a complete sky atlas featuring all of the modern celestial catalogs (stars, moon, galaxies, planets, and more). A special "eyepiece mode" allows the user to identify an object and then focus a telescope on those celestial coordinates. Budget conscious? **Luminos** for the iPad provides a low-cost but fully functioning astronomy simulator.

Looking for general information about the heavens? **Astronomy Picture of the Day**, aka **APOD**, has a working web page and free apps. Each day, APOD features a new image of the heavens along with explanatory material provided by an expert. The **Deep Sky Browser** app provides elegant digitized images from the Digitized Sky Survey, such as galaxies and Messier objects. Also quite wonderful is the free **NASA** app for iPad, which features information about every aspect of space and the U.S. space program along with real-time video and more.

Apps for Studying the Moon

Are you, as a magick user, interested in learning more about the moon's rhythms, its zodiacal procession, and the ways it affects our lives on Earth? **Deluxe Moon HD** is an iPad app that not only shows moon rise, set, age (from new) and phase, but also the moon's location in the zodiac and how its current position and lighting affect everything from finances to personal relationships to menstrual cycles to gardening. Touch controls allow you to rotate the moon to advance or roll back the date. A moon compass is included; your viewing location is shown by longitude/latitude and is set via automatic GPS. The app is rich with animation (including a moving zodiac) and the images are gorgeous, with a black background, white font, and moon renderings in shades of blue, gray, and soft white.

Deluxe Moon Basic is a free iPhone version of **Deluxe Moon HD**, including many of the same wonderful features. Moon is another free app that furnishes simple information about the current moon phase as well as presenting a set of "fun facts."

Another excellent app is **MoonPhase – Moon Info,** which provides basic lunar details for any date between 1900 and 2100, including moon phases, rise and set times, zodiacal positions, full moon names, and more. One of the niftiest aspects of this app is its display of a full set of monthly calendar pages, each with a superimposed moon of the correct phase. And just for fun, you can display the moon in normal, cartoon, or "cheese" formats.

Looking for ultra-simple lunar apps? Try **Luan – Lunar Calendar**. You'll get moon phases, moon rise and set times, and animated transitions. Or take a look at **Moon Calendar**, which provides a full color moon calendar with phases and rise and set times for any month and any location.

Would you like to study more about the moon's geography and geology? Take a look at **Moon Atlas.** This iPad app provides a fully rendered (via satellite and laser altimeter data) 3D globe of the moon, complete with labeled features and details about space explorations. Or try **Moon Globe**, also featuring a fully rendered

3D globe that can be twirled and spun with one finger, while providing information about spaceflights, topography, and more.

Interested in simply looking at pretty pictures of the moon? Try **Moon!**, an app with hundreds of gorgeous lunar photographs, each of which can be used as wallpaper.

If you'd like more detail about the moon's magickal and arcane traditions, try the **New Age Moon Calendar**. This app really isn't a calendar, but it's full of goodies, including full moon names, lunar gods and goddesses, moon lore, and eclipses. **Moon Sign** is a fun little app that tells what sign the moon was in when you were born and shares details of your resulting personal characteristics. **iLuna** notes the moon's phase and its current position in the zodiac as well as when the moon is void of course. Detailed explanations are given for each data point.

Apps for Studying the Sun

Solar Walk allows detailed navigation and examination of the sun, planets, and man-made satellites within our solar system. With a pair of 3D red/cyan glasses, you can use the app's 3D display—which also works on 3D-enabled television.

Sun Seeker: 3D Augmented Reality Viewer shows the solar path, rise and set times, and directions for any daylight hour. It can also zoom in on an image of any location, showing the location and direction of solar exposure. This is a rather technical app but could be quite useful if your magickal works involve working with the sun's directions.

The free app **3D Sun** presents a 3D view of the sun and provides detail information about solar flares, sunspots, and other solar activity. The free **SoHo Viewer** features the latest images of the sun's surface as taken by the Solar and Heliospheric Observatory. This app includes a nifty zoom feature.

Apps for Studying the Planets

To visit and explore your favorite planets up close and personal, try the iPad apps **Venus**, **Mars**, **Jupiter**, or **Saturn Atlas**. These provide fully rendered 3D globes of the planets, complete with elegant physical details. Or try the **Mars Globe**, a free app furnishing a gorgeous 3D map of the planet Mars. You might also check out the incredible **Solar Walk**, described earlier.

Apps for Studying the Stars

One of my favorite dedicated iPad apps is **Star Walk**. Hold your iPad up to the sky and the onscreen image will display what you're seeing in the night sky and will tell you exactly what you're looking at. It can show you what the sky looks like at any time in the past, present, or future and provides an excellent search function. It also tracks satellites and the International Space Station. This app provides a red-tinted night-viewing option to protect your night vision.

Sky View is a free app that functions like a smaller and less detailed version of Star Walk. **Planisphere** provides a basic star map that can be used to explore the clear night sky. In addition to showing stellar positions, it also marks asterisms (constellations), galaxies, and more.

Apps for Studying Astrology

Celeste 1.0 creates a complete 2D natal chart with a detailed interpretation. If you're looking for something more complex, **Astrologo** delivers an elegant birth chart and interpretation, offering twenty popular house systems, both the Tropical and Sidereal methods, and additional bells, whistles, and options. An interactive Orrery view is provided, and the graphics are outstanding. The comprehensive Planetlab app goes even further and is designed for the serious astrologer or astrology student.

Terrific Arcane Apps (These Are Just Plain Fun!)

The iPad app **Analemma** provides an introduction to the analemma-shaped movements of sun, moon, and planets via images and animations. **Planetary 2D** shows a 2D Orrery, displaying the orbital movements of the solar system. **Pocket Sundial** renders a working 2D sundial, showing the current time. Just for fun, you can choose different views and styles.

Sun Clock Detailed is an iPad app that models a 300-year old Louis the Fourteenth clock, featuring sun rise and set times and a spherical moon phase indicator. Julian time displays at the bottom. **Astrolabe Clock** is an astronomical clock based on the astrolabe, an ancient instrument used to tell time and to follow and predict positions of the celestial bodies. It provides moon phases, sunrise and set, planetary transit times, eclipses, and more. And it looks really cool, too. **Emerald Observatory** for the iPad provides a unique chronometer-style display of clock time, sunrise and set, planetary movements, twilight stages, the eclipses, seasons, and more. It also features an Orrery, showing the actual planetary dance.

Enjoy!

Santería Survival

by Dallas Jennifer Cobb

Cuban Santería is a fascinating spiritual practice. With origins in the Yoruba culture of West Africa, Santeria grew out of the traditional practices of slaves imported to Cuba to labor on sugar plantations and in mines in the 1800s. While enslaved, the West Africans were forced to convert to Catholicism, the predominant religion of the Spanish nationals.

To ensure their physical survival, the slaves had to appear to be practicing Catholicism, the religion of their oppressor. But, with a stronger will to ensure their cultural survival, the West Africans found ways to keep the knowledge and practice of their Yoruba culture alive through *syncretism*, the practice of depicting their Yoruban deities

(called *orishas*) as Roman Catholic saints. In substituting the Catholic icons for West African deities, the gods and goddesses of the Yoruban tradition survived.

Like the Cuban people, Santería has survived many waves of oppression, plus significant cultural and political change. Disguised as Catholic saints, knowledge of the orishas survived and was passed on for generations. Not only has it preserved traditional cultural knowledge, spiritual beliefs and practices, but Santería has evolved from the original religious practice, taking on a life of its own.

Survival

Blending the animistic beliefs of West Africa, the dance and drum traditions of the Yoruba, and the structures and icons of Catholicism, Santería is a product of the melting pot of nations and cultures that converged in Cuba during Colonialism. After the abolition of slavery, Santería survived and grew in Cuban communities, which were strongly Afro-Cuban. Primarily an agricultural society, animistic beliefs and practices fit well with the life of the average Cuban. Santería was commonly practiced in villages and homes throughout Cuba.

But with the advent of the Cuban Revolution, another strong wave of spiritual repression and religious intolerance swept through the country. Long experienced with adaptation and disguise of their traditional beliefs, Cubans again disguised Santería, and it survived the resultant era of communist propaganda. This time the orishas and spiritual ceremonies were hidden within commonly allowed social expressions, including music, drumming, dancing, and poetry.

Known for its investment in arts and culture, communist Cuba has produced world-class musicians, dancers, painters, and writers. Within their life work, many Cubans have preserved the knowledge of Santería, hiding sacred images and practices in drumming and dance, theater, and works of visual art.

Santería Simplified

An animistic practice, Santeria holds that there is a life force, or *Ashe,* within each of us, and in every aspect of our universe. Song, dance, drumming, and community celebrations increase Ashe, so much of the practice of Santería is about increasing the blessing of life force within the community.

A fundamental belief is that each person has a guardian saint, or orisha, who watches over them, and who should be worshiped throughout life. These guardian saints are the focal point of the rituals and rites of Santería. *Casas de santos* or "houses of saints" are organized for the followers of a particular saint or orisha. Within these houses a *padrino* or *madrino,* godfather or godmother, takes on the responsibility of passing along traditional teachings to newcomers. Because Santería is an oral tradition, the customs are learned by watching, listening, and taking part in ceremonies. Children learn Santería songs, stories, dances, rhythms, and the structure of rituals from their elders.

Like many other Pagan practices, Santerían rituals, rites, and spells involve the use of herbs, roots, candles, divination tools, sacred chants, and music. Some practitioners also engage in the ritualistic sacrifice of birds and animals, used to "feed" the patron saint. *Ebbo* is the practice of sacrifice or offering to an orisha. It could be something simple like a candle, flowers, or fruit, or on important occasions, it could involve animal sacrifice in which the Ashe or life force of an animal is offered to the orisha.

Similarly, Santería is primarily an earth-based spiritual practice used for good, though a small number of people veer into the practice of using it for malevolent purposes.

A *santero* or *santera* is a priest or priestess of Santería. A high priest is known as a *babalawo*. Priests and priestesses lead ritual ceremonies, perform spells for protection, divine the future, and interpret omens to guide the practitioner. The ancestors, called *Egun,* are always invoked in Santería ceremonies. Like the oral tradition that is handed down, the Egun are remembered and honored.

While each Santería ceremony is different, all involve communication with the orishas and the Egun. Drumming, dancing, and singing are a central part of all Santería ceremonies, and while they were often thought to be simple "entertainment" practiced by the slaves (or "comrades" under the communist regime), these forms of communication served as a way to send messages not just to the ancestors and gods, but to other believers in the area. A simple rhythm could carry the message of hope, resilience, and fortitude, unbeknownst to the oppressors.

The Orishas

With hundreds of gods and goddesses, Santería has a patron orisha that embodies every aspect of nature and human nature. With both positive and negative qualities, humans often have one primary orisha, but possess character traits from many others. Practitioners continually strive to become in balance with their human nature, and by doing so to fulfill the destiny that they were born to.

Each orisha has his or her own specific colors, numbers, elements, rhythms, dance steps, images, and saint, all of which are used ceremonially.

While there are literally hundreds of gods and goddess, a few of the main deities include Obatala, Yemaya, Eleggua, Oggun, Oshun, and Chango.

Obatala is the father of all gods and goddesses, and the god of peace. He created earth and humans and is often depicted as a wise old man or woman.

Yemaya is the great mother, goddess of motherhood and the seas. She symbolizes virtue, prudence, intelligence, and fulfillment.

Eleggua is the divine messenger who oversees new beginnings, choice, and the crossroads. He is the guardian of the crossroads, but he can be mischievous and a bit of a trickster. Because of this, Eleggua is always the first invoked at any ceremony so he is appeased.

Oggun is a warlike god who governs tools and weapons, anything made of iron. He symbolizes the worker, toiling the field with a pick, or pounding iron with a hammer.

Oshun is the goddess of love and lust, sensuality and sexuality. She is also goddess of fresh water, the rivers, lakes, and lagoons, and of all things beautiful.

Chango is the god of thunder and lightning, drums and dance, and is a great warrior king filled with virility, strength, and sexuality.

Communication with the Orishas

Communication with the orishas occurs through *Ifa* or ceremonial possession.

Ita is the practice of divination used by santeros, that employs sixteen cowry shells, thrown repeatedly. Each time they are thrown the number of shells landing "mouth down" or "mouth up" is noted. This is called a number, sign, or letter, each of which has a traditional story or saying associated with it. In this manner the santero or santera contacts an orisha, then brings their message to the petitioner. When they are first initiated, newcomers will receive Ita to divine their past, present, and future and suggest best how to play the cards life has dealt them in order to influence outcomes and fulfill their destiny.

During a Santería ceremony, orishas visit through possession of an initiate. The initiate dances in motions that symbolize the orisha, such as the undulating wave-like movements of Yemaya. Possession is seen as proof that an orisha is present at the ceremony.

Santería ceremonies feature the use of several kinds of percussion instruments that perform specific rhythms for specific orishas. For the most sacred rituals the *bata*, a set of three hourglass-shaped drums, are played. *Bembe* drums and *shekeres* (gourd shakers) are used for other, less sacred ceremonies.

Initiation

Often children learn Santería songs, dances, rhythms and rituals in their home. But while families can pass on much of the traditional knowledge, the process of initiation into Santería is an intense one involving many ceremonies over a long period of time.

Initially people join a *casa de santos* after showing an affinity or connection to a particular orisha. Here they

would receive a beaded necklace in the color particular to their orisha or patron saint. Wearing that necklace, the person is considered "marked" by their orisha. While many people are happy to be part of a spiritual house and to have a patron saint, there are some who choose to undergo a long and involved process in order to become an initiate, entering into the realm of sacred teachings that would eventually make them a santero or santera.

For detailed information on the steps and ceremonies taken to become a *Santero* visit: www.orishanet.org/initiate.html

Santería Survival

Cuba is facing rapid change and growth, affected by factors like the fall of Russian Communism and the disappearance of their primary trading partner; increased trade with neighboring South American countries; an increase in free market economic activity within the country; a gradual liberalization of politics and society;

and the opportunity for Cuban Nationals from the United States to visit Cuba.

While Cuba seems to be emerging from over fifty years of social isolation, the movement is slow and cautious. While many people, and countries, wonder what direction Cuba will go in after the death of Fidel Castro, one thing is for sure. The Cuban people are survivors, and like their ancestors the Yoruban slaves, they know what to protect, to teach, and to pass on to the generations to come. The traditional knowledge and practices of Santería will continue to flourish in Cuba, and in any country where Cubans live.

In my travels to Cuba (seven times in the past ten years), I have seen slow and gradual changes taking place. Where once there was no free enterprise, now there are artists and farmers selling their wares along the roadside. But underneath this window dressing, there is something that has not changed. Regardless of the political or economic climate of their country, Cubans continue to ensure that what matters most to them will survive.

I have seen the Ashe (life force) of the Cuban people, and it cannot be enslaved or oppressed. Like their sacred Santería, what matters most to the average Cuban is what is at the heart of Santería—life force, the ancestors, their families and communities, and the ceremonies that affirm, bless, and raise the life force within the community.

Viva Santería survival.

Pagan Home Libraries

by Blake Octavian Blair

Pagans and magickal folk are well-known as book lovers. This isn't at all surprising, as books are magickal objects with their own mystique in and of themselves. A first glance upon entering any devoted Pagan's home will usually result in seeing at least several dozen volumes. And more tomes generally reside throughout the home. Books about basic witchcraft and tarot are almost a given, but usually you'll find an array of topics including Buddhism, hoodoo, ceremonial magick, incense making, encyclopedias, gardening, classical literature, romance novels—anything that piques the owner's interest. Many Pagans undoubtedly possess what we'd accurately term to be home libraries. And for the well-versed and well-read Pagan, a well-stocked, organized, and accessible library can enhance your practice. Organization is especially important if more than one person regularly uses the home library. In fact, the practicality and the joy of a Pagan home library can by extension lead to reading circles, book clubs, and coven libraries. So let's take a stroll through the stacks and explore the possibilities for Pagan home libraries, shall we?

Most Pagans have a wide variety of interests and often have a very pluralistic spiritual worldview. This is reflected in their book collections. If books are a particular passion, the number of them in your home can escalate quite rapidly. While this is not necessarily a bad thing, you're going to need to develop a method of organization and storage. The last thing you want is to need a quick answer on what herb to use for an emergency, spur of the moment spell and have to dig through a pile of books on auras and Greek mythology to find your copy of *Cunningham's Encyclopedia of Magical Herbs*.

Organizing Methods

There are a few options for small- to moderate-sized home libraries. One option is to group books by subject, for example all the divination books together, all your shamanism books together, herbalism together, etc. This can serve as a practical way to locate certain information if you do not have a specific book in mind. You could further choose to subdivide within the topic categories by author name. For example, my herb-related books by Scott Cunningham are shelved together in my herb and plant magick section, but my copy of *The Magical Household* by Cunningham and Harrington is shelved in a separate section related to hearth, home, and cottage witchery. For books that are part of a series, it might make sense logically to group them together. However, some feel that a disadvantage to this system is breaking up the works of a particular and/or prolific author. For example, if you remember that you read something by Christopher Penczak regarding working with archangels for a particular purpose but you cannot recall the title, you may have to search several areas to locate the information. Despite the possible cons, grouping books by subject is popular and is my preferred method for organizing my own growing magickal home library.

Another option is to simply organize by author name. Some practitioners prefer this method, especially if they know the title and author of a specific book they have in mind. This system eliminates any confusion regarding where to shelve books that could fit into more than one subject category. If you want to find more information on an angelic name that came to you during a meditation and you know that you want to check your copy of Richard Webster's *Encyclopedia of Angels*, you can head to the "W" shelf and then to Webster and, voilà. The downside, of course, is that if you are doing general research and browsing a topic for ideas and not specific answers, you now have to pick through several areas to pull all the books you may need.

When one's home library approaches the larger end of the spectrum, many believe it's time for a cataloging method. There are a few ways to do this. One is to create a physical card catalog This is done with a stack of index cards and a recipe box and then affixing a corresponding label to the spine of each book. You will want to create your own version of how to arrange and label the books, so each book will have an officially assigned "home position," and you can use the cards in the recipe box to locate it. Of course, in our technological age, software programs can create a digital database. My husband and I are beginning to catalog our books and experiment with such a program for our own home library. You can even purchase a bar-code scanner that will instantly upload information about your books such as price, publisher, ISBN, author, and even a short description into the program and allow you to enter its physical location in your library!

Grow Your Library

You might be wondering how you can begin growing your own Pagan home library on a budget. In hard economic times, books remain a wonderful investment toward both entertainment and education, but they do indeed still cost money. While I may be biased, please remember that when you spend your hard-earned money on Pagan-related books you are supporting your favorite authors and allowing them to continue writing, which in turn benefits the Pagan community at large. However, I'd now like to share a few creative and affordable ways to obtain volumes for your library. One is to check out the metaphysical section at your

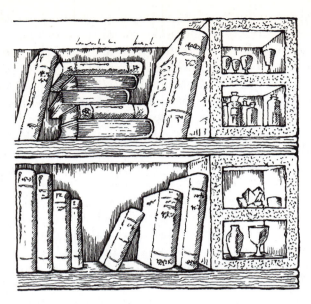

local used bookstore. (I always recommend trying to support small locally owned businesses!) Take a trip around the sale and remainder tables and you may be surprised what you can find, including rare out-of-print titles at amazingly low prices. Don't rule out digging through book piles at thrift stores and yard sales, as there are hidden treasures to be found. Lastly, don't forget to visit your favorite publishers online; Llewellyn's website allows you to sign up for e-mail newsletters on new titles and sales alerts. Take advantage of these frequent sales and deals to broaden the scope of your library at a discounted cost!

Once you begin to amass a number of books, your thoughts will soon turn to where to put them all. Commercially available bookcases from department stores are often affordable but are usually made of low-quality particleboard and are not of great long-term durability. Quality bookcases made of real wood are quite expensive, making owning even a couple of them a pricey affair. The solution relies upon creativity! My husband and I took a trip to a home-improvement warehouse store shortly after moving into our current apartment. We bought the materials to make several custom bookcases out of cinder blocks and white-wood boards. The key to turning these primitive dorm-reminiscent materials into stylish bookcases lies in a few overlooked tips. First, for durability sake, select solid wooden boards for shelves rather than plywood, which will warp and sag in short order. The next secret is to buy latex paint to coat your cinder blocks. The paint not only fills in and smooths out the slightly rough porous blocks, it gives you a nice finished product that can match your décor! (You may choose to paint or stain your boards depending upon your tastes.) We went with forest green for the blocks for our bedroom bookcase and black for the office and living room. We receive many compliments on our ultra-affordable bookcases. They actually look quite polished and have a sort of industrial-chic feel. Furthermore, we spent less than $200 in supplies to produce about 70 linear feet of bookshelves—pretty magickal in itself! Other affordable options include milk and file crates turned on their side, thrift store finds, yard sales, Craigslist, and used furniture stores.

Enhance the Space

A library should be inviting—like a classic old reading room. Many people like to use their library areas to display artwork, statuary, and crystals. Whether you concentrate your library in one area or you spread it throughout your home (like mine), this lends a wonderfully magickal ambiance to your environment. With mindful selection of the items, the décor can energetically assist you in your studies. One perk to our affordable block-and-board bookcases is that the cinder block's cubbyholes provide a great place to display such items. In fact, we have a Shiva shrine in one cubby of our office bookcase. Statues and art of deities relating to knowledge, academics, writing, and the written word, as well as patrons of members of the household are excellent choices to display in your library. Furthermore, spare ritual tools such as chalices, extra candlesticks, and wands can make artful display items. The décor would not be complete without at least a few crystals to boost the studious vibes of the space. Citrine for retention of intellectual information, apatite for stimulating creativity, or perhaps one of my personal favorites—fluorite for processing information and preventing disorganization. Make your space inviting—it can have a library meets gallery feel. Do not forget to add a comfortable place to sit and read!

Sharing the Wealth

The magickal book lover will undoubtedly love to share great reads with their comrades. Forming a magickal book club or study group is a great way to do so. These groups can range from just a few close likeminded friends, your circle or coven, or even take place on a greater community scale. Starting out smaller is usually better. Have an initial meeting to discuss what books to read and develop a reading timeline and meeting schedule. You might try meeting on New Moons or perhaps near each sabbat. Whatever is decided upon should be convenient and work for all participants. For a simple book discussion group, choose a book that can be read straight through and make sure any exercises can be easily completed in a solitary setting. Books with multiple exercises, meditations, or group work are better suited for the study group because they will require more meetings at closer intervals to practice and experience the exercises together. In either situation, when multiple copies of a book are necessary, for ease of acquisition it is best to stick with titles that are currently in print. A beneficial side effect to these types of social gatherings is that they also lend themselves extremely well to potlucks and finger foods! Remember, this should be an enjoyable experience.

Leaders of a coven or organized circle may find themselves thinking about creating a coven library. Effectively, this opens the library to group members for education, study, and research by allowing them to "check out" and take home books. With this arrangement arises an obligatory mention of a few important

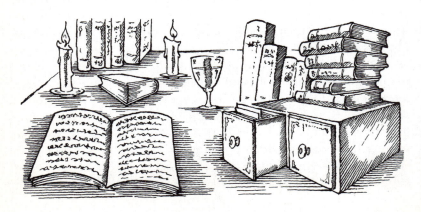

points. First, a cataloging system that also allows you to keep track of who has what book becomes mandatory. The second point stems from the first—magickal books have a habit of not finding their way home. Take a poll among your magickal friends about who has lent or borrowed a magick-related book with the best of intentions only to never see it return. A self-depleting library is not a pleasant occurrence to deal with. So you will have to set up and make clear a set of lending terms that your group can agree upon. A properly managed coven library can be a wonderful resource. You always have the option of taking the approach that I have to lending magick-related books: I don't. I tell my friends that my library is like the reference floor at the public library— you can browse and read all you want at my home, but the book isn't leaving with you! They usually understand, and it provides a nice occasion for a cup of tea with a friend while they are visiting. If there are a couple books in particular you frequently recommend to people, another approach you might consider is keeping a few inexpensive used copies that you can give out and not worry about their return.

E-books

With advancing technology I would be remiss not to mention a bit about electronic books (e-books) and some of the pros and cons when compared to hard copy versions. I will be the first to admit that I far prefer hard copy books over e-books. For me, nothing replaces the sheer character of a physical volume or the sensory experience of reading a physical book—the touch, the smell, the feel of the paper and cover in your hands. The energy the tome emits simply sitting in your library awaiting your eager perusal. Additionally, for research I like being able to have several books open side by side while I am working. Personal opinions aside, e-books do have some unique benefits that add to the reading experience. They are virtually weightless and thousands of books can be stored on a single device, making it appealing for travel. They also often have hyperlinks for cross-referencing, and the text is searchable for certain words or phrases, making for the speedy location of facts and informational tidbits. In the end, the hard copy vs. e-book debate amounts to personal preference. I suspect the future safely holds a place for both.

A Pagan home library is an invaluable resource. Aside from the importance of having books on hand you will need to reference often or relate to a specialized interest you may have, another reason to have a diverse and well-stocked Pagan home library is that public libraries often lack books in our particular fields of interest. While it is unfortunate that many public libraries in more conservative areas will not stock books related to Pagan or occult topics, it is important to know that this isn't always the reason their metaphysical section might be thin. Many libraries attempt to stock these topics but have trouble preventing the books from turning up missing either due to delinquent borrowers or people committing theft to prevent the library from stocking books of their nature. However, you can always request a title via interlibrary loan or ask that they order a title to add to their collection—especially if you don't feel you would reference the book often enough to merit purchase.

So whether you're a bargain-book shopper, an e-reader, or avid researcher looking for the next tome for your collection, hopefully you are well on your way to assembling your Pagan home library. Take a stroll through your stacks, pick an enchanting volume, sit in your favorite comfy spot, and enjoy a good read!

For Further Study
Hall, Judy. *The Crystal Bible: A Definitive Guide to Crystals.* Cincinnati, OH: Walking Stick Press, 2003.

Epstein, Edward. "U.S. Libraries Checking Out Book Theft/'Most-Stolen' List Will Help Curb Crime." SFGate. http://articles.sfgate.com/2001-05-15/news/17597485_1_libraries-books-gay-issues (accessed August 23, 2011).

Gonfalons:
Show Your I.D. Proudly

by Emyme

From ancient times to present day, like-minded people band together. Conversely, from ancient times to present day, individuals appreciate recognition of their uniqueness. For protection and out of pride, it was, and continues to be, necessary to identify a community or individual to the world, other communities, or other individuals. In addition to our names, tribes and clans create physical manifestations of their origin, history, strengths, purpose, education, or goal(s). The symbols and form chosen are infinitely varied. Just two examples are the tartan fabrics of Scotland and the totem poles of Native Americans, ancient identifications that carry on through hundreds of years.

In medieval Italy, neighborhoods were identified by flags. Community meetings were known as *gonfaloni*, and the name of the banners evolved into *gonfalon* or *gonfalone*. Constructed of cloth, gonfalon were painted or embroidered with the symbols of the community. The top was attached to a crossbar at the end of a long pole, the bottom was swallow-tailed or hung with streamers. These banners were carried at the front of processions and displayed at community gatherings. Symbolism, ceremony, and ritual being cornerstones of the overall Pagan belief system, a gonfalon is an innovative way to represent your particular corner of the Wiccan world. The following are just a few ways in which to use a gonfalon—adapt them as you wish.

Coven

You gather for sabbats and full moon rituals. You convene to celebrate handfastings, welcome newborns, cleanse and bless homes and vehicles, and assist members with personal issues. You perform community service and disseminate local and world news and information as it relates to your group. The creation of the standard by which your coven is known is a worthy project for any coven—be it newly formed, well established, or transitioning.

Whatever your chosen school of belief—Faerie Tradition or British Traditional or Stregheria, to name just a few—it is helpful to be identified when you meet with other covens. You may go simple and uncomplicated with two symbols on a field of color divided diagonally. Or you can choose a more traditional style of meaningful symbols presented in the quarters of a coat of arms. Alternatively, this may be the time for intricate detail—your group motto embroidered in metallic thread, a characterized history of the coven formation in stick figures, or a dazzling fabric portrait of your patron god or goddess. Consider trimming the borders with the group motto and/or commemorative dates. Covens can be fluid in membership and leadership roles. Removable streamers pinned from the bottom hem can be rearranged as needed. In this fashion, each member has the opportunity to participate in the formation of the banner by creating their own representative streamer, thereby adding ever-changing and unique personality to the permanent flag.

Solitary

You have read every book you can find. You have researched the Internet until your eyes blur. You have purchased ingredients from local (and not so local) herb and health-food shops. You have written spells and performed castings in the quiet of your sacred space, drawn down the moon and worshipped the sun, read the cards, discovered your spirit animal, and created your magickal name. In or out of the broom closet—after years of self-training or perhaps only the requisite year and a day—you find yourself ready to move on and solidify your standing as a solitary Wiccan. A gonfalon is one object, one physical talisman, of your hard work; a symbol of "graduation," so to speak.

If you are an herbal or garden Witch, you may wish to include a pot of herbs or a favorite flower on your banner. On the other side of a diagonal line, place a silhouette of your spirit animal.

Another design idea may incorporate a shield, similar to a coat of arms, divided into three or more sections. This allows you to include more characters: possibly some combination of flora and fauna that call to you, a rune and/or glyph, and your chosen god or goddess. As in the coven gonfalon, feel free to be as minimal or highly crafted as you wish. Using fabrics and trim that hold special meaning for you, your magical name above, in any language and size you deem appropriate—and you have a fitting representation of your journey.

For those of you who may be concerned about your degree of fabric artistry talent—do not despair. Seek out local craft and fabric shops and inquire after their class schedule. If sewing is not for you, consider fabric paints, or iron-on letters and patches. Sequins, jewels, beads, feathers … trim options are vast. There are a variety of fabric glues available—hot and cold. Quite literally, a banner can be created without using one stitch of thread. Most covens are blessed with at least one seamstress or tailor. Those fabric artists need no further instructions, just direction. And of course, all the previous nonsewing ideas can be intertwined with traditional needlework. Especially in the case of individual streamers, fabric craft may need to be less thread-specific.

~

Flags fly from crossbars at renaissance fairs. Multicolored and ornate, the ends swallow-tailed or decorated with streamers, they are carried in processions and hang outside shop entrances. Banners wave in the great hall. Tasseled or fringed: lion, snake, badger, and eagle—since 1997 these representations of four school houses play a part in the books and movies about Witches and wizards coming of age in the United Kingdom. At scout camps and jamborees, banners are staked in front of the cabins of each troop. At college gradation ceremonies, they denote the school from which a diploma is received. At meetings of civic clubs and organizations whose intention is to accomplish good deeds, flags stand next to the podium. At the kitchen door of a solitary Hedge Witch, at the entrance to a coven's sacred space—gonfalons readily identify history and purpose to others. A medieval symbol of community and identity, reinvented and brought into our modern times, a gonfalon is an imaginative way to honor Pagan beliefs.

Magick in Your Toolbox

by Melanie Marquis

Do potpourri and scented candles leave you feeling a bit ... fluffy? When we're not in tune with the implements used to carry out our spellwork, the magick suffers. If you want your spells to work their best, finding methods and mediums that suit your own unique spirit and personality is crucial. So too is mastering the art of versatility, learning new ways to cast familiar magick. When we try out different techniques, our skill set expands and we give ourselves the opportunity to discover the full range of our abilities. Whether it's experimenting with an atypical ritual format or using a blade of grass instead of a wand, such experiences boost our creativity and our magickal

power as we find out firsthand what works for us and what doesn't. Such a sentiment led me one day to a hypothesis: if we can cast spells with magickal tools, perhaps we can work equal magick with regular, everyday tools, too. So I picked up a hammer, some nails, and a few pieces of scrap wood, and I began the process of building a whole new style of magickal technique. I'm not much of a carpenter myself; I'm hoping for woodworking enthusiasts with greater talents than I to take these ideas and run with them, expanding on the basics and illuminating additional ideas and methods through experimentation, intuition, and good old trial and error. I've hammered out the basics to get you started; brush up on your woodworking safety, grab your toolbox, and get ready for something different.

The Hammer

A hammer and nail can be used effectively to magickally join, bind, and fuse two energies together. Such a technique

is desirable when you wish for the energies and elements involved to be brought together while remaining virtually intact and unchanged. Reuniting estranged friends, manifesting a positive collaboration, or simply bringing new resources to the table are a few examples of magickal goals one might accomplish with this simple form of toolbox magick.

Choose two pieces of wood to symbolize the energies you wish to unite.

You might select a different type of wood for each component, using mahogany as a symbol of wealth, for instance, or choosing oak as a symbol of strength. If you prefer, the wood can be infused with your intentions through the use of glyphs, words, or oils, or through the straightforward process of energy transference from mind into matter, simply thinking of the symbolic link you wish to create and sending this feeling out through your palm, fingertips, or wand point and into the object.

Once the wood is prepared, each piece now representing one of the energies you aim to bring together, select a nail that is long and sturdy enough to hammer completely through both pieces. Infuse the nail with an energy of love, success, strength, or unity—use a permanent marker to create an appropriate glyph on the nail head to infuse it with the desired essence. Stack the two pieces of wood and hammer the nail into the center, visualizing the energies coming closer together with each blow.

The Screwdriver

The screwdriver is another handy tool to use in your spellwork. Try this technique the next time you have a need for a little extra magick in your life. You'll need a small piece of wood (scrap wood is fine), a screwdriver, and a screw. Although a flat head screwdriver works just fine, I personally favor the Phillips head screwdriver because the "X" shaped head can symbolize the four elements, the four directions, and the convergence and cooperation of these magickal forces.

This type of spellwork operates on the principle of insertion—by introducing a new energetic vibration into the situation at hand, transformation occurs as existing energies adjust to match the pattern of the new energy inserted by the magick. First, charm the wood. Draw or write on the wood pictures or words to represent the current situation that you would like to change. For example, you might write the word "unemployed," or draw a glyph of a broken heart—whatever you feel best matches your situation. If you like, rub the wood with appropriate essential oils, potions, or herbs to strengthen the symbolism. Next, enchant the screw. Hold it in your hands and visualize and feel the essence of the energy you wish to insert into your life, be it more money, true romance, or greater happiness. Send this energy into the screw and "name" it through the process of magickal identification to complete the enchantment: make an assertive statement that affirms the screw's new identity. For example, if it's a job you're after, you would hold the screw in your hands while visualizing and experiencing the feeling of employment, then after sending this energy into the screw, you might say, "This is no longer a screw. This is a job." It's not enough to think of the screw as merely *representing* the thing you desire; for your spell to have maximum impact,

the screw needs to actually *become* your desire through the process of magickal identification. Anoint the screw with oils or potions appropriate to your goal to add more power to the charm. Now all that's left to do is the spell itself: insert the screw into the wood while imagining the new energy infusing and changing your situation with each turn of the screwdriver. The spell complete once the screw is firmly in place, keep your creation intact until your wish is fulfilled.

The Rasp

When you have a need for magick to dissolve negativity or diminish misfortune, pull out your rasp and try this spell to file away your woes. Using a marker or pencil, decorate a piece of wood with an appropriate symbolic representation of the energies you wish to banish. If you prefer subtlety, empower some wood stain to match the ill fate you want to escape, and use this to color the wood. Once the wood is thus enchanted, hold the rasp in your hands and think of your own personal power, your ability to take charge and set your own standards of what is and isn't acceptable in your life. Fill the rasp with your power, and if you like, call on divine energies and elemental forces to enter the tool and help along your spell. Now rub the rasp back and forth across the wood, scraping away the symbolized bane. Once the pictures, words, or wood stain is completely filed away and no longer visible, the spell is complete. Throw away the shavings and reuse the wood if possible.

The Level

Are there areas of imbalance in your life? Too much work and no play, or too much play and no work, can be disorienting and taxing on our magickal abilities. To regain your natural balance and reclaim your power, try this handy spell that makes use of a level to put things back on the level. You'll also need a picture frame and a piece of paper sized to fit. Draw a line down the center of the paper. On one side, create a list of all the excesses currently plaguing your life, and on the other side, write down all the things you wish you had a little more of, be it time, peace, or playfulness. Place the paper in the frame and hang it on the wall. Step back from the picture and place the level on the flat of your palm. Take a moment to envision your life in perfect balance and harmony. Shift your gaze between the picture and the level. As soon as the level is balanced and your visualizations are clear, place the tool on the top edge of the picture frame. Carefully adjust the tilt of the picture until the level indicates perfect balance. Leave the picture and the level in place for a week or so while the spell takes effect and you adjust to a new routine. Where logical changes in habits back powerful magickal actions, a more harmonious existence is quick to follow.

Blueprint for the Future

Now that you've explored the basics, challenge yourself to take this new form of magick even farther. Try creating whole projects with your toolbox magick; you might build a piece of furniture or even an entire house to encapsulate and cast your spell. Come up with ways to use other tools in your spellwork. How might a drill be used for magick? What about a saw, or a wrench? Your magick doesn't have to be limited to the traditional tools and trappings. The power of the Witch comes from within the heart of Nature, and it is not the tools we use, so much as it is the truths we weave.

Almanac Section

Calendar

Time Changes

Lunar Phases

Moon Signs

Full Moons

Sabbats

World Holidays

Incense of the Day

Color of the Day

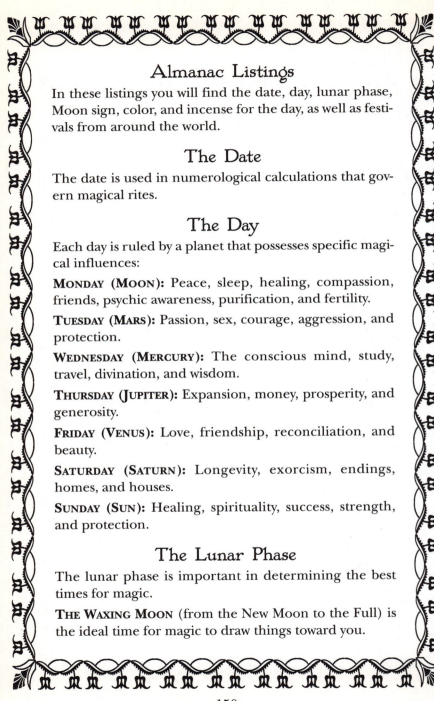

Almanac Listings

In these listings you will find the date, day, lunar phase, Moon sign, color, and incense for the day, as well as festivals from around the world.

The Date

The date is used in numerological calculations that govern magical rites.

The Day

Each day is ruled by a planet that possesses specific magical influences:

MONDAY (MOON): Peace, sleep, healing, compassion, friends, psychic awareness, purification, and fertility.

TUESDAY (MARS): Passion, sex, courage, aggression, and protection.

WEDNESDAY (MERCURY): The conscious mind, study, travel, divination, and wisdom.

THURSDAY (JUPITER): Expansion, money, prosperity, and generosity.

FRIDAY (VENUS): Love, friendship, reconciliation, and beauty.

SATURDAY (SATURN): Longevity, exorcism, endings, homes, and houses.

SUNDAY (SUN): Healing, spirituality, success, strength, and protection.

The Lunar Phase

The lunar phase is important in determining the best times for magic.

THE WAXING MOON (from the New Moon to the Full) is the ideal time for magic to draw things toward you.

THE FULL MOON is the time of greatest power.

THE WANING MOON (from the Full Moon to the New) is a time for study, meditation, and little magical work (except magic designed to banish harmful energies).

The Moon's Sign

The Moon continuously "moves" through the zodiac, from Aries to Pisces. Each sign possesses its own significance.

ARIES: Good for starting things, but lacks staying power. Things occur rapidly, but quickly pass. People tend to be argumentative and assertive.

TAURUS: Things begun now last the longest, tend to increase in value, and become hard to alter. Brings out appreciation for beauty and sensory experience.

GEMINI: Things begun now are easily changed by outside influence. Time for shortcuts, communication, games, and fun.

CANCER: Stimulates emotional rapport between people. Pinpoints need, supports growth and nurturance. Tends to domestic concerns.

LEO: Draws emphasis to the self, central ideas, or institutions, away from connections with others and other emotional needs. People tend to be melodramatic.

VIRGO: Favors accomplishment of details and commands from higher up. Focuses on health, hygiene, and daily schedules.

LIBRA: Favors cooperation, social activities, beautification of surroundings, balance, and partnership.

SCORPIO: Increases awareness of psychic power. Precipitates psychic crises and ends connections thoroughly. People tend to brood and become secretive.

Sagittarius: Encourages flights of imagination and confidence. This is an adventurous, philosophical, and athletic Moon sign. Favors expansion and growth.

Capricorn: Develops strong structure. Focus on traditions, responsibilities, and obligations. A good time to set boundaries and rules.

Aquarius: Rebellious energy. Time to break habits and make abrupt changes. Personal freedom and individuality is the focus.

Pisces: The focus is on dreaming, nostalgia, intuition, and psychic impressions. A good time for spiritual or philanthropic activities.

Color and Incense

The color and incense for the day are based on information from *Personal Alchemy* by Amber Wolfe, and relate to the planet that rules each day. This information can be taken into consideration along with other factors when planning works of magic or when blending magic into mundane life. Please note that the incense selections listed are not hard and fast. If you cannot find or do not like the incense listed for the day, choose a similar scent that appeals to you.

Festivals and Holidays

Festivals are listed throughout the year. The exact dates of many of these ancient festivals are difficult to determine; prevailing data has been used.

Time Changes

The times and dates of all astrological phenomena in this almanac are based on **Eastern Standard Time (EST)**. If you live outside of the Eastern time zone, you will need to make the following changes:

PACIFIC STANDARD TIME: Subtract three hours.

MOUNTAIN STANDARD TIME: Subtract two hours.

CENTRAL STANDARD TIME: Subtract one hour.

ALASKA: Subtract four hours.

HAWAII: Subtract five hours.

DAYLIGHT SAVING TIME (ALL ZONES): Add one hour.

Daylight Saving Time begins at 2 am on March 10, 2013, and ends at 2 am on November 3, 2013.

Please refer to a world time zone resource for time adjustments for locations outside the United States.

2013 Sabbats and Full Moons

January 26	Leo Full Moon 11:38 pm
February 2	Imbolc
February 25	Virgo Full Moon 3:26 pm
March 27	Libra Full Moon 5:27 am
March 20	Ostara (Spring Equinox)
April 25	Scorpio Full Moon 3:57 pm
May 1	Beltane
May 25	Sagittarius Full Moon 12:25 am
June 23	Capricorn Full Moon 7:32 am
June 20	Midsummer (Summer Solstice)
July 22	Aquarius Full Moon 2:16 pm
August 1	Lammas
August 20	Aquarius Full Moon 9:45 pm
September 19	Pisces Full Moon 7:13 am
September 22	Mabon (Fall Equinox)
October 18	Aries Full Moon 7:38 pm
October 31	Samhain
November 17	Taurus Full Moon 10:16 am
December 17	Gemini Full Moon 4:28 am
December 21	Yule (Winter Solstice)

*All times are Eastern Standard Time (EST)
or Eastern Daylight Time (EDT)*

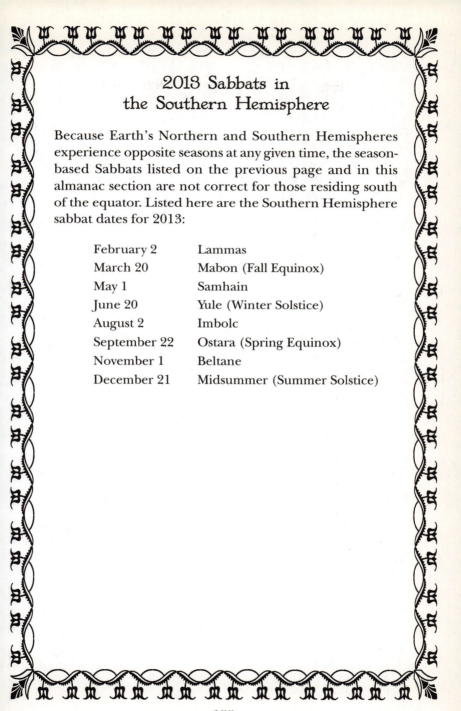

2013 Sabbats in the Southern Hemisphere

Because Earth's Northern and Southern Hemispheres experience opposite seasons at any given time, the season-based Sabbats listed on the previous page and in this almanac section are not correct for those residing south of the equator. Listed here are the Southern Hemisphere sabbat dates for 2013:

February 2	Lammas
March 20	Mabon (Fall Equinox)
May 1	Samhain
June 20	Yule (Winter Solstice)
August 2	Imbolc
September 22	Ostara (Spring Equinox)
November 1	Beltane
December 21	Midsummer (Summer Solstice)

January

1

Tuesday

New Year's Day • Kwanzaa ends
Waning Moon
Moon phase: Third Quarter 1:15 am
Color: Red

Moon Sign: Leo
Moon enters Virgo 12:35 pm
Incense: Cinnamon

2

Wednesday

First Writing Day (Japanese)
Waning Moon
Moon phase: Third Quarter
Color: Brown

Moon Sign: Virgo
Incense: Lilac

3

Thursday

St. Genevieve's Day
Waning Moon
Moon phase: Third Quarter
Color: Purple

Moon Sign: Virgo
Moon enters Libra 8:11 pm
Incense: Balsam

4

Friday

Frost Fairs on the Thames
Waning Moon
Moon phase: Fourth Quarter 10:58 pm
Color: White

Moon Sign: Libra
Incense: Thyme

5

Saturday

Epiphany Eve
Waning Moon
Moon phase: Fourth Quarter
Color: Gray

Moon Sign: Libra
Incense: Ivy

6

Sunday

Epiphany
Waning Moon
Moon phase: Fourth Quarter
Color: Gold

Moon Sign: Libra
Moon enters Scorpio 1:09 am
Incense: Hyacinth

7

Monday

Rizdvo (Ukrainian)
Waning Moon
Moon phase: Fourth Quarter
Color: Gray

Moon Sign: Scorpio
Incense: Rosemary

January

8 **Tuesday**
Midwives' Day
Waning Moon
Moon phase: Fourth Quarter
Color: Black

Moon Sign: Scorpio
Moon enters Sagittarius 3:28 am
Incense: Ginger

9 **Wednesday**
Feast of the Black Nazarene (Filipino)
Waning Moon
Moon phase: Fourth Quarter
Color: White

Moon Sign: Sagittarius
Incense: Honeysuckle

10 **Thursday**
Business God's Day (Japanese)
Waning Moon
Moon phase: Fourth Quarter
Color: Purple

Moon Sign: Sagittarius
Moon enters Capricorn 3:54 am
Incense: Myrrh

☽ **Friday**
Carmentalia (Roman)
Waning Moon
Moon phase: New Moon 2:44 pm
Color: Rose

Moon Sign: Capricorn
Incense: Violet

12 **Saturday**
Revolution Day (Tanzanian)
Waxing Moon
Moon phase: First Quarter
Color: Black

Moon Sign: Capricorn
Moon enters Aquarius 4:01 am
Incense: Rue

13 **Sunday**
Twentieth Day (Norwegian)
Waxing Moon
Moon phase: First Quarter
Color: Yellow

Moon Sign: Aquarius
Incense: Almond

14 **Monday**
Feast of the Ass (French)
Waxing Moon
Moon phase: First Quarter
Color: Lavender

Moon Sign: Aquarius
Moon enters Pisces 5:49 am
Incense: Narcissus

15 Tuesday
Birthday of Martin Luther King, Jr. (actual)
Waxing Moon
Moon phase: First Quarter
Color: Gray

Moon Sign: Pisces
Incense: Ylang-ylang

---

16 Wednesday
Apprentices's Day
Waxing Moon
Moon phase: First Quarter 4:08 am
Color: Brown

Moon Sign: Pisces
Moon enters Aries 11:07 am
Incense: Marjoram

---

17 Thursday
St. Anthony's Day (Mexican)
Waxing Moon
Moon phase: First Quarter
Color: Turquoise

Moon Sign: Aries
Incense: Carnation

◖ Friday
Assumption Day
Waxing Moon
Moon phase: Second Quarter 6:45 pm
Color: Purple

Moon Sign: Aries
Moon enters Taurus 8:36 pm
Incense: Vanilla

---

19 Saturday
Kitchen God Feast (Chinese)
Waxing Moon
Moon phase: Second Quarter
Color: Brown

Moon Sign: Taurus
Sun enters Aquarius 4:52 pm
Incense: Sage

---

20 Sunday
Inauguration Day
Waxing Moon
Moon phase: Second Quarter
Color: Orange

Moon Sign: Taurus
Incense: Marigold

---

21 Monday
Birthday of Martin Luther King, Jr. (observed)
Waxing Moon
Moon phase: Second Quarter
Color: White

Moon Sign: Taurus
Moon enters Gemini 9:04 am
Incense: Hyssop

January

22 Tuesday
Saint Vincent's Day (French)
Waxing Moon
Moon phase: Second Quarter
Color: Red

Moon Sign: Gemini
Incense: Basil

23 Wednesday
St. Ildefonso's Day (French)
Waxing Moon
Moon phase: Second Quarter
Color: Topaz

Moon Sign: Gemini
Moon enters Cancer 10:00 pm
Incense: Lavender

24 Thursday
Alasitas Fair (Bolivian)
Waxing Moon
Moon phase: Second Quarter
Color: Crimson

Moon Sign: Cancer
Incense: Mulberry

25 Friday
Burns' Night (Scottish)
Waxing Moon
Moon phase: Second Quarter
Color: Pink

Moon Sign: Cancer
Incense: Cypress

☺ Saturday
Republic Day (Indian)
Waxing Moon
Moon phase: Full Moon 11:38 pm
Color: Indigo

Moon Sign: Cancer
Moon enters Leo 9:20 am
Incense: Pine

27 Sunday
Vogelgruff (Swiss)
Waning Moon
Moon phase: Third Quarter
Color: Amber

Moon Sign: Leo
Incense: Heliotrope

28 Monday
St. Charlemange's Day
Waning Moon
Moon phase: Third Quarter
Color: Silver

Moon Sign: Leo
Moon enters Virgo 6:27 pm
Incense: Lily

29 **Tuesday**
Australia Day
Waning Moon
Moon phase: Third Quarter
Color: White

Moon Sign: Virgo
Incense: Cedar

---

30 **Wednesday**
Three Hierarchs Day (Eastern Orthodox)
Waning Moon
Moon phase: Third Quarter
Color: Yellow

Moon Sign: Virgo
Incense: Bay laurel

---

31 **Thursday**
Independence Day (Nauru)
Waning Moon
Moon phase: Third Quarter
Color: Green

Moon Sign: Virgo
Moon enters Libra 1:36 am
Incense: Clove

New Year, New Way

Tired of making New Year's resolutions only to break them? Try something new this year and make resolutions you'll actually enjoy keeping. Basing your goals on what you want to do rather than on what you don't want to do makes it easier to expect success, fueling your innate magical powers to transform yourself in big and bold ways. Instead of making a list of "don't"s, make a list of "do"s: activities you will try, actions you will take, goals and dreams you will pursue. Put your list in a special place in your home to act as a talisman to attract opportunity and promote success.

–Melanie Marquis

February

1   Friday
St. Brigid's Day (Irish)
Waning Moon
Moon phase: Third Quarter
Color: White

Moon Sign: Libra
Incense: Alder

---

2   Saturday
Imbolc • Groundhog Day
Waning Moon
Moon phase: Third Quarter
Color: Gray

Moon Sign: Libra
Moon enters Scorpio 7:02 am
Incense: Sandalwood

---

3   Sunday
St. Blaise's Day
Waning Moon
Moon phase: Fourth Quarter 8:56 am
Color: Orange

Moon Sign: Scorpio
Incense: Frankincense

---

4   Monday
Independence Day (Sri Lankan)
Waning Moon
Moon phase: Fourth Quarter
Color: Gray

Moon Sign: Scorpio
Moon enters Sagittarius 10:45 am
Incense: Neroli

---

5   Tuesday
Festival de la Alcaldesa (Italian)
Waning Moon
Moon phase: Fourth Quarter
Color: White

Moon Sign: Sagittarius
Incense: Geranium

---

6   Wednesday
Bob Marley's Birthday (Jamaican)
Waning Moon
Moon phase: Fourth Quarter
Color: Brown

Moon Sign: Sagittarius
Moon enters Capricorn 12:55 pm
Incense: Marjoram

---

7   Thursday
Full Moon Poya (Sri Lankan)
Waning Moon
Moon phase: Fourth Quarter
Color: Purple

Moon Sign: Capricorn
Incense: Apricot

February

8   **Friday**
Mass for Broken Needles (Japanese)
Waning Moon
Moon phase: Fourth Quarter
Color: Rose

Moon Sign: Capricorn
Moon enters Aquarius 2:16 pm
Incense: Orchid

---

9   **Saturday**
St. Marion's Day (Lebanese)
Waning Moon
Moon phase: Fourth Quarter
Color: Black

Moon Sign: Aquarius
Incense: Patchouli

---

10   **Sunday**
Chinese New Year (snake)
Waning Moon
Moon phase: New Moon 2:20 am
Color: Amber

Moon Sign: Aquarius
Moon enters Pisces 4:20 pm
Incense: Eucalyptus

---

11   **Monday**
Foundation Day (Japanese)
Waxing Moon
Moon phase: First Quarter
Color: White

Moon Sign: Pisces
Incense: Clary sage

---

12   **Tuesday**
Mardi Gras
Waxing Moon
Moon phase: First Quarter
Color: Red

Moon Sign: Pisces
Moon enters Aries 8:51 pm
Incense: Bayberry

---

13   **Wednesday**
Ash Wednesday
Waxing Moon
Moon phase: First Quarter
Color: Yellow

Moon Sign: Aries
Incense: Lavender

---

14   **Thursday**
Valentine's Day
Waxing Moon
Moon phase: First Quarter
Color: Green

Moon Sign: Aries
Incense: Jasmine

February

15 Friday
Lupercalia (Roman)
Waxing Moon
Moon phase: First Quarter
Color: Pink

Moon Sign: Aries
Moon enters Taurus 5:08 am
Incense: Yarrow

---

16 Saturday
Fumi-e (Japanese)
Waxing Moon
Moon phase: First Quarter
Color: Indigo

Moon Sign: Taurus
Incense: Magnolia

◐ Sunday
Quirinalia (Roman)
Waxing Moon
Moon phase: Second Quarter 3:31 pm
Color: Yellow

Moon Sign: Taurus
Moon enters Gemini 4:50 am
Incense: Juniper

---

18 Monday
Presidents' Day (observed)
Waxing Moon
Moon phase: Second Quarter
Color: Silver

Moon Sign: Gemini
Sun enters Pisces 7:02 am
Incense: Rosemary

---

19 Tuesday
Pero Palo's Trial (Spanish)
Waxing Moon
Moon phase: Second Quarter
Color: Maroon

Moon Sign: Gemini
Incense: Cedar

---

20 Wednesday
Installation of the New Lama (Tibetan)
Waxing Moon
Moon phase: Second Quarter
Color: Topaz

Moon Sign: Gemini
Moon enters Cancer 5:45 am
Incense: Bay laurel

---

21 Thursday
Feast of Lanterns (Chinese)
Waxing Moon
Moon phase: Second Quarter
Color: Crimson

Moon Sign: Cancer
Incense: Nutmeg

February

22 Friday
Caristia (Roman)
Waxing Moon
Moon phase: Second Quarter
Color: Coral

Moon Sign: Cancer
Moon enters Leo 5:12 pm
Incense: Mint

23 Saturday
Terminalia (Roman)
Waxing Moon
Moon phase: Second Quarter
Color: Brown

Moon Sign: Leo
Incense: Sage

24 Sunday
Purim
Waxing Moon
Moon phase: Second Quarter
Color: Gold

Moon Sign: Leo
Incense: Marigold

☺ Monday
Saint Walburga's Day (German)
Waxing Moon
Moon phase: Full Moon 3:26 pm
Color: Ivory

Moon Sign: Leo
Moon enters Virgo 1:52 am
Incense: Hyssop

26 Tuesday
Zamboanga Festival (Filipino)
Waning Moon
Moon phase: Third Quarter
Color: Black

Moon Sign: Virgo
Incense: Basil

27 Wednesday
Threepenny Day
Waning Moon
Moon phase: Third Quarter
Color: White

Moon Sign: Virgo
Moon enters Libra 8:02 am
Incense: Lilac

28 Thursday
Kalevala Day (Finnish)
Waning Moon
Moon phase: Third Quarter
Color: Purple

Moon Sign: Libra
Incense: Clove

March

1 Friday
Matronalia (Roman)
Waning Moon
Moon phase: Third Quarter
Color: Purple

Moon Sign: Libra
Moon enters Scorpio 12:33 pm
Incense: Rose

---

2 Saturday
St. Chad's Day (English)
Waning Moon
Moon phase: Third Quarter
Color: Gray

Moon Sign: Scorpio
Incense: Patchouli

---

3 Sunday
Doll Festival (Japanese)
Waning Moon
Moon phase: Third Quarter
Color: Yellow

Moon Sign: Scorpio
Moon enters Sagittarius 4:11 pm
Incense: Almond

◑ Monday
St. Casimir's Day (Polish)
Waning Moon
Moon phase: Fourth Quarter 4:53 pm
Color: Lavender

Moon Sign: Sagittarius
Incense: Neroli

---

5 Tuesday
Isis Festival (Roman)
Waning Moon
Moon phase: Fourth Quarter
Color: Gray

Moon Sign: Sagittarius
Moon enters Capricorn 7:14 pm
Incense: Cinnamon

---

6 Wednesday
Alamo Day
Waning Moon
Moon phase: Fourth Quarter
Color: Topaz

Moon Sign: Capricorn
Incense: Honeysuckle

---

7 Thursday
Bird and Arbor Day
Waning Moon
Moon phase: Fourth Quarter
Color: Turquoise

Moon Sign: Capricorn
Moon enters Aquarius 10:01 pm
Incense: Carnation

March

8 Friday
International Women's Day
Waning Moon
Moon phase: Fourth Quarter
Color: Rose

Moon Sign: Aquarius
Incense: Vanilla

---

9 Saturday
Forty Saints' Day
Waning Moon
Moon phase: Fourth Quarter
Color: Brown

Moon Sign: Aquarius
Incense: Rue

---

10 Sunday
Daylight Saving Time begins
Waning Moon
Moon phase: Fourth Quarter
Color: Orange

Moon Sign: Aquarius
Moon enters Pisces 1:19 am
Incense: Juniper

☽ Monday
Feast of the Gauri (Hindu)
Waning Moon
Moon phase: New Moon 3:51 pm
Color: White

Moon Sign: Pisces
Incense: Lily

---

12 Tuesday
Receiving the Water (Buddhist)
Waxing Moon
Moon phase: First Quarter
Color: Black

Moon Sign: Pisces
Moon enters Aries 7:17 am
Incense: Bayberry

---

13 Wednesday
Purification Feast (Balinese)
Waxing Moon
Moon phase: First Quarter
Color: Brown

Moon Sign: Aries
Incense: Lavender

---

14 Thursday
Mamuralia (Roman)
Waxing Moon
Moon phase: First Quarter
Color: Green

Moon Sign: Aries
Moon enters Taurus 3:08 pm
Incense: Myrrh

March

15 Friday
Phallus Festival (Japanese)
Waxing Moon
Moon phase: First Quarter
Color: Pink

Moon Sign: Taurus
Incense: Yarrow

16 Saturday
St. Urho's Day (Finnish)
Waxing Moon
Moon phase: First Quarter
Color: Black

Moon Sign: Taurus
Incense: Sandalwood

17 Sunday
St. Patrick's Day
Waxing Moon
Moon phase: First Quarter
Color: Gold

Moon Sign: Taurus
Moon enters Gemini 2:09 am
Incense: Hyacinth

18 Monday
Sheelah's Day (Irish)
Waxing Moon
Moon phase: First Quarter
Color: Gray

Moon Sign: Gemini
Incense: Narcissus

◑ Tuesday
St. Joseph's Day (Sicilian)
Waxing Moon
Moon phase: Second Quarter 1:27 pm
Color: Red

Moon Sign: Gemini
Moon enters Cancer 2:55 pm
Incense: Ylang-ylang

20 Wednesday
Ostara • Spring Equinox • Int'l Astrology Day
Waxing Moon
Moon phase: Second Quarter
Color: White

Moon Sign: Cancer
Sun enters Aries 7:02 am
Incense: Lilac

21 Thursday
Juarez Day (Mexican)
Waxing Moon
Moon phase: Second Quarter
Color: Purple

Moon Sign: Cancer
Incense: Balsam

March

22 **Friday**
Hilaria (Roman)
Waxing Moon
Moon phase: Second Quarter
Color: Coral

Moon Sign: Cancer
Moon enters Leo 2:50 am
Incense: Violet

---

23 **Saturday**
Pakistan Day
Waxing Moon
Moon phase: Second Quarter
Color: Blue

Moon Sign: Leo
Incense: Ivy

---

24 **Sunday**
Palm Sunday
Waxing Moon
Moon phase: Second Quarter
Color: Amber

Moon Sign: Leo
Moon enters Virgo 11:49 am
Incense: Frankincense

---

25 **Monday**
Tichborne Dole (English)
Waxing Moon
Moon phase: Second Quarter
Color: Silver

Moon Sign: Virgo
Incense: Rosemary

---

26 **Tuesday**
Passover begins
Waxing Moon
Moon phase: Second Quarter
Color: Maroon

Moon Sign: Virgo
Moon enters Libra 5:32 pm
Incense: Ginger

☺ **Wednesday**
Smell the Breezes Day (Egyptian)
Waxing Moon
Moon phase: Full Moon 5:27 am
Color: Yellow

Moon Sign: Libra
Incense: Marjoram

---

28 **Thursday**
Oranges and Lemons Service (English)
Waning Moon
Moon phase: Third Quarter
Color: Green

Moon Sign: Libra
Moon enters Scorpio 8:53 pm
Incense: Nutmeg

March

29 Friday
Good Friday
Waning Moon
Moon phase: Third Quarter
Color: White

Moon Sign: Scorpio
Incense: Orchid

30 Saturday
Seward's Day (Alaskan)
Waning Moon
Moon phase: Third Quarter
Color: Indigo

Moon Sign: Scorpio
Moon enters Sagittarius 11:13 pm
Incense: Pine

31 Sunday
Easter
Waning Moon
Moon phase: Third Quarter
Color: Yellow

Moon Sign: Sagittarius
Incense: Eucalyptus

Three's a Charm

It's widely known that carrying a four-leaf clover will bring good luck, but what can you do with all those three-leaf ones? This common botanical is not only edible, it's also magical. Three is a sacred number associated with the Moon and goddess energies, and three-leaf clovers are nearly as powerful as their rarer four-leaf siblings when it comes to bringing love, wealth, and good fortune. Add a few leaves to a salad or soup to promote success, or steep three dried flowers in water to create a tea to attract love. You can also use clover to ward off misfortune; just scatter the leaves or flowers around your home, car, and office.

–Melanie Marquis

April

♈

1   **Monday**
April Fools' Day
Waning Moon
Moon phase: Third Quarter
Color: White

Moon Sign: Sagittarius
Incense: Lily

---

2   **Tuesday**
Passover ends
Waning Moon
Moon phase: Third Quarter
Color: Black

Moon Sign: Sagittarius
Moon enters Capricorn 1:35 am
Incense: Geranium

---

3   **Wednesday**
Thirteenth Day (Iranian)
Waning Moon
Moon phase: Fourth Quarter 12:37 am
Color: Yellow

Moon Sign: Capricorn
Incense: Bay laurel

---

4   **Thursday**
Megalesia (Roman)
Waning Moon
Moon phase: Fourth Quarter
Color: Crimson

Moon Sign: Capricorn
Moon enters Aquarius 4:41 am
Incense: Jasmine

---

5   **Friday**
Tomb-Sweeping Day (Chinese)
Waning Moon
Moon phase: Fourth Quarter
Color: Rose

Moon Sign: Aquarius
Incense: Thyme

---

6   **Saturday**
Chakri Day (Thai)
Waning Moon
Moon phase: Fourth Quarter
Color: Blue

Moon Sign: Aquarius
Moon enters Pisces 9:00 am
Incense: Magnolia

---

7   **Sunday**
Festival of Pure Brightness (Chinese)
Waning Moon
Moon phase: Fourth Quarter
Color: Orange

Moon Sign: Pisces
Moon enters Scorpio 11:18 am
Incense: Heliotrope

April

♈

8 **Monday**
Buddha's Birthday
Waning Moon
Moon phase: Fourth Quarter
Color: Silver

Moon Sign: Pisces
Moon enters Aries 3:02 pm
Incense: Narcissus

9 **Tuesday**
Valour Day (Filipino)
Waning Moon
Moon phase: Fourth Quarter
Color: Maroon

Moon Sign: Aries
Incense: Bayberry

☽ **Wednesday**
The Tenth of April (English)
Waning Moon
Moon phase: New Moon 5:35 am
Color: White

Moon Sign: Aries
Moon enters Taurus 11:22 pm
Incense: Honeysuckle

11 **Thursday**
Heroes Day (Costa Rican)
Waxing Moon
Moon phase: First Quarter
Color: Purple

Moon Sign: Taurus
Incense: Apricot

12 **Friday**
Cerealia (Roman)
Waxing Moon
Moon phase: First Quarter
Color: Pink

Moon Sign: Taurus
Incense: Myrrh
Incense: Alder

13 **Saturday**
Thai New Year
Waxing Moon
Moon phase: First Quarter
Color: Brown

Moon Sign: Taurus
Moon enters Gemini 10:13 am
Incense: Rue

14 **Sunday**
Sanno Festival (Japanese)
Waxing Moon
Moon phase: First Quarter
Color: Gold

Moon Sign: Gemini
Incense: Pine
Incense: Juniper

April

15 Monday
Plowing Festival
Waxing Moon
Moon phase: First Quarter
Color: Lavender

Moon Sign: Gemini
Moon enters Cancer 10:49 pm
Incense: Clary sage

16 Tuesday
Zurich Spring Festival (Swiss)
Waxing Moon
Moon phase: First Quarter
Color: White

Moon Sign: Cancer
Incense: Ginger

17 Wednesday
Yayoi Matsuri (Japanese)
Waxing Moon
Moon phase: First Quarter
Color: Topaz

Moon Sign: Cancer
Incense: Marjoram

Thursday
Flower Festival (Japanese)
Waxing Moon
Moon phase: Second Quarter 8:31 am
Color: Turquoise

Moon Sign: Cancer
Moon enters Leo 11:13 am
Incense: Clove

19 Friday
Cerealia last day (Roman)
Waxing Moon
Moon phase: Second Quarter
Color: Purple

Moon Sign: Leo
Sun enters Taurus 6:03 pm
Incense: Rose

20 Saturday
Drum Festival (Japanese)
Waxing Moon
Moon phase: Second Quarter
Color: Black

Moon Sign: Leo
Moon enters Virgo 9:08 pm
Incense: Pine

21 Sunday
Tiradentes Day (Brazilian)
Waxing Moon
Moon phase: Second Quarter
Color: Amber

Moon Sign: Virgo
Incense: Marigold

April

22 Monday
Earth Day
Waxing Moon
Moon phase: Second Quarter
Color: Gray

Moon Sign: Virgo
Incense: Hyssop

23 Tuesday
St. George's Day (English)
Waxing Moon
Moon phase: Second Quarter
Color: Red

Moon Sign: Virgo
Moon enters Libra 3:25 am
Incense: Basil

24 Wednesday
St. Mark's Eve
Waxing Moon
Moon phase: Second Quarter
Color: White

Moon Sign: Libra
Incense: Lavender

☺ Thursday
Robigalia (Roman)
Waxing Moon
Moon phase: Full Moon 3:57 pm
Color: Green

Moon Sign: Libra
Moon enters Scorpio 6:25 am
Incense: Mulberry

26 Friday
Arbor Day
Waning Moon
Moon phase: Third Quarter
Color: Coral

Moon Sign: Scorpio
Incense: Cypress

27 Saturday
Humabon's Conversion (Filipino)
Waning Moon
Moon phase: Third Quarter
Color: Indigo

Moon Sign: Scorpio
Moon enters Sagittarius 7:32 am
Incense: Patchouli

28 Sunday
Floralia (Roman)
Waning Moon
Moon phase: Third Quarter
Color: Yellow

Moon Sign: Sagittarius
Incense: Frankincense

April

29 **Monday**
Green Day (Japanese)
Waning Moon
Moon phase: Third Quarter
Color: Ivory

Moon Sign: Sagittarius
Moon enters Capricorn 8:21 am
Incense: Neroli

30 **Tuesday**
Walpurgis Night • May Eve
Waning Moon
Moon phase: Third Quarter
Color: Gray

Moon Sign: Capricorn
Incense: Geranium

Springtime Bud Magic

The sun is shining and leaf and flower buds are opening and blooming; welcome some of this brightness and growth into your own life by mixing up a batch of magical springtime potpourri. Select a handful of partially opened leaf buds and several freshly bloomed flowers. Set them in the sunshine or hang them from string in an airy place to dry. Sprinkle the buds and flowers with an essential oil of your choice, adding a few drops of oil at a time and mixing until the desired fragrance is achieved. Charged with the essence of spring, simmering this potpourri in a pot of hot water creates a light, positive, and fertile atmosphere conducive to creativity, productivity, and joy.

–Melanie Marquis

May

1   **Wednesday**
Beltane • May Day
Waning Moon
Moon phase: Third Quarter
Color: Brown

Moon Sign: Capricorn
Moon enters Aquarius 10:20 am
Incense: Lilac

2   **Thursday**
Big Kite Flying (Japanese)
Waning Moon
Moon phase: Fourth Quarter 7:14 am
Color: Turquoise

Moon Sign: Aquarius
Incense: Clove

3   **Friday**
Orthodox Good Friday
Waning Moon
Moon phase: Fourth Quarter
Color: White

Moon Sign: Aquarius
Moon enters Pisces 2:25 pm
Incense: Mint

4   **Saturday**
Bona Dea (Roman)
Waning Moon
Moon phase: Fourth Quarter
Color: Gray

Moon Sign: Pisces
Incense: Ivy

5   **Sunday**
Cinco de Mayo (Mexican) • Orthodox Easter
Waning Moon
Moon phase: Fourth Quarter
Color: Gold

Moon Sign: Pisces
Moon enters Aries 9:03 pm
Incense: Eucalyptus

6   **Monday**
Martyrs' Day (Lebanese)
Waning Moon
Moon phase: Fourth Quarter
Color: Gray

Moon Sign: Aries
Incense: Narcissus

7   **Tuesday**
Pilgrimage of St. Nicholas (Italian)
Waning Moon
Moon phase: Fourth Quarter
Color: White

Moon Sign: Aries
Incense: Cinnamon

175

May

8 **Wednesday**
Liberation Day (French)
Waning Moon
Moon phase: Fourth Quarter
Color: Topaz

Moon Sign: Aries
Moon enters Taurus 6:09 am
Incense: Honeysuckle

9 **Thursday**
Lemuria (Roman)
Waning Moon
Moon phase: New Moon 8:28 pm
Color: Purple

Moon Sign: Taurus
Incense: Apricot

10 **Friday**
Census Day (Canadian)
Waxing Moon
Moon phase: First Quarter
Color: Coral

Moon Sign: Taurus
Moon enters Gemini 5:21 pm
Incense: Vanilla

11 **Saturday**
Ukai Season opens (Japanese)
Waxing Moon
Moon phase: First Quarter
Color: Indigo

Moon Sign: Gemini
Incense: Sage

12 **Sunday**
Mother's Day
Waxing Moon
Moon phase: First Quarter
Color: Orange

Moon Sign: Gemini
Incense: Heliotrope

13 **Monday**
Pilgrimage to Fatima (Portuguese)
Waxing Moon
Moon phase: First Quarter
Color: White

Moon Sign: Gemini
Moon enters Cancer 5:57 am
Incense: Lily

14 **Tuesday**
Carabao Festival (Spanish)
Waxing Moon
Moon phase: First Quarter
Color: Gray

Moon Sign: Cancer
Incense: Ylang-ylang

May

15 Wednesday
Shavuot
Waxing Moon
Moon phase: First Quarter
Color: Brown

Moon Sign: Cancer
Moon enters Leo 6:38 pm
Incense: Bay laurel

16 Thursday
St. Honoratus' Day
Waxing Moon
Moon phase: First Quarter
Color: Crimson

Moon Sign: Leo
Incense: Jasmine

17 Friday
Norwegian Independence Day
Waxing Moon
Moon phase: First Quarter
Color: Rose

Moon Sign: Leo
Incense: Yarrow

◐ Saturday
Las Piedras Day (Uruguayan)
Waxing Moon
Moon phase: Second Quarter 12:35 am
Color: Black

Moon Sign: Leo
Moon enters Virgo 5:33 am
Incense: Sandalwood

19 Sunday
Pilgrimage to Treguier (French)
Waxing Moon
Moon phase: Second Quarter
Color: Amber

Moon Sign: Virgo
Incense: Pine
Incense: Almond

20 Monday
Pardon of the Singers (British)
Waxing Moon
Moon phase: Second Quarter
Color: Silver

Moon Sign: Virgo
Moon enters Libra 1:07 pm
Sun enters Gemini 5:09 pm
Incense: Rosemary

21 Tuesday
Victoria Day (Canadian)
Waxing Moon
Moon phase: Second Quarter
Color: Black

Moon Sign: Libra
Incense: Cedar

May
♊

22 Wednesday
Heroes' Day (Sri Lankan)
Waxing Moon
Moon phase: Second Quarter
Color: White

Moon Sign: Libra
Moon enters Scorpio 4:55 pm
Incense: Lavender

23 Thursday
Tubilustrium (Roman)
Waxing Moon
Moon phase: Second Quarter
Color: Green

Moon Sign: Scorpio
Incense: Nutmeg

24 Friday
Culture Day (Bulgarian)
Waxing Moon
Moon phase: Second Quarter
Color: Pink

Moon Sign: Scorpio
Moon enters Sagittarius 5:49 pm
Incense: Orchid

☺ Saturday
Urbanas Diena (Latvian)
Waxing Moon
Moon phase: Full Moon 12:25 am
Color: Brown

Moon Sign: Sagittarius
Incense: Magnolia

26 Sunday
Pepys' Commemoration (English)
Waning Moon
Moon phase: Third Quarter
Color: Yellow

Moon Sign: Sagittarius
Moon enters Capricorn 5:28 pm
Incense: Hyacinth

27 Monday
Memorial Day (observed)
Waning Moon
Moon phase: Third Quarter
Color: Ivory

Moon Sign: Capricorn
Incense: Hyssop

28 Tuesday
St. Germain's Day
Waning Moon
Moon phase: Third Quarter
Color: Maroon

Moon Sign: Capricorn
Moon enters Aquarius 5:48 pm
Incense: Geranium

29 Wednesday
Royal Oak Day (English)
Waning Moon
Moon phase: Third Quarter
Color: Topaz

Moon Sign: Aquarius
Incense: Honeysuckle

30 Thursday
Memorial Day (actual)
Waning Moon
Moon phase: Third Quarter
Color: Turquoise

Moon Sign: Aquarius
Moon enters Pisces 8:30 pm
Incense: Balsam

☽ Friday
Flowers of May
Waning Moon
Moon phase: Fourth Quarter 2:58 pm
Color: Purple

Moon Sign: Pisces
Incense: Vanilla

Petal Power

When flowers burst into full bloom, take advantage of their beauty and magic by crafting some pretty and powerful pressed flower candles. Select flowers appropriate for your magical intent: rose petals for love, daisies for friendship, pansies for healing and purity. Press the flowers between the pages of a heavy book and allow them to dry. Choose a large wax candle and place it upright on a heatproof surface. Heat the surface of the candle with a lighter or hairdryer, just until the wax begins to melt. Carefully press the flowers into the hot wax and allow it to dry. Seal the blossoms more securely by painting over them with a thin layer of melted wax from an uncolored candle.

–Melanie Marquis

June ♊

1   Saturday
National Day (Tunisian)
Waning Moon
Moon phase: Fourth Quarter
Color: Brown

Moon Sign: Pisces
Incense: Rue

---

2   Sunday
Rice Harvest Festival (Malaysian)
Waning Moon
Moon phase: Fourth Quarter
Color: Amber

Moon Sign: Pisces
Moon enters Aries 2:33 am
Incense: Frankincense

---

3   Monday
Memorial to Broken Dolls (Japanese)
Waning Moon
Moon phase: Fourth Quarter
Color: Lavender

Moon Sign: Aries
Incense: Neroli

---

4   Tuesday
Full Moon Day (Burmese)
Waning Moon
Moon phase: Fourth Quarter
Color: Scarlet

Moon Sign: Aries
Moon enters Taurus 11:53 am
Incense: Basil

---

5   Wednesday
Constitution Day (Danish)
Waning Moon
Moon phase: Fourth Quarter
Color: Yellow

Moon Sign: Taurus
Incense: Bay laurel

---

6   Thursday
Swedish Flag Day
Waning Moon
Moon phase: Fourth Quarter
Color: Green

Moon Sign: Taurus
Moon enters Gemini 11:32 pm
Incense: Myrrh

---

7   Friday
St. Robert of Newminster's Day
Waning Moon
Moon phase: Fourth Quarter
Color: Pink

Moon Sign: Gemini
Incense: Rose

June

♊

🌙 **Saturday**
St. Medard's Day (Belgian)
Waning Moon
Moon phase: New Moon 11:56 am
Color: Gray

Moon Sign: Gemini
Incense: Ivy

9 Sunday
Vestalia (Roman)
Waxing Moon
Moon phase: First Quarter
Color: Yellow

Moon Sign: Gemini
Moon enters Cancer 12:16 pm
Incense: Eucalyptus

10 Monday
Time-Observance Day (Chinese)
Waxing Moon
Moon phase: First Quarter
Color: Ivory

Moon Sign: Cancer
Incense: Clary sage

11 Tuesday
Kamehameha Day (Hawaiian)
Waxing Moon
Moon phase: First Quarter
Color: Black

Moon Sign: Cancer
Incense: Cinnamon

12 Wednesday
Independence Day (Filipino)
Waxing Moon
Moon phase: First Quarter
Color: White

Moon Sign: Cancer
Moon enters Leo 12:58 am
Incense: Marjoram

13 Thursday
St. Anthony of Padua's Day
Waxing Moon
Moon phase: First Quarter
Color: Purple

Moon Sign: Leo
Incense: Carnation

14 Friday
Flag Day
Waxing Moon
Moon phase: First Quarter
Color: Rose

Moon Sign: Leo
Moon enters Virgo 12:26 pm
Incense: Yarrow

June

---

15 **Saturday**
St. Vitus' Day Fires
Waxing Moon
Moon phase: First Quarter
Color: Indigo

Moon Sign: Virgo
Incense: Pine

☾ **Sunday**
Father's Day
Waxing Moon
Moon phase: Second Quarter 1:24 pm
Color: Gold

Moon Sign: Virgo
Moon enters Libra 9:19 pm
Incense: Almond

---

17 **Monday**
Bunker Hill Day
Waxing Moon
Moon phase: Second Quarter
Color: Gray

Moon Sign: Libra
Incense: Lily

---

18 **Tuesday**
Independence Day (Egyptian)
Waxing Moon
Moon phase: Second Quarter
Color: Red

Moon Sign: Libra
Incense: Bayberry

---

19 **Wednesday**
Juneteenth
Waxing Moon
Moon phase: Second Quarter
Color: Brown

Moon Sign: Libra
Moon enters Scorpio 2:38 am
Incense: Lilac

---

20 **Thursday**
Midsummer • Summer Solstice
Waxing Moon
Moon phase: Second Quarter
Color: Turquoise

Moon Sign: Scorpio
Incense: Mulberry

---

21 **Friday**
U.S. Constitution ratified
Waxing Moon
Moon phase: Second Quarter
Color: White

Moon Sign: Scorpio
Sun enters Cancer 1:04 am
Incense: Cypress
Moon enters Sagittarius 4:31 am

June

22 Saturday
Rose Festival (English)
Waxing Moon
Moon phase: Second Quarter
Color: Blue

Moon Sign: Sagittarius
Incense: Magnolia

Sunday
St. John's Eve
Waxing Moon
Moon phase: Full Moon 7:32 am
Color: Orange

Moon Sign: Sagittarius
Moon enters Capricorn 4:08 am
Incense: Hyacinth

24 Monday
St. John's Day
Waning Moon
Moon phase: Third Quarter
Color: White

Moon Sign: Capricorn
Incense: Narcissus

25 Tuesday
Fiesta of Santa Orosia (Spanish)
Waning Moon
Moon phase: Third Quarter
Color: Gray

Moon Sign: Capricorn
Moon enters Aquarius 3:27 am
Incense: Ylang-ylang

26 Wednesday
Pied Piper Day (German)
Waning Moon
Moon phase: Third Quarter
Color: Topaz

Moon Sign: Aquarius
Incense: Lavender

27 Thursday
Day of the Seven Sleepers (Islamic)
Waning Moon
Moon phase: Third Quarter
Color: Crimson

Moon Sign: Aquarius
Moon enters Pisces 4:32 am
Incense: Jasmine

28 Friday
Paul Bunyan Day
Waning Moon
Moon phase: Third Quarter
Color: Coral

Moon Sign: Pisces
Incense: Violet

June

29 **Saturday**
Feast of Saints Peter and Paul
Waning Moon
Moon phase: Third Quarter
Color: Brown

Moon Sign: Pisces
Moon enters Aries 9:07 am
Incense: Sage

○ **Sunday**
The Burning of the Three Firs (French)
Waning Moon
Moon phase: Fourth Quarter 12:54 am
Color: Yellow

Moon Sign: Aries
Incense: Heliotrope

Sunshine and Roses

If you can't beat the heat, use it! Magical Sunshine and Roses Tea is a great way to make thrifty use of positive and powerful solar energies. Fill a large glass jar with cool water and a bag or two of your favorite tea. Add a handful of fresh rose petals. Place the jar outside in direct light and let the sunshine brew the tea. Remove the roses and let the petals dry in the sun. Pour the tea over ice and drink to beat the heat and recharge, and use the dried rose petals in herbal sachets and potpourri to magically energize and freshen your home.

–Melanie Marquis

July

1 Monday
Climbing Mount Fuji (Japanese)
Waning Moon
Moon phase: Fourth Quarter
Color: Silver

Moon Sign: Aries
Moon enters Taurus 5:43 pm
Incense: Hyssop

2 Tuesday
Heroes' Day (Zambian)
Waning Moon
Moon phase: Fourth Quarter
Color: White

Moon Sign: Taurus
Incense: Ginger

3 Wednesday
Indian Sun Dance (Native American)
Waning Moon
Moon phase: Fourth Quarter
Color: Yellow

Moon Sign: Taurus
Incense: Lilac

4 Thursday
Independence Day
Waning Moon
Moon phase: Fourth Quarter
Color: Green

Moon Sign: Taurus
Moon enters Gemini 5:21 am
Incense: Balsam

5 Friday
Tynwald (Nordic)
Waning Moon
Moon phase: Fourth Quarter
Color: Purple

Moon Sign: Gemini
Incense: Mint

6 Saturday
Khao Phansa Day (Thai)
Waning Moon
Moon phase: Fourth Quarter
Color: Black

Moon Sign: Gemini
Moon enters Cancer 6:14 pm
Incense: Patchouli

7 Sunday
Weaver's Festival (Japanese)
Waning Moon
Moon phase: Fourth Quarter
Color: Gold

Moon Sign: Cancer
Incense: Juniper

July

Monday
St. Elizabeth's Day (Portuguese)
Waning Moon
Moon phase: New Moon 3:14 am
Color: Gray

Moon Sign: Cancer
Incense: Neroli

9 Tuesday
Ramadan begins
Waxing Moon
Moon phase: First Quarter
Color: Black

Moon Sign: Cancer
Moon enters Leo 6:48 am
Incense: Cedar

10 Wednesday
Lady Godiva Day (English)
Waxing Moon
Moon phase: First Quarter
Color: White

Moon Sign: Leo
Incense: Bay laurel

11 Thursday
Revolution Day (Mongolian)
Waxing Moon
Moon phase: First Quarter
Color: Crimson

Moon Sign: Leo
Moon enters Virgo 6:12 pm
Incense: Myrrh

12 Friday
Lobster Carnival (Nova Scotian)
Waxing Moon
Moon phase: First Quarter
Color: Rose

Moon Sign: Virgo
Incense: Alder

13 Saturday
Festival of the Three Cows (Spanish)
Waxing Moon
Moon phase: First Quarter
Color: Brown

Moon Sign: Virgo
Incense: Rue

14 Sunday
Bastille Day (French)
Waxing Moon
Moon phase: First Quarter
Color: Yellow

Moon Sign: Virgo
Moon enters Libra 3:41 am
Incense: Marigold

July

◐ Monday
St. Swithin's Day
Waxing Moon
Moon phase: Second Quarter 11:18 pm
Color: White

Moon Sign: Libra
Incense: Clary sage

---

16 Tuesday
Our Lady of Carmel
Waxing Moon
Moon phase: Second Quarter
Color: Red

Moon Sign: Libra
Moon enters Scorpio 10:24 am
Incense: Bayberry

---

17 Wednesday
Rivera Day (Puerto Rican)
Waxing Moon
Moon phase: Second Quarter
Color: Topaz

Moon Sign: Scorpio
Incense: Marjoram

---

18 Thursday
Gion Matsuri Festival (Japanese)
Waxing Moon
Moon phase: Second Quarter
Color: Green

Moon Sign: Scorpio
Moon enters Sagittarius 1:54 pm
Incense: Mulberry

---

19 Friday
Flitch Day (English)
Waxing Moon
Moon phase: Second Quarter
Color: Coral

Moon Sign: Sagittarius
Incense: Thyme

---

20 Saturday
Binding of Wreaths (Lithuanian)
Waxing Moon
Moon phase: Second Quarter
Color: Gray

Moon Sign: Sagittarius
Moon enters Capricorn 2:39 pm
Incense: Sandalwood

---

21 Sunday
National Day (Belgian)
Waxing Moon
Moon phase: Second Quarter
Color: Amber

Moon Sign: Capricorn
Incense: Almond

☺ **Monday**
St. Mary Magdalene's Day
Waxing Moon
Moon phase: Full Moon 2:16 pm
Color: Lavender

Moon Sign: Capricorn
Sun enters Leo 11:56 pm
Incense: Rosemary
Moon enters Aquarius 2:07 pm

---

23 **Tuesday**
Mysteries of Santa Cristina (Italian)
Waning Moon
Moon phase: Third Quarter
Color: Gray

Moon Sign: Aquarius
Incense: Ylang-ylang

---

24 **Wednesday**
Pioneer Day (Mormon)
Waning Moon
Moon phase: Third Quarter
Color: Brown

Moon Sign: Aquarius
Moon enters Pisces 2:22 pm
Incense: Honeysuckle

---

25 **Thursday**
St. James' Day
Waning Moon
Moon phase: Third Quarter
Color: Purple

Moon Sign: Pisces
Incense: Apricot

---

26 **Friday**
St. Anne's Day
Waning Moon
Moon phase: Third Quarter
Color: Pink

Moon Sign: Pisces
Moon enters Aries 5:29 pm
Incense: Rose

---

27 **Saturday**
Sleepyhead Day (Finnish)
Waning Moon
Moon phase: Third Quarter
Color: Indigo

Moon Sign: Aries
Incense: Pine

---

28 **Sunday**
Independence Day (Peruvian)
Waning Moon
Moon phase: Third Quarter
Color: Orange

Moon Sign: Aries
Incense: Frankincense

July

○ **Monday**
Pardon of the Birds (French)
Waning Moon
Moon phase: Fourth Quarter 1:43 pm
Color: White

Moon Sign: Aries
Moon enters Taurus 12:43 am
Incense: Narcissus

30 Tuesday
Micman Festival of St. Ann
Waning Moon
Moon phase: Fourth Quarter
Color: Black

Moon Sign: Taurus
Incense: Geranium

31 Wednesday
Weighing of the Aga Kahn
Waning Moon
Moon phase: Fourth Quarter
Color: Yellow

Moon Sign: Taurus
Moon enters Gemini 11:42 am
Incense: Lilac

Hot as Ice

When the weather gets hot this summer, cool off and make things interesting with an icy magical fruit drink to increase passion and romance. Wash a handful of strawberries and cherries, removing the leaves, pits, and stems. Empower the fruits to bring out their unique energies: charge the strawberries for love and the cherries for passion. Place the fruit in a blender with ice, and add a little orange juice to give the drink extra power. Mix until the ice is evenly crushed. Pour into glasses and share this refreshing drink with someone special to heat up your love life while cooling you down.

–Melanie Marquis

August

1   **Thursday**
Lammas
Waning Moon
Moon phase: Fourth Quarter
Color: Purple

Moon Sign: Gemini
Incense: Nutmeg

---

2   **Friday**
Porcingula (Native American)
Waning Moon
Moon phase: Fourth Quarter
Color: White

Moon Sign: Gemini
Incense: Violet

---

3   **Saturday**
Drimes (Greek)
Waning Moon
Moon phase: Fourth Quarter
Color: Black

Moon Sign: Gemini
Moon enters Cancer 12:29 am
Incense: Sage

---

4   **Sunday**
Cook Islands Constitution Celebration
Waning Moon
Moon phase: Fourth Quarter
Color: Gold

Moon Sign: Cancer
Incense: Eucalyptus

---

5   **Monday**
Benediction of the Sea (French)
Waning Moon
Moon phase: Fourth Quarter
Color: Silver

Moon Sign: Cancer
Moon enters Leo 12:58 pm
Incense: Hyssop

---

6   **Tuesday**
Hiroshima Peace Ceremony
Waning Moon
Moon phase: New Moon 5:51 pm
Color: Red

Moon Sign: Leo
Incense: Cedar

---

7   **Wednesday**
Ramadan ends
Waxing Moon
Moon phase: First Quarter
Color: White

Moon Sign: Leo
Moon enters Virgo 11:57 pm
Incense: Honeysuckle

August

8 **Thursday**
Dog Days (Japanese)
Waxing Moon
Moon phase: First Quarter
Color: Turquoise

Moon Sign: Virgo
Incense: Carnation

---

9 **Friday**
Nagasaki Peace Ceremony
Waxing Moon
Moon phase: First Quarter
Color: Pink

Moon Sign: Virgo
Incense: Cypress

---

10 **Saturday**
St. Lawrence's Day
Waxing Moon
Moon phase: First Quarter
Color: Indigo

Moon Sign: Virgo
Moon enters Libra 9:08 am
Incense: Rue

---

11 **Sunday**
Puck Fair (Irish)
Waxing Moon
Moon phase: First Quarter
Color: Yellow

Moon Sign: Libra
Incense: Hyacinth

---

12 **Monday**
Fiesta of Santa Clara
Waxing Moon
Moon phase: First Quarter
Color: White

Moon Sign: Libra
Moon enters Scorpio 4:18 pm
Incense: Neroli

---

13 **Tuesday**
Women's Day (Tunisian)
Waxing Moon
Moon phase: First Quarter
Color: Gray

Moon Sign: Scorpio
Incense: Ginger

☽ **Wednesday**
Festival at Sassari
Waxing Moon
Moon phase: Second Quarter 6:56 am
Color: Topaz

Moon Sign: Scorpio
Moon enters Sagittarius 9:04 pm
Incense: Lavender

August

15 Thursday
Assumption Day
Waxing Moon
Moon phase: Second Quarter
Color: Green

Moon Sign: Sagittarius
Incense: Clove

16 Friday
Festival of Minstrels (European)
Waxing Moon
Moon phase: Second Quarter
Color: Purple

Moon Sign: Sagittarius
Moon enters Capricorn 11:25 pm
Incense: Orchid

17 Saturday
Feast of the Hungry Ghosts (Chinese)
Waxing Moon
Moon phase: Second Quarter
Color: Brown

Moon Sign: Capricorn
Incense: Ivy

18 Sunday
St. Helen's Day
Waxing Moon
Moon phase: Second Quarter
Color: Orange

Moon Sign: Capricorn
Incense: Marigold

19 Monday
Rustic Vinalia (Roman)
Waxing Moon
Moon phase: Second Quarter
Color: Lavender

Moon Sign: Capricorn
Moon enters Aquarius 12:07 am
Incense: Lily

Tuesday
Constitution Day (Hungarian)
Waxing Moon
Moon phase: Full Moon 9:45 pm
Color: Black

Moon Sign: Aquarius
Incense: Cinnamon

21 Wednesday
Consualia (Roman)
Waning Moon
Moon phase: Third Quarter
Color: Yellow

Moon Sign: Aquarius
Moon enters Pisces 12:43 am
Incense: Marjoram

August ♍

22 Thursday
Feast of the Queenship of Mary (English)
Waning Moon
Moon phase: Third Quarter
Color: Crimson

Moon Sign: Pisces
Sun enters Virgo 7:02 pm
Incense: Myrrh

23 Friday
National Day (Romanian)
Waning Moon
Moon phase: Third Quarter
Color: Rose

Moon Sign: Pisces
Moon enters Aries 3:13 am
Incense: Mint

24 Saturday
St. Bartholomew's Day
Waning Moon
Moon phase: Third Quarter
Color: Gray

Moon Sign: Aries
Incense: Magnolia

25 Sunday
Feast of the Green Corn (Native American)
Waning Moon
Moon phase: Third Quarter
Color: Amber

Moon Sign: Aries
Moon enters Taurus 9:13 am
Incense: Heliotrope

26 Monday
Pardon of the Sea (French)
Waning Moon
Moon phase: Third Quarter
Color: Gray

Moon Sign: Taurus
Incense: Clary sage

27 Tuesday
Summer Break (English)
Waning Moon
Moon phase: Third Quarter
Color: White

Moon Sign: Taurus
Moon enters Gemini 7:08 pm
Incense: Basil

◐ Wednesday
St. Augustine's Day
Waning Moon
Moon phase: Fourth Quarter 5:35 am
Color: Brown

Moon Sign: Gemini
Incense: Bay laurel

August ♍

29 **Thursday**
St. John's Beheading
Waning Moon
Moon phase: Fourth Quarter
Color: Purple

Moon Sign: Gemini
Incense: Balsam

30 **Friday**
St. Rose of Lima Day (Peruvian)
Waning Moon
Moon phase: Fourth Quarter
Color: Coral

Moon Sign: Gemini
Moon enters Cancer 7:33 am
Incense: Thyme

31 **Saturday**
Unto These Hills Pageant (Cherokee)
Waning Moon
Moon phase: Fourth Quarter
Color: Blue

Moon Sign: Cancer
Incense: Patchouli

Spelling on a Budget

As kids stock up on new supplies for back to school time, take advantage of all the broken crayons, old erasers, and short pencils that would otherwise be tossed aside or left on a shelf to collect dust. Melt and recycle broken crayons into customizable effigies and magical candles to boost energy and creativity, and crumble up old erasers to use in diminishing, curse-breaking, and banishing powders. Keep a few short pencils in your car to use for written spells on the go, or grind the graphite into an energy-boosting dust to use in your wandcraft.

–Melanie Marquis

September ♍

1 Sunday
Greek New Year
Waning Moon
Moon phase: Fourth Quarter
Color: Yellow

Moon Sign: Cancer
Moon enters Leo 8:01 pm
Incense: Juniper

2 Monday
Labor Day
Waning Moon
Moon phase: Fourth Quarter
Color: Silver

Moon Sign: Leo
Incense: Rosemary

3 Tuesday
Founder's Day (San Marino)
Waning Moon
Moon phase: Fourth Quarter
Color: Scarlet

Moon Sign: Leo
Incense: Ginger

4 Wednesday
Los Angeles' Birthday
Waning Moon
Moon phase: Fourth Quarter
Color: Topaz

Moon Sign: Leo
Moon enters Virgo 6:43 am
Incense: Marjoram

5 Thursday
Rosh Hashanah • First Labor Day (1882)
Waning Moon
Moon phase: New Moon 7:36 am
Color: Crimson

Moon Sign: Virgo
Incense: Jasmine

6 Friday
The Virgin of Remedies (Spanish)
Waxing Moon
Moon phase: First Quarter
Color: Coral

Moon Sign: Virgo
Moon enters Libra 3:12 pm
Incense: Vanilla

7 Saturday
Festival of the Durga (Hindu)
Waxing Moon
Moon phase: First Quarter
Color: Black

Moon Sign: Libra
Incense: Sandalwood

September ♍

8 Sunday
Birthday of the Virgin Mary
Waxing Moon
Moon phase: First Quarter
Color: Gold

Moon Sign: Libra
Moon enters Scorpio 9:44 pm
Incense: Hyacinth

9 Monday
Chrysanthemum Festival (Japanese)
Waxing Moon
Moon phase: First Quarter
Color: White

Moon Sign: Scorpio
Incense: Neroli

10 Tuesday
Festival of the Poets (Japanese)
Waxing Moon
Moon phase: First Quarter
Color: Red

Moon Sign: Scorpio
Incense: Bayberry

11 Wednesday
Coptic New Year
Waxing Moon
Moon phase: First Quarter
Color: Yellow

Moon Sign: Scorpio
Moon enters Sagittarius 2:36 am
Incense: Lavender

Thursday
National Day (Ethiopian)
Waxing Moon
Moon phase: Second Quarter 1:08 pm
Color: Green

Moon Sign: Sagittarius
Incense: Mulberry

13 Friday
The Gods' Banquet (Roman)
Waxing Moon
Moon phase: Second Quarter
Color: Rose

Moon Sign: Sagittarius
Moon enters Capricorn 5:56 am
Incense: Alder

14 Saturday
Yom Kippur
Waxing Moon
Moon phase: Second Quarter
Color: Gray

Moon Sign: Capricorn
Incense: Magnolia

September ♍

15 Sunday
Birthday of the Moon (Chinese)
Waxing Moon
Moon phase: Second Quarter
Color: Orange

Moon Sign: Capricorn
Moon enters Aquarius 8:05 am
Incense: Marigold

16 Monday
Mexican Independence Day
Waxing Moon
Moon phase: Second Quarter
Color: Lavender

Moon Sign: Aquarius
Incense: Clary sage

17 Tuesday
Von Steuben's Day
Waxing Moon
Moon phase: Second Quarter
Color: White

Moon Sign: Aquarius
Moon enters Pisces 9:58 am
Incense: Cedar

18 Wednesday
Sukkot begins
Waxing Moon
Moon phase: Second Quarter
Color: Brown

Moon Sign: Pisces
Incense: Bay laurel

☻ Thursday
St. Januarius' Day (Italian)
Waxing Moon
Moon phase: Full Moon 7:13 am
Color: Purple

Moon Sign: Pisces
Moon enters Aries 12:58 pm
Incense: Carnation

20 Friday
St. Eustace's Day
Waning Moon
Moon phase: Third Quarter
Color: Pink

Moon Sign: Aries
Incense: Yarrow

21 Saturday
UN International Day of Peace
Waning Moon
Moon phase: Third Quarter
Color: Brown

Moon Sign: Aries
Moon enters Taurus 6:33 pm
Incense: Patchouli

22 Sunday
Mabon • Fall Equinox
Waning Moon
Moon phase: Third Quarter
Color: Amber

Moon Sign: Taurus
Sun enters Libra 4:44 pm
Incense: Frankincense

---

23 Monday
Shubun no Hi (Chinese)
Waning Moon
Moon phase: Third Quarter
Color: Ivory

Moon Sign: Taurus
Incense: Lily

---

24 Tuesday
Schwenkenfelder Thanksgiving (German-American)
Waning Moon
Moon phase: Third Quarter
Color: Gray

Moon Sign: Taurus
Moon enters Gemini 3:34 am
Incense: Ylang-ylang

---

25 Wednesday
Sukkot ends
Waning Moon
Moon phase: Third Quarter
Color: White

Moon Sign: Gemini
Incense: Honeysuckle

◐ Thursday
Feast of Santa Justina (Mexican)
Waning Moon
Moon phase: Fourth Quarter 11:55 pm
Color: Turquoise

Moon Sign: Gemini
Moon enters Cancer 3:24 pm
Incense: Apricot

---

27 Friday
Saints Cosmas and Damian's Day
Waning Moon
Moon phase: Fourth Quarter
Color: Purple

Moon Sign: Cancer
Incense: Mint

---

28 Saturday
Confucius's Birthday
Waning Moon
Moon phase: Fourth Quarter
Color: Indigo

Moon Sign: Cancer
Incense: Pine

September

29 Sunday
Michaelmas
Waning Moon
Moon phase: Fourth Quarter
Color: Yellow

Moon Sign: Cancer
Moon enters Leo 3:57 am
Incense: Heliotrope

30 Monday
St. Jerome's Day
Waning Moon
Moon phase: Fourth Quarter
Color: Gray

Moon Sign: Leo
Incense: Rosemary

Leave It to the Leaves

Looking for low-cost ways to make your living space more stylish and magical this fall? Add a few leaf-inspired touches to your décor and let Nature's autumn beauty shine indoors. Fill a glass bowl with colorful leaves chosen for their magical attributes and use as a table decoration to bring a special atmosphere to your gatherings. Tuck fresh autumn leaves into napkin rings to add pizzazz and natural power to your dining room. To make an autumn-themed altar cloth, dip leaves in paint and drop them onto a large piece of fabric to create a pattern; carefully press the leaves flat, then slowly peel them off.

–Melanie Marquis

October

1 Tuesday
Armed Forces Day (South Korean)
Waning Moon
Moon phase: Fourth Quarter
Color: White

Moon Sign: Leo
Moon enters Virgo 2:52 pm
Incense: Cinnamon

2 Wednesday
Old Man's Day (Virgin Islands)
Waning Moon
Moon phase: Fourth Quarter
Color: Yellow

Moon Sign: Virgo
Incense: Lilac

3 Thursday
Moroccan New Year's Day
Waning Moon
Moon phase: Fourth Quarter
Color: Turquoise

Moon Sign: Virgo
Moon enters Libra 10:59 pm
Incense: Clove

☽ Friday
St. Francis' Day
Waning Moon
Moon phase: New Moon 8:35 pm
Color: Coral

Moon Sign: Libra
Incense: Violet

5 Saturday
Republic Day (Portuguese)
Waxing Moon
Moon phase: First Quarter
Color: Blue

Moon Sign: Libra
Incense: Rue

6 Sunday
Dedication of the Virgin's Crowns (English)
Waxing Moon
Moon phase: First Quarter
Color: Gold

Moon Sign: Libra
Moon enters Scorpio 4:33 am
Incense: Eucalyptus

7 Monday
Kermesse (German)
Waxing Moon
Moon phase: First Quarter
Color: White

Moon Sign: Scorpio
Incense: Narcissus

October

8 Tuesday
Okunchi (Japanese)
Waxing Moon
Moon phase: First Quarter
Color: Red

Moon Sign: Scorpio
Moon enters Sagittarius 8:21 am
Incense: Geranium

9 Wednesday
Alphabet Day (South Korean)
Waxing Moon
Moon phase: First Quarter
Color: Brown

Moon Sign: Sagittarius
Incense: Bay laurel

10 Thursday
Health Day (Japanese)
Waxing Moon
Moon phase: First Quarter
Color: Purple

Moon Sign: Sagittarius
Moon enters Capricorn 11:17 am
Incense: Nutmeg

◖ Friday
Medetrinalia (Roman)
Waxing Moon
Moon phase: Second Quarter 7:02 pm
Color: Rose

Moon Sign: Capricorn
Incense: Alder

12 Saturday
National Day (Spanish)
Waxing Moon
Moon phase: Second Quarter
Color: Black

Moon Sign: Capricorn
Moon enters Aquarius 2:00 pm
Incense: Sage

13 Sunday
Fontinalia (Roman) begins
Waxing Moon
Moon phase: Second Quarter
Color: Yellow

Moon Sign: Aquarius
Incense: Juniper

14 Monday
Columbus Day (observed)
Waning Moon
Moon phase: Second Quarter
Color: Gray

Moon Sign: Aquarius
Moon enters Pisces 5:06 pm
Incense: Hyssop

October

15 Tuesday
The October Horse (Roman)
Waxing Moon
Moon phase: Second Quarter
Color: Black

Moon Sign: Pisces
Incense: Basil

16 Wednesday
The Lion Sermon (British)
Waxing Moon
Moon phase: Second Quarter
Color: White

Moon Sign: Pisces
Moon enters Aries 9:18 pm
Incense: Lavender

17 Thursday
Pilgrimage to Paray-le-Monial
Waxing Moon
Moon phase: Second Quarter
Color: Crimson

Moon Sign: Aries
Incense: Mulberry

☺ Friday
Brooklyn Barbecue
Waxing Moon
Moon phase: Full Moon 7:38 pm
Color: Pink

Moon Sign: Aries
Incense: Rose

19 Saturday
Our Lord of Miracles Procession (Peruvian)
Waning Moon
Moon phase: Third Quarter
Color: Brown

Moon Sign: Aries
Moon enters Taurus 3:27 am
Incense: Ivy

20 Sunday
Colchester Oyster Feast
Waning Moon
Moon phase: Third Quarter
Color: Orange

Moon Sign: Taurus
Incense: Almond

21 Monday
Feast of the Black Christ
Waning Moon
Moon phase: Third Quarter
Color: Lavender

Moon Sign: Taurus
Moon enters Gemini 12:14 pm
Incense: Lily

October

22 Tuesday
Goddess of Mercy Day (Chinese)
Waning Moon
Moon phase: Third Quarter
Color: White

Moon Sign: Gemini
Moon enters Aquarius 1:02 am
Incense: Bayberry

23 Wednesday
Revolution Day (Hungarian)
Waning Moon
Moon phase: Third Quarter
Color: Topaz

Moon Sign: Gemini
Sun enters Scorpio 2:10 am
Incense: Marjoram
Moon enters Cancer 11:36 pm

24 Thursday
United Nations Day
Waning Moon
Moon phase: Third Quarter
Color: Green

Moon Sign: Cancer
Incense: Balsam

25 Friday
St. Crispin's Day
Waning Moon
Moon phase: Third Quarter
Color: Purple

Moon Sign: Cancer
Incense: Vanilla

☾ Saturday
Quit Rent Ceremony (English)
Waning Moon
Moon phase: Fourth Quarter 7:40 pm
Color: Gray

Moon Sign: Cancer
Moon enters Leo 12:12 pm
Incense: Sandalwood

27 Sunday
Feast of the Holy Souls
Waning Moon
Moon phase: Fourth Quarter
Color: Amber

Moon Sign: Leo
Incense: Marigold

28 Monday
Ochi Day (Greek)
Waning Moon
Moon phase: Fourth Quarter
Color: White

Moon Sign: Leo
Moon enters Virgo 11:45 pm
Incense: Neroli

October ♏

29 Tuesday
Iroquois Feast of the Dead
Waning Moon
Moon phase: Fourth Quarter
Color: Scarlet

Moon Sign: Virgo
Incense: Cinnamon

30 Wednesday
Meiji Festival (Japanese)
Waning Moon
Moon phase: Fourth Quarter
Color: Yellow

Moon Sign: Virgo
Incense: Honeysuckle

31 Thursday
Halloween • Samhain
Waning Moon
Moon phase: Fourth Quarter
Color: Purple

Moon Sign: Virgo
Moon enters Libra 8:22 am
Incense: Apricot

Seedy Spellwork

After carving up those pumpkins, don't just throw the seeds away or eat them all. In each little pumpkin seed lies a large store of natural energy. Save seeds to bring magic to your life year-round. They're great for increasing strength, promoting prosperity, encouraging health, and enhancing growth and expansion. Grind them to include in incense and magical powders, carry one in your pocket for a good luck talisman, or tie a few inside a small square of fabric to make a charm to promote peace and balance in the home. You can even use pumpkin seeds to create your own set of biodegradable runes—just use a pen and some natural ink to make the glyphs.

–Melanie Marquis

November

1 Friday
All Saints' Day
Waning Moon
Moon phase: Fourth Quarter
Color: White

Moon Sign: Libra
Incense: Orchid

---

2 Saturday
All Souls' Day
Waning Moon
Moon phase: Fourth Quarter
Color: Blue

Moon Sign: Libra
Moon enters Scorpio 1:35 pm
Incense: Ivy

Sunday
Daylight Saving Time ends
Waning Moon
Moon phase: New Moon 7:50 am
Color: Yellow

Moon Sign: Scorpio
Incense: Juniper

---

4 Monday
Mischief Night (British)
Waxing Moon
Moon phase: First Quarter
Color: Silver

Moon Sign: Scorpio
Moon enters Sagittarius 3:14 pm
Incense: Clary sage

---

5 Tuesday
Election Day (general) • Islamic New Year
Waxing Moon
Moon phase: First Quarter
Color: Black

Moon Sign: Sagittarius
Incense: Ylang-ylang

---

6 Wednesday
Leonard's Ride (German)
Waxing Moon
Moon phase: First Quarter
Color: Brown

Moon Sign: Sagittarius
Moon enters Capricorn 4:44 pm
Incense: Bay laurel

---

7 Thursday
Mayan Day of the Dead
Waxing Moon
Moon phase: First Quarter
Color: Green

Moon Sign: Capricorn
Incense: Carnation

November ♏

8   **Friday**
The Lord Mayor's Show (English)
Waxing Moon
Moon phase: First Quarter
Color: Coral

Moon Sign: Capricorn
Moon enters Aquarius 6:30 pm
Incense: Thyme

---

9   **Saturday**
Lord Mayor's Day (British)
Waxing Moon
Moon phase: First Quarter
Color: Gray

Moon Sign: Aquarius
Incense: Pine

◐   **Sunday**
Martin Luther's Birthday
Waxing Moon
Moon phase: Second Quarter 12:57 am
Color: Gold

Moon Sign: Aquarius
Moon enters Pisces 9:36 pm
Incense: Heliotrope

---

11   **Monday**
Veterans Day
Waxing Moon
Moon phase: Second Quarter
Color: White

Moon Sign: Pisces
Incense: Narcissus

---

12   **Tuesday**
Tesuque Feast Day (Native American)
Waxing Moon
Moon phase: Second Quarter
Color: Red

Moon Sign: Pisces
Incense: Geranium

---

13   **Wednesday**
Festival of Jupiter (Roman)
Waxing Moon
Moon phase: Second Moon 5:08 pm
Color: Yellow

Moon Sign: Pisces
Moon enters Aries 2:39 am
Incense: Marjoram

---

14   **Thursday**
The Little Carnival (Greek)
Waxing Moon
Moon phase: Second Quarter
Color: Purple

Moon Sign: Aries
Incense: Nutmeg

November ♏

15 Friday
St. Leopold's Day
Waxing Moon
Moon phase: Second Quarter
Color: Rose

Moon Sign: Aries
Moon enters Taurus 9:49 am
Incense: Cypress

---

16 Saturday
St. Margaret of Scotland's Day
Waxing Moon
Moon phase: Second Quarter
Color: Black

Moon Sign: Taurus
Incense: Magnolia

☺ Sunday
Queen Elizabeth's Day
Waxing Moon
Moon phase: Full Moon 10:16 am
Color: Amber

Moon Sign: Taurus
Moon enters Gemini 7:07 pm
Incense: Almond

---

18 Monday
St. Plato's Day
Waning Moon
Moon phase: Third Quarter
Color: Gray

Moon Sign: Gemini
Incense: Rosemary

---

19 Tuesday
Garifuna Day (Belizean)
Waning Moon
Moon phase: Third Quarter
Color: Scarlet

Moon Sign: Gemini
Incense: Cedar

---

20 Wednesday
Revolution Day (Mexican)
Waning Moon
Moon phase: Third Quarter
Color: White

Moon Sign: Gemini
Moon enters Cancer 6:23 am
Incense: Honeysuckle

---

21 Thursday
Repentance Day (German)
Waning Moon
Moon phase: Third Quarter
Color: Turquoise

Moon Sign: Cancer
Sun enters Sagittarius 10:48 pm
Incense: Myrrh

November

22 Friday
St. Cecilia's Day
Waning Moon
Moon phase: Third Quarter
Color: Pink

Moon Sign: Cancer
Moon enters Leo 6:56 pm
Incense: Yarrow

23 Saturday
St. Clement's Day
Waning Moon
Moon phase: Third Quarter
Color: Brown

Moon Sign: Leo
Incense: Sage

24 Sunday
Feast of the Burning Lamps (Egyptian)
Waning Moon
Moon phase: Third Quarter
Color: Orange

Moon Sign: Leo
Incense: Eucalyptus

◐ Monday
St. Catherine of Alexandria's Day
Waning Moon
Moon phase: Fourth Quarter 2:28 pm
Color: Lavender

Moon Sign: Leo
Moon enters Virgo 7:11 am
Incense: Hyssop

26 Tuesday
Festival of Lights (Tibetan)
Waning Moon
Moon phase: Fourth Quarter
Color: White

Moon Sign: Virgo
Incense: Ginger

27 Wednesday
Saint Maximus' Day
Waning Moon
Moon phase: Fourth Quarter
Color: Topaz

Moon Sign: Virgo
Moon enters Libra 5:00 pm
Incense: Lilac

28 Thursday
Thanksgiving Day • Hanukkah begins
Waning Moon
Moon phase: Fourth Quarter
Color: Crimson

Moon Sign: Libra
Incense: Clove

29 Friday

Tubman's Birthday (Liberian)
Waning Moon
Moon phase: Fourth Quarter
Color: Purple

Moon Sign: Libra
Moon enters Scorpio 11:03 pm
Incense: Violet

30 Saturday

St. Andrew's Day
Waning Moon
Moon phase: Fourth Quarter
Color: Indigo

Moon Sign: Scorpio
Incense: Patchouli

Sweater Magic

When the air gets chilly, it's time to dig out your sweaters, hats, and scarves and bundle up. Don't let all those extra clothes get you down, though—make the most of it by adding a dash of magic to your cold weather wardrobe. Draw pentacles on clothing tags to attract wealth, anoint zippers with magically attuned essential oils, decorate sweater buttons with meaningful sigils. Pin small pieces of herbs onto hats: pine for prosperity, holly for protection, fir for extra energy and a youthful glow. You can even charm your favorite scarf to encourage good cheer—choose beads in a "happy" color like blue or yellow, add your own symbols to the beads using a permanent marker, and tie them onto the scarf with yarn.

–Melanie Marquis

December

1 **Sunday**
Big Tea Party (Japanese)
Waning Moon
Moon phase: Fourth Quarter
Color: Amber

Moon Sign: Scorpio
Incense: Hyacinth

☽ **Monday**
Republic Day (Loatian)
Waning Moon
Moon phase: New Moon 7:22 pm
Color: Ivory

Moon Sign: Scorpio
Moon enters Sagittarius 1:31 am
Incense: Clary sage

---

3 **Tuesday**
St. Francis Xavier's Day
Waxing Moon
Moon phase: First Quarter
Color: Gray

Moon Sign: Sagittarius
Incense: Basil

---

4 **Wednesday**
St. Barbara's Day
Waxing Moon
Moon phase: First Quarter
Color: Yellow

Moon Sign: Sagittarius
Moon enters Capricorn 1:49 am
Incense: Lavender

---

5 **Thursday**
Hanukkah ends
Waxing Moon
Moon phase: First Quarter
Color: Purple

Moon Sign: Capricorn
Incense: Jasmine

---

6 **Friday**
St. Nicholas' Day
Waxing Moon
Moon phase: First Quarter
Color: Pink

Moon Sign: Capricorn
Moon enters Aquarius 1:53 am
Incense: Mint

---

7 **Saturday**
Burning the Devil (Guatemalan)
Waxing Moon
Moon phase: First Quarter
Color: Blue

Moon Sign: Aquarius
Incense: Rue

December

8 **Sunday**
Feast of the Immaculate Conception
Waxing Moon
Moon phase: First Quarter
Color: Yellow

Moon Sign: Aquarius
Moon enters Pisces 3:34 am
Incense: Frankincense

---

9 **Monday**
St. Leocadia's Day
Waxing Moon
Moon phase: Second Quarter 10:12 am
Color: Gray

Moon Sign: Pisces
Incense: Hyssop

---

10 **Tuesday**
Nobel Day
Waxing Moon
Moon phase: Second Quarter
Color: White

Moon Sign: Pisces
Moon enters Aries 8:06 pm
Incense: Bayberry

---

11 **Wednesday**
Pilgrimage at Tortugas
Waxing Moon
Moon phase: Second Quarter
Color: Brown

Moon Sign: Aries
Incense: Lilac

---

12 **Thursday**
Fiesta of Our Lady of Guadalupe (Mexican)
Waxing Moon
Moon phase: Second Quarter
Color: Crimson

Moon Sign: Aries
Moon enters Taurus 3:40 pm
Incense: Carnation

---

13 **Friday**
St. Lucy's Day (Swedish)
Waxing Moon
Moon phase: Second Quarter
Color: Rose

Moon Sign: Taurus
Incense: Thyme

---

14 **Saturday**
Warriors' Memorial (Japanese)
Waxing Moon
Moon phase: Second Quarter
Color: Black

Moon Sign: Taurus
Incense: Sandalwood

December

15 Sunday
Consualia (Roman)
Waxing Moon
Moon phase: Second Quarter
Color: Gold

Moon Sign: Taurus
Moon enters Gemini 1:40 am
Incense: Juniper

16 Monday
Posadas (Mexican)
Waxing Moon
Moon phase: Second Quarter
Color: White

Moon Sign: Gemini
Incense: Rosemary

⊙ Tuesday
Saturnalia (Roman)
Waxing Moon
Moon phase: Full Moon 4:28 am
Color: Black

Moon Sign: Gemini
Moon enters Cancer 1:17 pm
Incense: Geranium

18 Wednesday
Feast of the Virgin of Solitude
Waning Moon
Moon phase: Third Quarter
Color: Topaz

Moon Sign: Cancer
Incense: Bay laurel

19 Thursday
Opalia (Roman)
Waning Moon
Moon phase: Third Quarter
Color: Green

Moon Sign: Cancer
Incense: Clove

20 Friday
Commerce God Festival (Japanese)
Waning Moon
Moon phase: Third Quarter
Color: Coral

Moon Sign: Cancer
Moon enters Leo 1:48 am
Incense: Orchid

21 Saturday
Yule • Winter Solstice
Waning Moon
Moon phase: Third Quarter
Color: Brown

Moon Sign: Leo
Sun enters Capricorn 12:11 pm
Incense: Ivy

December

22 Sunday
Saints Chaeremon and Ischyrion's Day
Waning Moon
Moon phase: Third Quarter
Color: Orange

Moon Sign: Leo
Moon enters Virgo 2:19 pm
Incense: Hyacinth

23 Monday
Larentalia (Roman)
Waning Moon
Moon phase: Third Quarter
Color: Silver

Moon Sign: Virgo
Incense: Lily

24 Tuesday
Christmas Eve
Waning Moon
Moon phase: Third Quarter
Color: Red

Moon Sign: Virgo
Incense: Cedar

○ Wednesday
Christmas Day
Waning Moon
Moon phase: Fourth Quarter 8:48 am
Color: White

Moon Sign: Virgo
Moon enters Libra 1:17 am
Incense: Honeysuckle

26 Thursday
Kwanzaa begins
Waning Moon
Moon phase: Fourth Quarter
Color: Purple

Moon Sign: Libra
Incense: Myrrh

27 Friday
Boar's Head Supper (English)
Waning Moon
Moon phase: Fourth Quarter
Color: Pink

Moon Sign: Libra
Moon enters Scorpio 8:58 am
Incense: Rose

28 Saturday
Holy Innocents' Day
Waning Moon
Moon phase: Fourth Quarter
Color: Gray

Moon Sign: Scorpio
Incense: Sage

29 Sunday
Feast of St. Thomas Becket
Waning Moon
Moon phase: Fourth Quarter
Color: Amber

Moon Sign: Scorpio
Moon enters Sagittarius 12:37 pm
Incense: Juniper

30 Monday
Republic Day (Madagascan)
Waning Moon
Moon phase: Fourth Quarter
Color: Ivory

Moon Sign: Sagittarius
Incense: Neroli

31 Tuesday
New Year's Eve
Waning Moon
Moon phase: Fourth Quarter
Color: Black

Moon Sign: Sagittarius
Moon enters Capricorn 1:01 pm
Incense: Ginger

Super Cocoa!

Nothing beats the winter doldrums like a big cup of hot chocolate—except maybe a big cup of charmed hot chocolate! Add a dash of cinnamon to imbue your beverage with magical power, passion, or courage. Sprinkle in a little nutmeg to make a drink that will boost your psychic abilities. Stir in a splash of vanilla extract to create a hot chocolate to increase contentment and encourage affection. To make your cup of cocoa even more delicious and powerful, spoon on some whipped cream, then trace symbolic designs in the cream to match your magical intent.

–Melanie Marquis

Fire Magic

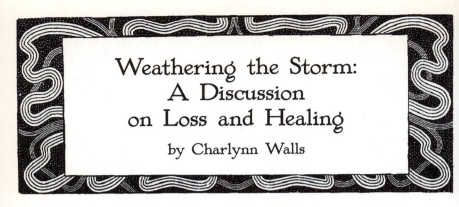

Weathering the Storm: A Discussion on Loss and Healing

by Charlynn Walls

Lightning, thunder, and the pounding rain—the pure intensity of the storm cuts through the atmosphere with surgical precision. The incredible heat, the flash of light, and the rumble of thunder reverberates through your entire being. Nothing is quite as exquisite as a thunderstorm.

They say lightning only strikes the same place once. So, too, do the most influential people in our lives. They are here one moment and gone the next. They leave an indelible mark on our psyche that encompasses the beauty and intensity of their moment in our lives.

That is why the death of a loved one can be so devastating. We've all experienced it, and each time it affects us a little differently. Very often, we—the Pagans, Witches, and Wiccans—are the ones people seek out for a sympathetic ear. But when we are the ones hit by the lightning of grief, how do we regain our own footing? How do we find our balance once again?

The Building Storm

In most instances when a loved one passes into the Summerlands, friends and family seek out the magickally inclined, as we tend to be empathetic and calm in the face of tragedy. We seem to know just what to say and do to comfort those left behind. Even though we are also saddened by the passing, we tend to be the voice of reason to those around us.

But when a close friend passed on, I found myself foundering. My typical thought patterns that included death as a natural progression of life were suddenly nothing but hollow words. Her passing left me in conflict with myself.

There are five generally accepted stages of grief, and I rolled through every one of them: denial, anger, bargaining, depression, and finally acceptance.

When we knew my friend was seriously ill, the last thing I wanted to do was acknowledge that she might die. I made myself scarce at the hospital so I didn't have to directly look at the fact that she was on the verge of death. Those around me knew I was in denial.

Once she passed on, I was furious that one of my dear sisters in the Craft had to leave our small, tightknit community. I was rocked to my spiritual core and unsure of what to do or how to move past that moment. I don't think I have ever felt that level of anger before. There was anger at the doctors for not doing more, anger at her for not trying harder, and anger at myself for not being there. When you're so full of one emotion, there is simply no room for anything else.

I bargained hard with the gods. If I could have traded places with her, I would have. She has a young daughter, after all, and a girl needs her mother. Surely, the universe wouldn't let something like this happen to her when she was still needed here and had so much more to give.

That's the moment when I lost myself. With no outlet for my grief, the depression set in, and once that had control, it seemed impossible to find myself again. The situation became self-perpetuating.

In the Eye of the Storm

Looking back, I did everything the wrong way. I withdrew from my friends and family. I ran from my dearest friends because I didn't want to burden them with my grief. I figured that if I didn't know how to deal with it, they wouldn't either. Or worse yet, they wouldn't want to deal with me as I tried to work through everything. It's very hard to see the big picture when you're in the middle of it.

I shut down and didn't talk out the feelings, which was emotionally exhausting. The more I tried to pretend that I was fine, the more I found myself in a torrent of pent-up emotions. Mentally, I knew I needed to let go and grieve, but actually putting that into practice seemed to be too hard of a challenge.

I sat with a heavy heart, pondering how to get past my block, while watching a thunderstorm pass. It was everything I felt. It was raw, intense, and unyielding. I felt like I could scream into the raging storm, and it would swallow up my words. There was some comfort in knowing that the storm was more powerful than me. It was a relief that I could vent, cry, or scream and not be criticized or denigrated for my loss of composure.

In that moment, I decided to do some weather witching to release all my built-up neglected emotion. Storms have an enormous amount of power, and it was time to tap into it. It was finally time to start healing.

I had found an outlet for my grief and a way toward accepting my new reality. It was fitting that it dealt with water as a conduit for change and understanding.

Ritual for Weathering the Storm

"Weathering the storm" is the perfect analogy for what I was feeling—the buildup of grief and anger, the release, and the eventual healing and growth. Each part is evident in the different parts of a storm and each is equally vital.

To do this ritual, you'll need a clear place to view a thunderstorm from your home. I find that a low window works best if you want to sit on the floor. If you have a window near a bed or comfortable chair, that will work as well. Please remember to keep yourself safe at all times.

If clear skies are in the forecast, you may want to find a recording of a storm to help you visualize the parts of this ritual and help focus your intent. Turn on the recording and set it to repeat. If you have a picture of your loved one, you may want to include that as well.

Once you have everything you need, make sure you are seated comfortably. I prefer to sit on the floor or in a window seat, so I can easily see the show that Mother Nature is putting on. No matter where you sit, make sure you have easy access to the window and that it's easy to open.

The first step will be to cast a simple circle. When I need to let go of negativity, I don't always feel the need for all the pomp and circumstance of a typical ritual. By closing my eyes and envisioning myself surrounded by a sphere of blue-white light, I can make my circle as small or large as I need. You'll want to do the same and make your circle comfortable. If possible, push the circle out just past the window. Once you have your circle in place, take a deep breath and exhale. This has a dual effect of setting the sacred space and grounding you at the same time.

Then call the quarters. Feel free to embellish on the versions I'm providing. Make sure they speak to you and what you want to accomplish. For my tradition, we typically begin in the north.

North: *Guardians of the north, let the rumble of the thunder be felt through me all the way to my core, helping ground and balance me. Welcome!*

East: *Guardians of the east, let your winds whip around me and dry my tears, bringing clarity and perspective. Welcome!*

South: *Guardians of the south, those forged in the heat of lightning, let me see past myself to those who love and need me. Welcome!*

West: *Guardians of the west, let your rain fall upon me and wash away the remaining anger and negativity and leave me ready for new growth. Welcome!*

Call to the God and Goddess. You can use any pantheon that you're comfortable with. I suggest using deities associated with storms, lightning, or rain.

Lord and Lady, gather near and offer your insight and counsel. Welcome!

When you can see a flash of lightning and hear the thunder in the distance, let the sound wash over you and through you. Close your eyes, and feel the rumbling pulse in your veins, building intensity. This is the anguish and anger you've held on to. It builds to a crescendo, and it must find a release or the pressure will rip you apart.

As the storm is reaching its peak, take some time to stop and look at the photo of your loved one. Reflect on what they meant to you. Take the time to connect to why you are reeling so profoundly from the loss.

You can yell into the storm to help rid yourself of your grief. If you are at a loss of words, you can repeat the following chant until you feel ready to release your burden to the God and Goddess. Let it build so that it reflects the enormity of your emotions. Chant:

Lord and Lady, hear my cries of anguish and despair,
Take from me my burden of pain and fear.

If you are able to open the window, you may want to do so now; if not, you can visualize the rain falling on your skin. Feel the rain as it drops onto your skin. Let the cool water soothe your anger. Cry if you can, and let the tears meld with the raindrops. Feel the release of the aggression and the hurt until there's nothing left to cry out. Allow the rain to cleanse and fill up the void that is left. Take the healing energy into you as if you were the earth soaking up the rain.

As the storm moves on and the sky begins to lighten, reflect on the spiritual journey you've just taken. Though things once looked dim, there is now a light on the horizon. The once oppressive and overwhelming feelings are just like the storm and will pass eventually. Take solace in the fact there is always a silver lining in every cloud.

Now, it is time to close the circle.

Lord and Lady, thank you for helping me shoulder my burden and for providing valuable insight. Stay if you will, go if you must.

West: *Guardians of the west, thank you for lending your cooling rain to temper my raw emotion. Farewell.*

South: *Guardians of the south, thank you for illuminating the issues that need work. Farewell.*

East: *Guardians of the east, thank you for the wind that comforted and cleansed. Farewell.*

North: *Guardians of the north, thank you for the stabilizing forces that give me strength to go on. Farewell.*

Now, close your eyes and hold in your mind the blue-white sphere of your sacred space. Watch it dissolve from above and below you into a thin line of a glowing circle around you. See the line weaken in intensity until it is completely gone. Take another

cleansing breath and exhale. The ritual is now complete. When you are ready and composed, you can start to move on.

Reflections on the Passing Storm

The beauty of this ritual is its simplicity. This practice let me focus on my feelings so I could see past the negativity to the healing and growth on the other side. Of course, it wasn't an overnight solution, but when I was ready to finally give up the hurt and anger, it was an invaluable part of being able to move forward.

Though not everyone will experience the stages of grief and healing the same way, we all go through the process. The important thing is to remember to honor yourself in addition to the person who passed so that you can heal. Lean on those you love and trust if you can and remember that deity will always listen. It is often a long journey, but it doesn't have to be filled with the heaviness of unexpressed hurt.

Everyday Totemism

by Lupa

Does everyone have a totem animal that stays with them their entire life? Some say yes, others say no. Regardless, totemism isn't just about those "primary" totems. The same person may have all kinds of different relationships and interactions with animal totems, and they don't all have to last a lifetime.

That has been my experience since I began working with animal totems in my spirituality since the 1990s. Rather than following what other people told me to do to connect with totems, I found my own path through that forest via a lot of trial and error. I quickly discovered was that there was no set number of totems a person could or should have and not every totem stuck around for a long time.

As I met and worked with more and more totem animals, I created an easy organizational system to help me describe some of these totemic relationships:

Primary totems are what most people think of when they talk about animal totems. These are your "life" totems, the ones who are around for the long haul, as it were.

Secondary totems are ones that come into your life on their own volition to help you through a stage of your life or a particular time period. Once their intent has been fulfilled, they generally leave your life, though some do make visits later on. But even then, they aren't as consistently present as primary totems.

Tertiary totems are totems that you approach to ask for help with something specific or simply to find out more about them. If you want help with a single ritual or untangling a problem in your life, you can find out what totem or totems may be best able to help you, and then approach them for that help.

Any totem animal can be a primary, secondary, or tertiary totem. It all depends on the nature of its relationship with that person. The particular totem itself isn't crucial—what matters is the intensity and duration of the connection between the totem and person.

This essay is about working with tertiary totems. While not everyone may have a primary totem, just about anyone can ask totems for help with more short-term goals, even if you've never worked with totems before.

Identify the Problem

The first thing you'll want to do is to figure out what you want help with. Here are some ideas:

• getting a boost in a job hunt or business endeavor, such as making the right connections with the right people or finding and making the most of resources available to you

• adding a spiritual component for treating existing medical problems or creating some magick to promote continued good health

• blessing and protecting a home, workplace, or other location

• making it through a particularly tough or challenging stage in your life, making a life passage or other transition

- staying focused and energized in activism, such as for the environment, animal welfare, human rights, etc.
- guidance and protection through a specific rite of passage or other ritual

Don't feel constrained by this list. Animal totems are a bridge between their species and the rest of the world, so they are not strangers to what we face, though the importance of our problems may need a little "translation."

For example, a number of years ago I was job hunting and wanted some help staying focused and motivated amid the sending of résumés and the receiving of "Sorry, we're hiring someone else" letters. So I asked American Badger for some aid in finding a job. I was inspired by Badger's tenacity first and foremost. However, Badger didn't quite understand what I was trying to achieve with this whole "employment" thing. So I explained to him that I wanted a bit of a boost finding the resources I need to maintain my den (apartment) and be able to acquire food (which to Badger, for some reason, looked like a huge pile of earthworms!). Once I was able to connect my job hunt to those concepts, it made a lot more sense Badger, and I got the help I needed.

So while you may need to do a similar bit of translation for more abstract concepts, don't be afraid to ask for what you need.

Identify the Totem

Once you have your need identified, you're going to need to determine what totem animal (or animals) may be able to help you. There are a few ways to go about doing this.

While I am not personally a huge fan of totem animal dictionaries, they are a record of how the authors have interacted with various totems. Most books on animal totemism have at least a brief dictionary, and some, such as Ted Andrews' *Animal-Speak*, are largely composed of dictionary entries detailing the totemic lore surrounding a variety of species. If you do choose the dictionary route, please be aware that the totem animal may not be willing or able to help you with the same things that the author writes about. Part of working with totems means creating individual relationships with them, even if only for a short time. Be open to what a totem has to say to you, even if it's not by the book.

You can also use a totem animal card deck. The main limitation is that only so many animals can fit in one deck. If the totem that's the best fit for your situation isn't in the deck, then you may not be able to identify her. On the other hand, with tertiary totems, there are usually multiple totems that can help with the same problem, so chances are good that at least one totem in the deck may be able to give you some assistance.[1]

The most direct method for identifying the relevant animal is to do a guided meditation. This allows you to be receptive to any totem that answers your request for help without expecting any specific animal to show up. There are a number of guided meditations that will work. Here's one brief example:

Visualize yourself going into a hole in the ground that leads into a tunnel, holding the problem or situation you would like help resolving. As you go through this tunnel, know that it will take you to a place where you can meet totem animals that may be able to assist you. As you come out of the tunnel, you find yourself in a natural place. Take time to explore this place and see if any animals appear. You may find one or more that come up to you; these will be the ones most likely to respond to your need. Take some time to speak with them and ask them why they've approached. Listen carefully and remember them for the next time you visit. Then come back to the waking world with the information you have gathered and write down as much as you can.

You can also use this meditation if you already know which totem you want to ask for help. She may be one that you have worked with before, or you may just feel intuitively that she's the one to speak with. Go into the

---

1. To address the limitations of totem animal card decks, I created "The Last Totem Card Deck You'll Ever Need." It is specifically designed to help you get in touch with literally any totem animal in the world, even extinct or mythological ones. You can find out more information in my book *DIY Totemism: Your Personal Guide to Animal Totems* (Megalithica Books, 2008).

tunnel with the intent of coming out to a place where you can meet that totem.

The meditation is also useful for continued visits to the totem. As with the previous example, enter the tunnel intending to meet the totem you're working with when you get to the other end.

Do be aware that this visualization doesn't work every time—a number of factors are at play. If no animal shows up or approaches, it may be that the animals present did not feel ready to help. Or you may not be able to focus well enough yet, especially if you haven't had much practice with guided meditation. And if you're really anticipating results, that anticipation can actually sabotage your efforts by making it too hard to relax into the meditation.

If this occurs, take a break of at least a week, if you can. Then come back and try again.

Asking for Help

Now that you've identified at least one totem animal who may be able to help you, it's time to ask for that help. I generally recommend some formality. You don't have to create a candlelit seven-course banquet with the totem's favorite foods; however, putting together a nice ritual often helps.

First, create a space to invite the totem to. This can be a small shrine on a shelf adorned with pictures and other images of the totem. If you have a dedicated ritual space, cleanse it and decorate it appropriately. Wear your ritual garments or at the very least, something nice that you can still perform ritual in.

An offering is also a good idea. If you offer food, make it something you can eat. Offer the spiritual essence to the totem while taking in the physical calories yourself. I don't recommend leaving the food out for wildlife because that encourages them to associate humans with food, which is a bad idea. Instead, think of it as a sharing—breaking bread together. Other offerings may include a favor to help the totem's physical counterparts (especially if they're endangered), composing a story or song in praise of the totem, or simply asking what the totem would like in exchange for helping you.

Once your sacred space and offering are prepared, it's time to call on the totem. You may go visit through guided meditation and ask the totem to come back to your space with you, or you can take the offering in spirit with you and offer it there. Or you can simply call the totem into your space; here's one short sample evocation:

[Name of totem], I invite you to this place
For I have a request, and a gift for you.
Grant me some of your time and space.
I need your help; there is work to do!

How will you know the totem has arrived? This varies from person to person. Some see shapes or movement out of the corner of their eye. Others notice a strange breeze or aroma. Sometimes it's purely intuitive; you can "feel" when the totem has arrived, changing the energy of a place.

Once the totem has arrived, explain what you need help with and make the offering. See how the totem responds. Just because you ask for help doesn't mean you're going to get it, at least not as requested. The totem may have other suggestions or requirements—or feel that a different totem is more able to help you. However, if the totem is able to help, you can now discuss what each of you needs to do to make things happen.

There have been times where a totem has made a special request of me in addition to the offering I made. Even tertiary totemic relationships are not one-way streets—we need to remember that totems are not just hanging around to make things happen for us. If the totem asks for your help with something in return, listen carefully and be honest about your ability to help. Under no circumstances should you promise something and then not follow through on it, especially if the totem upholds his end of the agreement!

Either way, at this point it's up to you and the totem to negotiate what each of you will do. There's no single right way to do this. Just take your time and do your best to both explain your end of things, and listen to what the totem says in response.

Making It Happen

So let's say all goes well and the totem has agreed to help you. He may have specific things you need to do on your end, such as daily meditations or spells, or working together to create another ritual aimed at manifesting what you desire into reality. Or you may simply carry around a small reminder of the totem to carry his energy, such as a necklace or charm, to help him influence your day-to-day life.

While all this is happening on a spiritual level, don't neglect the mundane activities! This is what the spiritual work is meant to augment, and if you aren't doing the mundane work, then the spiritual work has nowhere to go. So keep on job hunting, or visiting your doctor, or taking time out in a busy day for some self-care, and see how the spiritual work affects and even improves these seemingly routine everyday activities.

Of course, the end results may vary. Even with totemic help, you may still not get what you asked for. You may get nothing, or you might get something even better than you hoped for! No magic or other effort is a guarantee, but we do these things to try to increase the probability that we will achieve our goals. Eventually you will have to determine whether things are improving or not, and keep talking with the totem about the next plan of action as long as she is still willing to help.

What If It's More?

While tertiary totemic relationships are temporary, there are instances in which they can develop into something more long-lasting. You may find that you and the totem enjoy working together enough that you continue the connection. Or your act of asking for help might have been the invitation the totem needed to come into your life in a more interactive manner.

Again, the best practice is to ask what the totem would like from you. However, if you want to be proactive, try making a permanent shrine to the totem in your home, even if it's just one small shelf. You can also try daily meditation with the totem and even regular rituals celebrating the presence of the totem in your life. And the totem may be able to help you with other areas of your life besides your original request, as well as ask other things of you to help him out.

Either way, be open to the possibilities. Each totemic relationship is its own unique thing to be cherished and explored, whether it lasts a day or a lifetime.

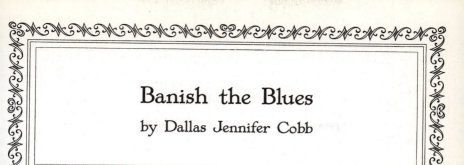

Banish the Blues
by Dallas Jennifer Cobb

Are you blue? Do you struggle with heavy energy and wish you could change it? Regardless of how resolved we are or how in harmony with family, nature, and the seasons, there are times when we are affected by sticky or depressing energy, commonly called "the blues."

While there are no instant solutions for major life challenges, and at times we need to retreat to express and heal strong emotions and powerful experiences, we can find proactive ways to "banish the blues." Pagan author Starhawk says, "Magic is the practice of changing your energy at will," and fortified with the knowledge of herbs, oils, techniques, foods, and spells that can help transform your energy, you can practice strong personal magic, and banish the blues.

This article is not intended to replace sound medical advice for extreme depression. If you have anything more serious than a case of "the blues," including but not limited to feeling suicidal or being unable to cope with daily life, seek professional help.

The Blues

Everybody gets the blues. A feeling of low energy, listlessness, and disinterest, a touch of sadness, betrayal, or even a broken heart can make us feel like retreating from life a little. It's not just emotional situations that can cause the blues, but physical, mental, spiritual, and environmental situations.

Physical reasons for feeling blue can include minor illnesses or imbalances; overindulgences in alcohol, drugs, or candy; a lack of sleep or downtime; and extreme physical wear and tear caused by overwork.

Mentally, periods of low self-esteem, social isolation, worry, and indecision can cause the blues. Overthinking, overanalyzing, and overreacting can all send us spiraling down.

Spiritually, a crisis of faith, feeling disconnected from Spirit or higher power, and even deep-rooted questions about good and evil in the universe create chaos. Blues that come from spiritual sources can shake us to our roots.

Almost everyone experiences the blues with the change of seasons: we say goodbye to summer friends, return to school or work, and change our hobbies, activities, and routines. Seasonal change is a well-known environmental factor affecting mood, especially the shift from summer to winter when we feel the effect of dwindling daylight. It causes low energy, a reticence to go outdoors, and sometimes a desire to stay curled up on the couch. Environmentally induced blues are not to be confused with SAD or Seasonal Affective Disorder, which is a profound medical depression associated with the lack of light.

Other environmental blues could include the heaviness that comes from working in a poorly lit conditions with little ventilation or fresh air, around a lot of electromagnetic energy, or even being around a bunch of people who are themselves very negative and heavy.

Banishing Techniques

There are many techniques and tools we can use to help transform our energy and banish the blues. And many of these tactics come from within—never underestimate the power of changing your own energy. It can have life-changing effects, and for this reason, do not take these techniques and tools too lightly. And as with all magic, harm no one.

While there are tons of banishing and evil hexing spells out there, I find the most profound magic occurs when I change my energy at will, so many of these tools and techniques focus on everyday practices you can do without a lot of specialty items, or too much preparation. They are "spells" of daily living, so they are easy to perform.

Changing your energy at will might sound hard, but there are a few really simple techniques you can use. As simple as the ABC's: awareness, breath, body, conditions, cognition, and spirit.

Awareness

Take a look at your life. In broad strokes, awareness is a powerful magical tool. A lack of balance in your life, bad relationships, and social isolation are very common causes for feeling blue. Are you getting enough sleep, eating well, and staying hydrated? Do you enjoy time outdoors in nature and have a supportive circle of friends and family? If you are aware of something you lack, consider addressing that deficiency in your life. Then expect that positive changes will come from this simple lifestyle adjustment.

Do your own diagnosis. When you feel blue, get out a pen and paper and write. Jot down everything that might be contributing to how you feel, no matter how small and insignificant it seems. Often, by the time you finish writing, you will have come to the "aha!" moment, realizing exactly what is contributing to feeling blue and how best to banish those blues.

Not just useful for intervention, awareness is one of the best and most effective preventative practices. Since prevention is easier than cure, incorporate "blues banishing" techniques into your daily life. If time for self-reflection, eating well, a full night's sleep, physical exercise, and time outdoors are all part of your daily routine, you have already laid a strong groundwork for blues prevention.

Breath

The power of breath is transformational. When I get rattled and need instant help, be it a need for calm, focus, or a feeling of safety, I pull the earth's energy up through my feet and into my body with a deep inhale. Exhaling, I send the energy cascading out the top of my head, flowing over my body and back to the earth. Usually, it only takes about three breaths before I feel tingling on the back of my neck, tightening of my scalp, and the elevation of spirit. Try it and be surprised by the efficacy of this simple technique.

Body

Sure, we hear so much about diet these days that we often tune out. But diet warrants attention if we want to banish the blues. By diet, I don't mean a restrictive method of reducing calories so you can lose weight, but simple awareness of what and how to eat, ensuring that a wide variety of foods in their most natural state possible is consumed. Eating small meals regularly helps keep blood-sugar levels balanced and provides ongoing fuel for the day. Fruits and vegetables are rich in antioxidants, which overcome the negative energy of free radicals. Avoiding overprocessed foods, trans-fats, simple sugars, additives, and dyes can significantly improve how we feel both physically and mentally, whereas overconsumption of these can overload the organs, making them to work overtime to process this "toxic" stuff, which can cause us to feel poorly.

Research provides clinical evidence to support the claim that exercise is related to positive mental health as indicated by relief in symptoms of depression and anxiety. Not only can exercise increase positive self-image and self-esteem, but it stimulates the production of endorphins, the feel-good hormones. You have heard about "runner's high," but all forms of exercise have the potential to uplift, not just improving mood, but lessening bodily aches and pains.

Sleep and mood are directly connected, so a practice of getting a good night's sleep every night (this varies and can change as a person develops, but is generally between seven and ten hours) will contribute to more even-keeled energy overall. Sleep in a really dark room, because when the eyes sense darkness, they trigger a gland in the brain to produce melatonin, which helps establish a positive sleep cycle. For many of us, avoiding caffeine, tobacco, and other unnatural stimulants is also necessary for normal sleep patterns.

Conditions

Take seasonal change into consideration: sit in the sun more because sunlight stimulates a gland in the brain to generate serotonin, which elevates mood and promotes wakefulness; get outdoors in the middle of the day, and engage in exercise to boost your level of feel-good endorphins; and if you can afford it, consider taking a winter vacation to the sunny south, or even doing light therapy with a special fluorescent light box.

Do what you can to modify work conditions or environments so they don't drain your good energy. Adding plants and water features and full-spectrum lighting will contribute to better air and light quality. As for the raft of negative coworkers, dose them with affirmations and positivity, surround yourself with protective energy, and at worst, avoid them as much as possible.

Cognition

I once read that we have about 60,000 thoughts a day, and over 80 percent of these are negative. If we tend to worry, obsess, or beat up on ourselves, think of the daily and cumulative effects of those thoughts!

Affirmation is a powerful tool for inserting positive messages into your conscious and subconscious mind, rewriting some of those 60,000 daily thoughts. Writing lines in the morning, singing or chanting a mantra, or posting notes that you read regularly throughout the day are all easy ways to generate positive messages. Write your own affirmation that addresses your personal situation, or use one of my favorites: "I am blessed by happiness"; "All is well in my world"; or "I now possess the time energy, money, and wisdom needed to accomplish all my desires."

Spirit

Some of the most effective blues banishers are techniques that are free and easy—prayer and meditation. You don't have to be religious to use prayer, and you don't need to get a guru to practice meditation. Think of prayer as asking or telling the universe (high power, nature, Goddess) what your problems are and where you need clarity, and think of meditation as listening. I use these techniques frequently in a variety of situations: walking vigorously for about thirty minutes (or until the endorphins kick in) usually brings clarity to my troubled mind; sitting on the rocks by the lake, aware of the beauty and wisdom in nature, often helps me to connect to the eternal metaphor of natural cycles and make sense of my life; and gathering with my circle for rituals and celebrations helps me to connect to different aspects of the elements, gods, and goddesses.

Of course, if you can also attend a church, synagogue, mosque, or otherwise connect with a spiritual community, you can ask for forgiveness, salvation, or hope and hear the answers in sacred scriptures or texts.

Other Banishing Tools

In addition to techniques that require few outside aids, there are tools you can use to help banish the blues, including the elements, herbs, and aromatherapy. When I am in a bad place and know I need outside help quickly, I usually reach for these to help shift my energy.

The Elements

When push comes to shove, get back to the basics. The elements are powerful tools for banishing the blues. Fire, water, earth, and air each can pull us out of that downward spiral.

Smudging is the use of fire energy and the smoke from sacred herbs, usually sweet grass or sage, to cleanse a space, object, or person of negative energy and recharge with positive. Herbs are burned in a fire-safe container, and the smoke is bathed over the entire object or through the entire space. Fire is a powerful purifier; the heat burns away negativity, which is carried up and away by the smoke.

Water's strong transformational energy can be easily used to banish the blues. If you feel out of sorts, run a warm bath. Add either two cups of sea salt (for cleansing negative energy and restoring balance) or a few drops of essential oil (to protect, uplift, and anoint). In an emergency situation, simply drink a glass of water while focusing on the calming and transformational energy as it seeps into you and is digested.

Visiting my in-laws one day, I felt self-conscious and insecure. For a quick intervention, I slipped into their backyard, placed my bare feet on the earth, grounded myself and drew from her sacred energy to restore my balance and feelings of self-worth.

Air can be used as breath (see page 236) or even as wind. Step outside and let all negativity be blown away.

Herbs

Many herbs can help transform energy and banish the blues, but herbs are powerful tools and should be prescribed by a certified

herbalist. Find one in your area to discuss your health and get advice. Even widely known and effective herbs, some of which are listed below, must be administered to meet the specific needs of each person.

St. John's wort (*Hypericum perferatum*) grows wild where I live. Flowering in the summer, it stores the vital energy of the sun in its brilliant yellow flowers as hypericin and hyperforin, both considered to be mood lifters. It relieves mild to moderate depression, calms, and is mildly sedative. Commercially prepared tinctures, tablets, and teas are available in most health-food stores, but there are a number of contraindications (situations in which you should not take St. John's wort), so consult an herbalist.

Passionflower (*Passiflora incarnata*) can be used to treat anxiety, as it has a calming effect on the nervous sytem. It's used in many teas that promote restful sleep.

Valerian root (*Valeriana officinalis*) is bitter tasting and strong smelling. The commercial drug Valium comes from it. While occasional use of valerian can calm jagged nerves and promote sleep, it shouldn't be used regularly as it disrupts natural sleep cycles.

Skullcap (*Scutilaria lateriflora*) is used to relieve headaches, anxiety, mild pain, and insomnia. It eases depression and is a general tonic for the nervous system.

While not an herb, folate, which occurs naturally in citrus fruit and dark green leafy vegetables, plays a role in healthy neurological functioning. Folate deficiency has been linked to depression and low energy. So eat well from a wide variety of foods and consider a multivitamin with folic acid to cover your nutritional needs.

Aromatherapy

Smell can trigger memories, stimulate emotions, and even help us focus or concentrate. Aromatherapy can stimulate the olfactory sense, affecting the physical body, emotions, and mind.

While everyone has favorite scents that hold positive associations, the most effective essential oils to banish the blues are common scents. Rose, clary sage, lavender, sandalwood, and jasmine are all effective in banishing blues. As with other powerful substances, consult a professional for guidance or purchase professionally crafted blends.

Dab on a diluted form of the oil as a body scent to be with you all day, add a few drops to a bath to provide a full-body blanket of protection, or set up a diffuser in your home to broadcast the therapeutic scent throughout.

Bye-Bye Blues

Armed with these simple tools and techniques, you have the power to transform your energy at will and banish the blues. While these are all highly effective, don't forget the power of gathering together in magical community to perform spell and ritual work and to celebrate.

There is amazing power in community that can uplift us even on the days when we feel to weak to banish our own blues. Don't forget to reach out for an element, a tool or technique, or the support of your community, and say "bye-bye" to the blues.

Dancing with Mercury, Backwards: Do More Than Just Survive Mercury Retrograde

by Lisa McSherry

I was talking with a woman at the gym the other day and she told me a story about trying to meet up with a friend coming in from out of town. It was a tale of missed calls, lost e-mails, and misunderstood words. When she was done, I commiserated, then asked her when this happened. Her reply matched with my suspicions, and I said, "Did you know you were doing all of that during Mercury retrograde?"

The basis of astrology (in extremely simple terms) is that a planet's energy influences matters here on Earth and that the different planets have energies that correspond with various gods and goddesses. So as a planet moves through its normal orbit, its energy changes and those changes are transmitted to us here on Earth. Three times a year, the planet Mercury goes retrograde for twenty-one to twenty-three days, and that "backwards" energy influences things on Earth in ways both subtle and gross. The planet isn't really moving backwards, but itappears to be because of the planetary motion created by the orbital rotation of Earth in relation to the other planets in our solar system. All the planets experience retrograde periods, but the one that gets the most attention is Mercury because its impact is the most noticeable in our modern world.

Mercury Mischief, Magic

The Roman god Mercury (Hermes to the Greeks) is the messenger of the gods—the link between spirit and matter, between soul and personality. Mercury symbolizes the power of communication, reasoning capacities, and the ability to perceive relationships and gather facts. Mercury narrates,

talks, argues, debates, writes, analyzes, memorizes, studies, travels, sells, reflects, and expresses itself through the hands as well as the tongue. Mercury is the magician and the trickster, two sides of the same coin, both inclined to be hard teachers. As a master of the hidden realms, Mercury confounds us with unexpected information and events and challenges our habitual perceptions. He also surprises us with unexpected gifts and new possibilities. If we like the surprises, we call it magic; if we don't, we call it bad luck. Either way, the result is to jar us from the inertia of our routines and move us out of the mundane. So when the planet is retrograde, we can expect things "ruled" by Mercury to go haywire; it's just another way Mercury is providing lessons.

Mercury retrograde periods are plagued by indecision, bad timing, delays, communication errors, and mechanical problems. Although many of us particularly notice computer problems during this time frame, Uranus is the planet that rules electronic devices, including computers. But since so much of our communication is conducted via computer, Mercury's influence has expanded.

For many of us, knowing when Mercury goes retrograde can be a sanity saver. We can mark retrograde periods on our calendars so we won't throw parties, write letters, buy electronics (or pets), sign contracts, or take a new job. If nothing else, it's a time to take extra care that what you say is understood as you meant it to be. For years, it was a time when I battened down the hatches and rode out the messed up energies.

No longer. Now I use the retrograde energies of Mercury in ways that the work like a kind of cosmic aikido move. Doing so has transformed nine weeks of my year into positive, productive times and my frustration level has decreased dramatically.

The key is to remember that Mercury retrograde is a time for "re" doing things. So it is a wonderful time for anything based on research, planning, examination of resources, and completing projects. You don't want to start anything new during Mercury retrograde, but if there is a project hanging out there that you haven't gotten around to finishing, this is the perfect time to return to it. Here are specific ideas to use Mercury's backwards energy to your advantage.

Review Your Resolutions
Pull out that list of goals you made and spend some time contemplating their value to you. Are they still relevant? Perhaps you wanted to learn Chinese because of that cute guy in the cafeteria. Are they achievable? Losing 100 pounds in three months is unhealthy. What has been blocking you from forward progress on them? What do you need to make the goals manifest? Perhaps you need more money, time, or privacy. This is a great time to examine whether these goals come from your truest desire, or whether you are trying to please someone else—which is often a major blockage to your success. You are not a fixed object, even if it feels like nothing changes in your

life; the truth is that there are many things changing constantly. Sticking with an outdated resolution, or one made in the heat of the moment, is just a waste of your time and attention. Use the three weeks of Mercury retrograde to dig in to your list of resolutions and make the changes you need to succeed.

Reorganize It (Closet, Junk Drawer, Basement, or …)

Been meaning to clean out your hall closet, the one you just cram things in and force the door closed? Or perhaps your "junk" drawer has gone beyond being useful. Or maybe you have a garage or basement that holds boxes of things, and you're not sure what? This is a great period to set aside time and clean it out. Take it in stages, especially if it's a really big job. You don't need to do it all at once. Get good music playing, make sure you've had a healthy meal (low sugar, lots of complex carbohydrates), and have a plan. (Personally, I like to have three piles: toss, recycle/sell, keep. The recycle/sell pile is the one I try to make the largest, I hate adding to landfill, and I don't want to keep everything I pull out.) Use labels and markers on the boxes you pack up and return to storage—you want to know what is in there in the future! If the task is really

huge, spend thirty minutes right at the beginning planning how you'll tackle the space and where your stopping point is, then take a break and do something else. Thereafter take breaks every fifteen minutes so you don't burn out.

Re-examine It

Mercury retrograde is a truly bad time to schedule a surgery because of the high probability of misunderstandings and poor communication—not what you want when you're unconscious! It is, however, a fantastic time to get diagnostic work taken care of. Have an odd crick in your neck for a while now? See the chiropractor or masseuse and ask them to look into it. Been meaning to have blood work done? Now is the time. Mercury's energies at this time trend toward introspection, so honor yourself by making sure you are as healthy as you can be.

Recycle It

Mercury retrograde is a great time to do anything related to cleaning and organizing. If you've been putting off getting rid of something, perhaps now is a good time to pass it along. I travel a lot, so I always bring home those mini-toiletries. One

set goes in the guest room just in case someone forgot something, but the others go to a local domestic violence shelter. If it's clean and functional, or can be with a little work, join your local Freecycle, post it on Craigslist, or make a run to your local donation store. Getting rid of the clutter in your life is very good for clearing out any stagnant energies—and it's a joy to have clean space where there once was a mess!

Renew It

Check your subscriptions and spend a little time thinking about whether you really want to keep each one. I find myself signing up for a lot of magazines when I am flush with cash and I can get crazy discounts for buying several years at a time. Some publications are still great after a year, but others just start feeling repetitive or boring.

This is also a great time to check the expiration date on all of your legal and social documentation. These are things like your driver's license, passport, memberships (social and political), and credit cards. If it has an expiration date on it, check it and decide whether you want to renew or drop it.

Repair It

I have a basket in my closet where I put clothes that need to be fixed—a missing button, a rip in the seam, a hem that needs lifting. These aren't big tasks, and not terribly difficult, but we usually don't make time. Mercury retrograde is a perfect time to take care of these small fixes. Other small fixes might be touching up the paint on your car (dealers sell small bottles of paint for just this task), fixing that broken headlight, straightening the wobbly table, mending the hole in the wall, or replacing the washer in that dripping faucet.

Revive It (Declutter Your Desk)

If you do nothing else during Mercury retrograde, clean your desk or workspace. My desk is where I spend easily as much time as I do at my day job. It's where I write, edit, talk, and play. I'm a pretty neat person, but I still make a point of clearing it all off and putting it back during Mercury retrograde. Taking everything off (and out) lets you reimagine the space and perhaps make changes that improve your habits. I'm a big fan of re-purposing shoeboxes (labeled, of course) to hold my office supplies. It takes just a moment to pull out the stapler or tape, and I don't use them all of the time. My desk normally holds just the piles of things I am working on, a notepad for making lists, and a pen (aside from my computer, that is). Everything I might need is stored in a bookcase behind me.

Review Your Links

I've been online since the mid-1990s and had collected literally thousands of links in my "favorites" folders. Most of them were sorted into fifty different subcategories, it's true, but there were so many I wasn't really using them—it was faster to just do another Web search. Then I was given a gift: during a reformatting of my hard drive, my favorites folder was accidentally wiped. It was gone. I could have restored it from a backup, but I decided to put that off and see if I'd need it. It's been a year, and I haven't restored them. Mercury retrograde is a great time to take a look at your saved information. Do you actually use those links? If you had them as part of a research project, maybe it's time to pull the data and put it into documents you can use? Do you really want to keep all of those broken links?

Re-up Your Warranties (or not)

This is a fun one. It seems like everything we buy comes with an instruction manual/warranty and if you're like me you just toss it in a drawer "just in case." Now the time to pull all of them out and sort through them. Keep the ones that might still be useful and recycle the rest. (Do you really need a manual on how to use your toaster?) For the ones you keep, try to find them online to download to your computer, then recycle the paper. (I have a folder called "warranties" just for these.)

Review

A great use of Mercury's retrograde energy is to spend time thinking about how you want your life to be and what you want to do going forward. Ask yourself if there is something missing that you'd like to manifest in your life or a change you think would be positive. This is a great time to review those decisions and look for hidden flaws and problems. Wait until Mercury goes direct to actually start any new projects or directions.

Reconcile It (Expect Miscommunication)

My husband and I spend a lot of extra time during Mercury retrograde checking in with each other and making sure that we understood what the other said. We've had plenty of times when one said yes and the other heard no, so we check, double-check and sometimes triple-check. We also completely forgive the other's mistake before an apology is proffered—it's not our fault. One way to cope with this aspect (which can be the most frustrating) is to slow down and really listen when people talk to you. You may want to take the time to repeat back the gist of what they said. Mostly, be patient and prepared to correct others' misunderstandings of what you said.

Relax!

This is an excellent time to catch up on your reading, especially the recreational reading. Above all, try to relax! Don't let the haywire energies cause you stress. Keep breathing, calmly and deeply, and give everything more time so you can correct mistakes before they become problems.

Mercury retrograde is not my favorite time of the year, but I'm a lot less stressed about it now that I've learned some strategies for using the backwards energy to my advantage.

For Further Study

Arroyo, Stephen. *Astrology, Psychology and the Four Elements*. Davis, CA: CRCS Publications, 1975.

deVore, Nicholas. *Encyclopedia of Astrology*. Philosophical Library, 1947.

Wilkinson, Robert, and Samuel Weiser. York Beach, ME: *A New Look at Mercury Retrograde*, 1997.

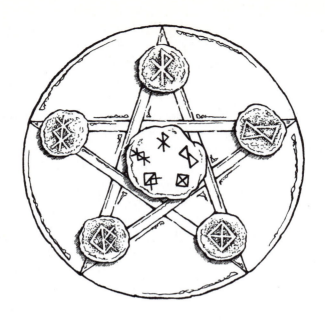

Five-Day Spellcasting

by Marion Sipe

Spellwork is most effective when both the mundane and magical paths to the goal can be seen and understood. This can be difficult for more complex or long-term goals, but you can make them easier to visualize by breaking them down into steps, so that each step becomes a goal in itself. Five-day spellwork forces you to consider what the steps toward your eventual goal are and to see them in a linear way.

This method of casting uses bindrunes (the traditional Nordic runes drawn in combined form to represent the day's goal) and the five elements (earth, air, fire, water, and spirit) to build up each step, forming in your mind and your spell object a map to lead the way to your goal.

The first day, call earth to lay the foundation and anchor your spell within your spell object. On the second day, call air to breath life into the goal. The third day call fire, because without passion and determination, we can't achieve anything. On the fourth day, call water to smooth the way, to wear away obstacles and acknowledge the emotional effects that the achieving of your goal will bring. On the last day, call spirit to send the spell out into the world, to bring the goal from the hypothetical world into the material one.

Materials

For this spellwork, the only materials you need are a spell object, a candle marked into five equal sections, a permanent marker, and five bindrunes to represent the daily goals of the spell. This sort of spellwork does not require elaborate ritual or tools; in fact, simplicity is preferable. I always perform this type of spell on a nearly bare altar—and once on a tea tray with the materials and few symbolic objects. Simplicity helps to control the influences you bring in on a day-to-day basis, so don't clutter the space or your mind. Use only those materials that are best suited to your purpose and in harmony with each day's goal.

The spell object is the thing onto which you'll be writing your bindrunes. It should be something like a stone or a bit of strong wood or metal—something solid and somewhat permanent. It will be a touchstone, something you can use to reinforce your spell, but also a representation of the spell itself. The candle is a timer, setting up the length of each day's spellwork and giving you a meditative focus that serves as a constant throughout your working. I generally use a white candle taper because the color works harmoniously with all energies.

Tailoring Your Spell

With each day's goal, the nature and qualities of the elements will change. In quelling wildfires, for instance, fire's part may be thought of as the pulling of heat from the situation. It's important to tailor your thoughts, tools, and actions to the spell's purpose. The more harmonious the elements you bring in, the better, but too many will clutter your thoughts. You want to represent your goal in the simplest, most straightforward terms. Because there are already five different aspects to the overall spell, keep extraneous decoration and symbolism to a minimum. That said, things that help you focus on the goals or bring forward the emotion you need to evoke can be helpful, especially if you have trouble with visualization.

Bindrunes

Bindrunes are the traditional Nordic runes combined into a single symbol to represent more complex concepts. For instance, a bindrune for help on an exam might consist of *thurisaz* (discipline, knowledge, study) with *kenaz* (inspiration, release of anxiety). When combining runes to form a bindrune, it is important that the original runes still be visible in the end result. However, they can be turned in any direction and the relative size of the runes is immaterial. Combine as many runes as necessary to describe your goal, but remember that the simpler the message, the more easily it's heard and understood. Refine each bindrune, each goal, into a single step along the path. Trying to skip ahead or take too many steps at once will only result in a fall.

The Ritual

The ritual itself is to be performed every day for five consecutive days. Each day will have a symbol and the symbols (bindrunes) will be added to the spell object, one per day until the end of the spell.

Ground and center.

Cast a circle, beginning with whichever quarter (determined by element) that you intend to call.

Call only the quarter of the element you're invoking. This limits the variables that you're introducing and focuses the working.

Light the candle, which will burn for as long as it takes to go through a marked section.

Place the spell object and permanent marker before the candle's base and invoke Divinity.

Meditation: Begin by focusing on the candle's flame. Set aside any thoughts that occur to you and let the flame fill your vision. Once you've reached a light trance state, begin a sustained period of visualization, building up an image that represents the completion of that day's goal. Work in as much detail as you can, even trying to conjure up smells and sounds as well as the visual image, but remember that the emotion of the moment is the most important. Even if you can't call to mind a clear image, work to bring up the emotion. How will it feel to accomplish that goal? What will it mean to you and to others? The image itself can change through the course of your visualization, but the overall circumstances (the accomplishment of the goal) must be the same. The changes in images can be used to review different emotions revolving around the same achievement. Or the fixed images of each day's visualization might combine on the final day in a sort of chronological picture show, revealing the many goals involved in the larger achievement.

Once you've achieved the visualization, hold it for as long as you can. When you lose it, simply re-ground and re-center and meditate on the candle flame until you feel ready to move forward.

Using the permanent marker, draw the day's symbol on the spell object. Spend the rest of the time linking your visualization to the bindrune and charging the rune with the emotion of that visualization.

Thank Divinity, thank the quarter, and close the circle.

Day One

The first day is about laying the groundwork, the subject and the situation. You call on earth not only because you're laying a foundation and anchoring the spell to an object, but also because you are planning to pull the desired results closer and to bring them into the "real," physical world. The bindrune for this first day should be a representation of the spell itself. It should encompass not only the end result, but the power and potential upon which you wish to call. It is your statement of intent to the universe.

Day Two

The second day is about the first phase of the change you wish to bring. It should be the first step toward your eventual goal, but should also represent an achievement in itself. Call on air as it represents the ideas and concepts, because that's what these are at this stage. It's through the spell that you'll convert them into a physical reality. The earth has already been invoked, and it grounds each of the following elements and solidifies them. Think carefully about what the first step to your goal is. Is it a change that must be made in yourself or in the physical world? What can you do to initiate that change? What steps can you take, both mystically and mundanely? ? The bindrune for this day represents your first goal. It may be small; in fact it should be something to get the ball rolling. As you create this bindrune, think of it as a snowball just beginning to roll downhill. What small goal could you reach to begin to see your spell working in the world and give yourself confidence in its power?

Day Three
The third day is about the second phase of the change. It should be the second step toward the eventual goal, but an achievement

that builds on and furthers the first. Call on fire, because now things have started moving and you need to keep them going with passion and energy. Now that you have a foundation on which to build, you can move more quickly, and now is the time to feel the fire, to be excited. The day's bindrune (and goal) should focus on picking up speed. What can you do to maintain the energy?

Day Four

The fourth day is about the third phase of the change, built on the previous achievements and in accord with the foundation. Call on water, because this is a time of nourishing and bounty, as well as a physical element that is still not quite a solid. It's transmutive and transformative. It's the next step in transforming your ideas into reality. The bindrune for this day should focus on the transformative nature of your goal and the emotions that you expect to feel because of the changes you're bringing into your life. How will this spell change you and your situation? How will it influence your future?

Day Five

The fifth day is about finalizing the symbols and sending the spell out into the world to work your will. This day's bindrune should be about the fulfillment of the goal overall. Call on spirit to draw on its endless potential. Take a moment to consider each day's visualization, put them together and visualize the finally result. The emotion you attach to the accomplishment of these goals creates energy and empowering your object with the emotions behind the bindrunes is vital to the success of your spell. Build energy through chanting, visualization, or any other method you prefer, push it into your object and through it out into the world to work your will, with harm to none.

Magical Authority: The Only Ingredient You Need

by Tess Whitehurst

It seems the longer I'm a Witch, the fewer spells I do and the more magic I weave into the fabric of my moment-to-moment existence. To put this another way, at first I transcended the illusion of powerlessness in short, intense bursts that required things like herbal ingredients and chanted words (e.g., spells and rituals). Now, while I love to do a spell or ritual every now and then, I am almost continuously conscious that I am walking between the worlds of form and spirit, which allows me to regularly delve beneath the surface of my perceptions, connect with the infinite power of the Divine, and direct my focus in ways that help shape my reality according to my will and desires.

This mindset, which we might call "magical authority," is in essence an alignment of our day-to-day awareness with the Divine, all-knowing consciousness, a.k.a. Who We Really Are. When we possess this alignment, everything in our life begins to work better because we are naturally working with our most ideal magical momentum and flow, and we are connected to our source of unlimited power. Not only that, wherever we are and whatever we do, we have all the magical ingredients we need: inner stillness, balance, confidence, trust in the Divine, alignment with our intuition, and a primordial sort of connection to the energy of love.

For most of us, consciously possessing magical authority every second of every day is an excellent goal, but it's not realistic. There will almost definitely be those times that we'll be sleep-deprived and then have to wait in line at the DMV forever and *then* our partner or sibling or parent will look at us sideways in what we're certain is an insulting manner (but they were not). Then we'll complain our heads off about our awful day and how powerless we felt to change it. And this is

just fine! There's no shame in being human. Besides, we would bore everyone to tears (including ourselves!) if we always approached everything in the most balanced and magically virtuous way possible.

Still, it's obviously ideal to do our best to first discover and cultivate this magical mindset, and then to stay in it as much as possible. That way, we can infuse our lives with magic and shape our lives according to our desires not only while we're sitting in front of our altars or dancing under the full moon, but also every minute of every day.

But how do we get into the natural flow of our magical authority, and stay there? Here are a few simple-yet-powerful methods that I've been lucky enough to discover.

Morning Tune-In Activities

The morning is when the magical momentum of our day is set into motion. So it's an especially powerful time for shaping the flavor of our day and the harmonics of our mood (i.e., the way we perceive and process our day). There are several tune-in exercises. Try them out, and once you find what works for you, do your best to make them as habitual as brushing your teeth.

First thing. As soon as you open your eyes and get ready to get out of bed, remind yourself that the day belongs to you. Also remind yourself that everything you do in this day will be a decision and a choice—that there is nothing that you do that you did not choose to do. (Even if it's something you don't want to do, recognize that you are still choosing to do it so that you can have a paycheck, a clean house, or whatever.) Then begin to visualize/feel/imagine/expect the conditions and occurrences you'd like to experience during the upcoming day *as well as the feelings that go along with them* (very important step).

During breakfast or coffee. Write down your intentions for the day in the present tense, as if they are already true. These may be feelings or actual occurrences. For example, you might write things like, "I love myself," "My cats are safe and happy," "I receive the such-and-such job offer or something better," "I'm wonderfully comfortable in my own skin," "The trip to the vet goes as smoothly as possible," "I am having a great hair day," "I am wealthy and receive generous sums of money from expected and unexpected sources," "I am awake to the magic of life," and/or "I embody the God/dess." You might write an entire page worth, and then write "Thank you, thank you, thank you. Blessed be. And so it is." And then sign and date.

Before you leave the house. I know you're busy, but this doesn't need to take longer than five minutes. Sit comfortably, relax, and call on your divine helper(s) of choice to clear, fine-tune, and shield your energy field. Visualize/imagine/feel this happening. Then consciously connect with the core of the earth and the cosmic light of the universe. You might do this by sending roots of light down into the earth and branches of light up into the sky. Draw golden earth light up from the earth and into your body/energy field, then draw sparkly rainbow light down from the cosmos and into your body/energy field. Think or say something like "I am one with the earth and sky. I am one with the God/dess, and I am in divine flow. All information is available to me. All power is available to me. I am always in the perfect place at the perfect time doing the perfect thing. I always know just what to do. Magical authority is mine."

Enhance Authority

Since you're on the magical path, chances are you have one or more patron deities, and a number of divine or magical beings that you like to call on for help. Although this is one of the simplest methods for aligning with your magical authority and shaping your reality according to your most ideal vision, it is also one of the most effective.

If you have a good working relationship with a being or group of beings, in most cases all you need to do is say or think something like, "Brighid, I call on you to bless this project! Thank you!" or "Dionysus, thank you for infusing my party with raucous fun!" (be careful with that one), or "Goddess, thank you for helping me get my car fixed swiftly and perfectly, and for a perfect price." And this really is all you need to do. In fact, it's important that you let go of the outcome after that. This doesn't mean don't be awake to or act on your intuition, it just means stop worrying about the outcome and know that just by remembering to tune in, you've already aligned your purposes and desires with divine wisdom and power.

Exercise

There is great power in your core (belly), and when you strengthen your belly, you intensify and hone your magical authority. So do those crunches, those sun salutations, that belly dancing, or whatever sort of abdominal workout you feel most drawn to. Just to be clear: bellies are beautiful in all shapes and sizes! This is not about having that conveniently (for marketers and magazines) elusive flat belly—it's just about getting stronger and possessing the fullness of your power.

Also, aerobic exercise helps align you with divine movement and flow, which means that it helps align you with your intuition and ideal life path (and of course your magical authority). While dancing is especially empowering because of its musical and magical nature, it matters less how you do it and more that you simply do it, so find an aerobic activity that feels fun and doable, and go for it.

Drink Lots of Water

Sounds simple and you've heard it a million times. But seriously, seriously: water is powerful stuff, and drinking at least half your body weight in ounces per day is an extremely potent way to clear your mind, body, and spirit, align with the divine flow, and shore up your magical authority. Think about it: everything is energy, and water is the physical manifestation of the energy of purity, cleansing, clarity, flow, joy, emotional connection, nourishment, and total well-being. So get yourself a beautiful (magical) water bottle and drink up!

Clear Clutter and Clean

If you've read anything else I've written, you've heard me extol the virtues of clearing clutter and cleaning. But I can't resist mentioning these things again because they are such powerful tools when it comes to regaining and retaining the fullness of your magical authority and power. Clearing clutter and cleaning will be especially important for you if you ever described yourself as "overwhelmed," "like things are getting away from you," or "stuck." Since everything you own is connected to you with a cord of energy, clearing and cleaning your space refines and purifies your energy field and lends clarity and direction to your mental and emotional landscapes.

Self-Care

When we feel gorgeous, radiant, and deliciously fragrant, we feel powerful. It might seem shallow, but it's not. Our internal and external environments are not only connected, they are a continuum, so one always affects the other. It follows that (no matter what your budget) taking the time to find clothes that flatter you and that you love, and engaging in self-care activities that accentuate your attractiveness and overall wellness, enhances your magical authority. After all, beauty and attractiveness are aspects of the God and Goddess, so when we cultivate these qualities in ways that nourish our spirits, we align ourselves more deeply with the divine.

Choosing to Be a Channel

Perhaps the most powerful of all magical authority enhancing methods is consciously choosing to be a channel of divine consciousness. In other words, when our overriding intention is to be a vessel for divine wisdom, beauty, and/or healing, and when we get our ego out of the way so that the Divine can shine through us, we couldn't be more in possession of our magical authority. To do this, all you need to do is simply choose to hold the space for the divine (in whatever form or incarnation feels right to you) to shine through you, as if you are a prism and the divine consciousness is the sun.

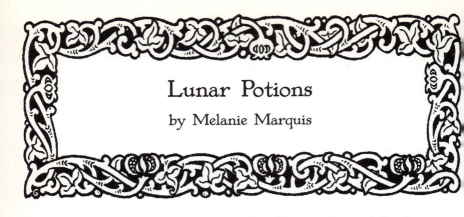

Lunar Potions

by Melanie Marquis

Magic and moonlight go together like candles and fire; lunar energy is a natural and efficient fuel for lighting up your life. Associated with Goddess energies, the power of the Moon shifts its character with each lunar phase. As the Moon begins its cycle and waxes to full, lunar energies are pulsing with abundance, growth, creativity, and attraction. After reaching its peak on the night of the Full Moon, the lunar light diminishes until it once more reaches the end of the cycle. This waning phase as the Moon turns from full to dark is optimal for banishing, purification, transformation, and communication between the astral and the physical, the mundane and the spiritual, the living and the dead.

The power of the Moon can be utilized in many ways. Not sure where to start? Consider trying your hand at some easy-to-learn, yet challenging-to-master lunar potion-making; you'll gain a foundation of experience and understanding that will kick-start your Moon magic. Here are a few basic formulas to try. Consider adding herbs, oils, or stones to personalize the recipes; just take care to use potions only externally unless you're absolutely certain about the composition, safety, and freshness of each ingredient.

Dark Moon Spirit Brew

Try this heated potion during the waning or Dark Moon to call on disembodied spirits and enhance communication between the living and the dead. Find a place outside where you can make a small fire. Place nine small stones around the perimeter of the fire. As the fire burns, think about the spirit or spirits you wish to summon; envision their form and remember their essence. Let the fire burn for a while so that the stones surrounding it become hot.

Fill a ceramic or other heat-resistant cup with clear, cool water. Hold the cup in both hands and lift it toward the sky. Call on the energies of the Dark Moon and present the water in the cup as an offering, expressing your gratitude as you sprinkle a bit of the water on the ground and take a small sip.

Now use a set of tongs to pull the nine stones from around the fire and place them one by one into the cup. Let the brew sit for a few minutes while you clear your mind and get into a state of heightened awareness, free from tension.

Use the tongs to remove the rocks from the potion. Hold your hand, palm facing downward, an inch or so above the cup. Use this chant to ask the Dark Moon goddess to ready the potion for use in spirit communication:

As the cauldron, so the cup.
As the cup, so the body.
Great Goddess, send your spirits unto me.
Dark Lady, make me your vessel; so mote it be!

Now think of the spirit or spirits you wish to contact, and call them by name. Invite the disembodied soul to enter the potion. Take a drink of the potion, welcoming the spirit into your body. Let go of your personality and ego and welcome the spirit to speak through you via direct mediumship. If that's a bit much, use a pen and paper and experiment with automatic writing, allowing your hand to be guided by the spirit with whom you are communicating.

You can also use the Dark Moon Spirit Brew to anoint and charge spirit communication tools such as talking boards, trumpets, séance tables, scrying orbs, tarot cards, or candles. If you have a personal item that belonged to the departed you wish to speak to, anoint the object with a little of the potion and place it in the area where you will be summoning the spirit. To give your mediumistic abilities a super boost, rub the potion on each of your chakras, or place a few drops into a relaxing bath.

Moon Maiden Magic Potion

This potion made under the light of the new or first quarter waxing Moon magnifies beauty and enhances romantic feelings. Fill a silver or clear crystal container with cool, pure water. Add three drops lavender oil while envisioning yourself youthful, beautiful,

loved. Go outside, taking the potion and a round mirror with you. Lay the mirror flat so that it reflects the moonlight. Place the potion on top of the mirror. Call on the Maiden Goddess, and ask her to enchant the potion with powers of beauty, youth, and love.

Place a drop of the potion on your cheeks, breasts, and navel to give yourself an irresistible glow. Anoint a candle with the potion and burn for an atmosphere conducive to romance and love. Use it to connect with the energies of the Maiden Goddess during rites, magical workings, and meditations.

Full Moon Manifestation Potion

Here's a versatile brew that can be used to create resources and reveal opportunities. Choose a symbol, sigil, or word to represent the thing you wish this potion to manifest. For example, if you want to manifest money, you might decide to use a dollar sign or a pentacle. Paint the symbol on the side of a clear glass jar while imagining the jar filled with the essence of your desire. Fill the jar with water and a handful of soil, then place it outside beneath a Full Moon. Gaze at the Moon and notice its expansive, creative energies. Ask these energies to enter and charge the water.

Sit quietly for thirteen minutes while the potion absorbs the moonlight. Swirl the jar clockwise thirteen times while visualizing the thing you wish to manifest, the fulfillment of your magical goal.

Use this potion to charm objects and places related to your goal. For example, if you want to manifest a new car, you might anoint your key ring with a bit of this brew. If greater creativity in your artwork is what you crave, sprinkle a few drops of the potion in your studio or on your art supplies.

Waning Moon Potion

This potion made over the course of the waning Moon is excellent for use in magic meant to diminish or banish. Begin making this potion three days after the Full Moon. Fill a dark, opaque container to the brim with cool water. Carefully place it outside under the moonlight. Take a few moments to meditate on the lunar cycle. Picture the Moon morphing from full to dark, slowly decreasing its glow until it is completely engulfed in shadow. Notice your feelings and thoughts. Is there something in your life you could do without, or do with less of? Do you feel as if you have obstacles to overcome, or negative energies to thwart? Envision any undesired elements diminishing, decreasing, fading away as surely as the Moon wanes. Pour out a tiny amount of the potion. Leave the container outside for at least a few hours each night, bringing it indoors before sunrise and storing it in a dark place. Repeat your visualizations and pour out a drop or two of the potion every night until the night of the Dark Moon. On the night of the Dark Moon, hold the potion skyward as you affirm its purpose, putting into your own words exactly what you expect of this magical mixture. Seal it tightly and keep it in a dark place away from direct sunlight until ready for use. Sprinkle the Waning Moon Potion where it's needed, be it in a specific place, on a symbolic object, or on a representational image or photo of the thing you wish to banish or decrease.

Waxing Moon Potion

A Waxing Moon Potion can be used in many types of abundance magic; its energies are perfect for attracting and increasing love, creativity, growth, and wealth. To make it, choose a clear or silver container and fill it about halfway to the top with water. Add a small piece of quartz crystal, then seal the container. Just when the New Moon shows its first sliver, place the potion outside. Call on the magnifying and magical energies of the Moon to enter the potion and infuse it with power. Allow the potion to remain outdoors during the nighttime, but be sure to bring it inside before sunrise. Every night, add a little more water to the potion and swirl the contents. On the night of the Full Moon, your potion is ready. Use the Waxing Moon Potion to add extra magickal power to your wardrobe, your ritual tools, or your sacred space. Anoint talismans and magickal candles with the potion to magnify and strengthen their effects.

Truth Revealing Lunar Potion

The Truth Revealing Lunar Potion fulfills a rare need in spellwork: it sweeps away illusion and deception to give the seeker clear insight into reality. When you feel there is falsity afoot, give this magical mixture a try. Fill a black stone bowl with water and place it outside in the daytime when the Moon is visible in the sky. Hold an ice cube in your hand and think of the matter in question, sending your thoughts and doubts into the ice. Put the ice cube in the center of the bowl of water, then look up at the Moon and make your petition: "Just as the sun reveals the Moon, so may the truth be shown to me soon." Leave the bowl in place. That night, when the Moon rises in the sky, return to the bowl. If the ice cube has not fully melted, hold a candle flame near it and let the water drip into the bowl. Place a lit candle several feet away from the bowl so that your surroundings will be only minimally illuminated. Sit comfortably in front of the bowl of Truth Revealing Lunar Potion and gaze into the liquid. Ask your question, then let your conscious mind go as you drift into a state of self-hypnosis. Look into the basin without fear and without expectation, and you may experience psychic sensations or see images appear in the potion. Analyze any visions you receive, then follow up with non-magical queries or appropriate actions. Don't jump the gun and assume the accuracy of any information gleaned through scrying!

If your scrying attempt was unsuccessful, pour the potion into a black bottle and seal it tightly. To use the potion, put it in contact with the person or persons you suspect of dishonesty: add a drop or two of the potion to food or drinks, spritz it around a

particular location, or lightly sprinkle it on a letter. Sooner rather than later, the truth will be revealed.

Making More Moon Magick

Now that you're familiar with some basics, try creating your own lunar potion recipes. Brainstorm ideas and then challenge yourself to come up with the best ways to make such potions. How might you make use of a lunar eclipse to craft a potion for transformation? Should a lunar potion for clarity be crafted only when the sky is clear? What ingredients might you include in a concealment blend best made when the Moon is obscured in clouds? When designing your concoctions, keep in mind the many ways a potion can be used, and see if you can think of a few more. Try adding a relaxing lunar potion to your bath, or water plants with a Moon-made potion to promote growth. Wash your altar with it, or use it to clean your scrying mirror. Follow your hunches, experiment, and discover the nuances of lunar potion-making for yourself. Formulating your own potion recipes will increase your creativity, boost your magical confidence, and provide you with the power to create the life you truly want. Like a wish on a star, a Moon potion works wonders.

Pagan Teens and Their Peers: A Story

by Calantirniel

As a single mother in the mid-1990s, when I was becoming more and more awakened (rather involuntarily), I realized that my belief systems were changing—a lot. It was changing the very core of my being that was reflecting more and more into my life. Without having access to books about alternative spiritual parenting available, I thought long and hard about how to properly include my elementary-aged children. For one, I did not wish to unduly influence their choices, as I wanted them to arrive independently to their right choices for themselves. But as much as I was excited to show them all I was learning, revealing my unfolding path to them was also risky in other ways.

At the time, we lived in the proverbial Bible Belt of North Carolina. I seriously questioned how much of my spellwork and spiritual practice could be safely revealed to them. I wondered if my children could comprehend the loving freedom of expression in our house to fully immerse in this paradigm, and yet at the same time be guarded and careful about sharing with other children (and more importantly their parents), who may not understand due to their security needs, upbringing, and worldview and thus display hostility. Other awakened types I managed to find did not have children, so it was difficult to seek advice. One awakened type who did have kids called herself Catholic, since most of her practice consisted of minor modifications to her upbringing. It was a perfect cover for her and her kids—but this was not my practice.

After much contemplation, I decided my children, although young, were smart enough to figure out for themselves how to be fully immersed along with me in a powerful yet unpopular belief system in a rigid, narrow-viewed outer world. I didn't wish to regret my decision, as even one accidental revealing to the wrong people could create a stigma that at a young

and sensitive age could be extremely difficult to handle, and in a small community nearly impossible for them to forget.

Both children became involved directly in my spellwork, since it often also concerned them, and always had phenomenal results in surprising ways. Together, we solved many types of problems through "concentrated prayer," in which objects like candles and tarot cards helped our focus. I carefully showed them proper ethics so that spells didn't backfire in undesirable ways, and they learned that it works really well, and sometimes a little too well!

At the same time, I knew they would wish to share this with others. Without holding back, I provided well-intentioned warnings about most people's upbringings and worldviews, be they Christian or of a more scientific nature, and I encouraged them to attend activities with these friends so they can understand the energy for themselves. I mentioned that while you would logically think people would be thrilled to know of such things, many people feel a deep need to be correct and therefore secure in their belief choices. Not only do they not like to be challenged, they may feel unsafe enough to ridicule or even outright attack you for your beliefs. Because of this, I told them to be careful when choosing friends, and to know them a long time before sharing such things, since it could be hard to reverse an attack if it were to happen. I thought they might struggle with this, but they rather instinctively figured out who was safe and who was not—how wonderful!

Many years passed, along with our collective experiences and two moves—one to Southern California (where I got remarried) and later to western Montana. I witnessed the kids turning into teenagers, showing wisdom in the most surprising ways! Nearly all the time, the friends they consciously chose were enthusiastic learners, and their parents were not only tolerant but warm, loving people.

We only had one close call. While in middle school, my daughter befriended a girl who had a fundamental Christian background. In hindsight, I also believe she was from a home with some type of trauma or abuse issues. (Disturbingly, I discovered this is a common combination.) When she visited our house, I was working for one of the phone/online psychic services at the time and she saw me doing tarot cards for a caller. She was appalled and asked my daughter if she knew I was going to hell for that! Suddenly, she confronted my daughter directly: "What do you believe?" Her answer was gracefully evasive: "What do you think?" She never said yes or no, even when being hard-pressed to do so.

Later, my daughter decided she had to end this so-called friendship because of this girl's extremely obsessive behavior, which consisted of, among other things, calling our house literally every ten minutes and feeling put off when asked, then told, not to call so often. I was really proud that my daughter did it entirely on her own, with kindness but firmness. Still, this did not go over well.

The next day, this girl came over after school, along with another one of their friends, and, in an act of revenge, decided to steal a few sets of my daughter's earrings when using our restroom! We created a recovery tarot ritual that night that could be performed the next morning. However, we didn't need to—the other friend unexpectedly arrived alone to pick up my daughter for the bus ride to school. My daughter was still upset and told her the whole story, including a thorough description of the earrings stolen. When they got off the bus at school, her friend helped her to immediately recover her earrings—directly from the thief's locker!

Furious at being thwarted, the girl was now deciding to spread rumors around the entire school that my daughter was a Witch. In this small, conservative town, that was not a good idea at all. This could have ended badly for my daughter, with so many more years of school left to face the multiple hostilities that could have been directed at her, and it could have really damaged her self-esteem. The good news was that understandably, not many people liked this girl; whereas many people liked my daughter.

So after everyone in the school came to my daughter to confirm (or deny) the "charges," my daughter decided to turn the tables and make a lighthearted joke about the whole thing. She said, "Oh sure, I am a Witch! Want to see the broom in my locker?" Everyone laughed and mentioned that they did not like the accusing girl at all! What a relief!

This story demonstrates the resiliency of someone who at a young age was able to really be present in her belief system while allowing others to be in theirs and to sidestep troublemakers. And I now realize more that these coping skills would not be what they are if I didn't educate them about the world around us—it is necessary for our kids to know how to operate in these environments, and they will deal with many of their peers later as adults.

Over time, when the kids were in high school, our home rather unexpectedly became a safe haven for other likeminded teens who lived in these strict and rigid families—and it still is. These kids are so hungry to ask questions that are forbidden in their homes, and perhaps we should start charging admission! Although I answer their questions in a way that beginners can understand, I also tell these kids that they must respect and obey their parents' wishes while they live in their home, but it doesn't mean that they cannot learn—they will have time to perfect their practice when they leave (this often seems like an eternity away to them at this young age).

I also emphasize that no matter what they practice, they must first align with love, not fear, and to fully think out any intentions for a higher good and purpose. I help them realize their parents love them and want the best for them. Despite their frustration, I show them the importance of loving and forgiving their parents, and although they may not realize it now, they need to learn something important from their family upbringing and development. I encourage them to do well in school, take care of their responsibilities, and not to be rebellious just because of this misunderstanding—this too shall pass, I say.

Sometimes, very challenging situations appeared. As an example, one of the kids was catching a cold, and we made her some hot herbal tea. Because she experienced immediate relief without groggy side effects, she asked if we could send some tea home with her so she could continue her healing and build her immune system, thwarting the cold. None of us, including the kid, had any idea that her parents would forbid herbs in their house. Their reasons? Their church told them that healing with plants was the devil's work, and that the dried herbs just looked too much like marijuana! The parents then immediately shoved immune-suppressing over-the-counter cold medicine into her (that in the long run made her more sick and miss school), and she was instructed to return the herbs. As frustrating as this scenario was, I wanted her to honor the parents' rule about no herbs entering their house. In the future, she devised ways around that rule. If she was feeling ill, she didn't tell her parents, and instead, just got their permission to visit our house. She then helped herself to the herbal tea cupboard and often stayed until her health returned. While this isn't the best scenario I could imagine, she did at least have permission to be at our house. (As for the herbs, they were all actually classified as food.)

Both of my kids flourished in high school. They had excellent teacher-student relations, healthy boundaries, and brought home excellent grades. They have developed many deep friendships that will likely last their lifetimes, and have been able to resist the negativity of others, without resorting to participation in negative behavior themselves. My daughter had even taken a liking to astrology and while not professional, she has given solid counsel to her many friends who needed relationship help, empowering them to make healthy choices.

Both kids are grown now. The current economy can be very disconcerting for many young people nowadays, with large student loans accompanied by no jobs being available years later upon graduation. My son is a computer programmer and loves his job. He is very self-reliant and has built a great reputation as a trustworthy person and as an excellent programmer in a very short time. Despite the fact my daughter's grades were good enough to enter college, as a free-flowing, artistic type and natural networker, she opted for her passion—she finished fourteen months of cosmetology school and did very well. She had yet to test for her license when she already lined up a wonderful first job—and her school's tuition has been paid in full to boot. She is already sharing her gift for gab in astrology with her hair clients, who appreciate receiving her "snippets" of advice that can help them feel really good about themselves, inside and out. What a great way to create return customers!

Why have I shared this story? The world is just the way it is, and I learned it is better to teach kids to work from a place of truth. I hope sharing my parental experiences inspires and empowers you and your families to live fully and authentically!

For Further Study

Forbes, Bronwen, *The Small Town Pagan's Survival Guide: How to Thrive in Any Community*. Woodbury, MN: Llewellyn Publications, 2011.

Madden, Kristin, *Pagan Parenting*, St. Paul, MN: Llewellyn Publications, 2000.

Renée, Janina, *Tarot Spells*, St. Paul, MN: Llewellyn Publications, 1998.

Winged Warriors

by Kristin Madden

In France, a family of snowy owls (*Nyctea scandiaca*) graces the wall of a cave covered with pictographs that date to Paleolithic times. In the southwestern United States, petroglyphs of doves and parrots were chipped in the desert varnish of lava boulders. And a common theme in ancient Egyptian funerary art was the inclusion of divine wings wrapped around the departed. More than any other bird, with the exception of corvids and vultures, eagles, hawks, and owls have captivated us. Legends of raptors as human ancestors, deities, and spirit guides fill our earliest history. While all birds have a wonderful ability to survive and protect themselves or their nests, raptors truly embody the energy of the warrior.

These birds often appear to be fearless. But what lies beneath that courageous exterior? Perhaps a unique ability to handle a crisis, a strength of character that does not shrink from a challenge, a fierce will to survive, or maybe a subconscious fear that leads to an intense need for self-protection. After all, what is courage but the ability to act consciously in the face of fear? These are some attributes that the winged warriors share. Humans with these allies should consider how these traits might manifest in their lives.

There is so much more to these birds than their ability to stalk prey. Like all creatures, they are individuals with personalities. They bond to a mate and a family. They feel stress and react to changes in their habitat. They can read you like a book and probably are more aware of your feelings toward them than you are. And although they will hide injury or sickness, they have no problem letting you know when you are doing something they don't like.

I have learned more than I can tell you from these birds. While reading about animal guides is useful, most of my lessons were brought through by the individual creatures themselves and their unique natural history. So I strongly encourage you to take your learning beyond the metaphysical books. Explore and commune and see what your winged warriors have to offer you.

In general, raptors have taught me to stay calm in the face of danger or confrontation. They have allowed me plenty of opportunities to endure pain, both physical and emotional, without losing my focus. They have also shown me how to be strong when I need to, to go after what I want with honor, and to know when the battle is just not worth fighting.

If the winged warriors attract you or have shown up in your life, I recommend learning as much as you can about the natural history of species you are connected with. Learn about their relationships with others of their species, their prey species, and their preferred habitats. Consider the energies they bring in and reflect to you. This article presents a brief overview of four of the most common types of raptor: eagles, hawks, falcons, and owls. As with all animal allies, be respectful in your interactions with them. Trust me; you don't want to feel their weapons.

Eagles

Eagles are massive, powerful birds that have rightly been revered throughout the world. The Steller's Sea Eagle can reach nearly four feet in length with a wingspan of almost eight feet. Harpy Eagles can exceed twenty pounds. The feet of the slightly smaller Golden Eagle exert a tremendous pressure, averaging 200 pounds per square inch. When I take hawks to education programs, many people ask if they are eagles. The truth is, there is no mistaking an eagle once you've seen one. There is nothing else quite like it.

Like all raptors, these iconic birds epitomize power, strength, and inspiration. But it is a rare raptor that approaches the sheer size and strength of an eagle. Eagles have forced me to acknowledge and accept my place as both predator and prey. When working with an eagle, one must face up to fear and conquer it. Like eagles, our only real predators in modern society are other humans. In spite of our false sense of power over the world, many of us have lost our personal power. Working with eagle energy can restore that power and offer unparalleled confidence and inner strength.

It is important to be completely honest when dancing with Eagle. Great power can blind a person to the effects of their actions on others. It can result in arrogance and a lack of compassion. While eagles can pick a fish from the sea or a monkey from a forest, they can also be notoriously opportunistic, frequenting garbage dumps and stealing food from other raptors. Eagle has a great deal to teach us about how we hold and wield power.

When you feel victimized, disempowered, or in danger, calling upon Eagle can provide the inner and outer power that you need to protect yourself. This is an ally that is supremely capable of helping you reclaim sovereignty over yourself and your life.

Falcons

Falcons are the speed demons of the raptor world. Unique adaptations allow falcons to achieve amazing speeds with ease. Peregrine falcons are the fastest animals, having been clocked at over 240 miles per hour in a dive.

This speed is something to consider when working with falcon energy. While your falcon spirit ally may not give you a choice in the matter, change and insight may come with breakneck speed. You need to prepare for this and deeply embody the agility and freedom that comes with falcon power. While challenging, this gift of Falcon allows us to perceive both opportunities and potential problems from a distance. With great skill, we are able to avoid problems and speed toward the issues we are ready to handle.

Falcons offer us a unique insight into how we live in our world. One of the main reasons the peregrine (and the bald eagle) was endangered was due to a pesticide that both killed adults and resulted in eggshells too thin to bring live chicks to hatching.

Falcon energy demands that we look at the toxicity in our own lives before it is too late. If something is out of balance, you can assume that some form of change will be swift. But in return for taking that leap into self-knowledge, we fly like no other can. We are one with the wind and the earth as we climb and dive and spiral with unsurpassed grace and intelligence.

One of the smaller falcons, the American kestrel, is a beautiful, charismatic bird. But it remains a serious raptor. Kestrels can drive off hawks more than twice their size. Kestrel energy teaches that even the smallest and sweetest of us possesses a strength that may not be immediately apparent. Each of us has the ability to rise to great heights, to stand up for what we believe in, and triumph against seemingly unbeatable odds.

Hawks

Probably the most commonly seen raptors, there are more than sixty hawk species worldwide. Hawks bring the regality and command of eagles to a more approachable level. Many hawk species adapt extremely well to sharing land with humans. Some even thrive in cities. Hawk energy teaches many things, but it truly speaks to how we interact with the human-impacted landscape.

If Hawk has entered your life, you might ask yourself how you are adapting to life as a modern human. This energy may also speak to you of freedom. All wild animals possess an innate need to be free. Some hawk species seem particularly invested in freedom. What might Hawk be telling you about freedom and wildness? Are you too urban, do you allow the modern world to tie you down too much? Are you perhaps too free and incapable of following through on commitments? Or is your freedom a façade to cover up fear? Hawk can help you identify your own wildness and keep it honest.

On the other hand, hawks tend to adapt to captivity well. Falconry and education hawks can develop exceptionally strong bonds to the humans they live with. They have the ability to move beyond species separations and instinct. Hawk allies have a way of reminding us that self-preservation can only take us so far. At some point, we need to put aside our defenses and embrace trust and love.

Owls

On soft wings, owls guide us to evoke great insights, make deep connections with the Divine, and face our own shadows. Awake predominantly at night and looking almost alien, owls seem to embody mystery and magic. Once revered as birds of wisdom and insight, some cultures now believe owls to be evil or bringers of death and destruction.

When you need strength to see what is hidden in your world or into your own shadows, Owl is the ideal spirit ally for you. Owl possesses an uncanny ability to perceive that which is shrouded in darkness. However, these adaptations can lead to a single-minded determination and an inability to see what lies on the periphery. Owls can turn their heads so far because their eyes are too large in their heads to allow the eyes themselves to turn. As a result, many get hit by cars while going after prey. If you work with Owl, you might periodically emerge from the shadows to gain perspective, take a break, and rest in the light for a time.

This silent hunter is truly a bird of stealth. Owl is a very different type of protector than Hawk, Falcon, or Eagle. While your owl allies will bring you distinctive strength and confidence, Owl prefers to sneak up on prey. You may find that you are more subtle, quieter, and very well camouflaged when you need to be.

This energy brings intuition, a need to look beyond the surface, and a need to go within for vision before taking action. Sometimes, quick illumination is not what you need. There are situations and shadows that require more time and a more understated plan of attack.

A Few Laws and Protections

Just as we can connect with deities through jewelry and statues, we can work with animal allies in similar ways. We honor and thank our spirit allies when we respect and conserve their physical manifestations. I have seen things done to live raptors for commercial and "religious" reasons that still bring tears to my eyes.

If you feel that a feather or talon is important, please explore the variety of museum replicas and painted feathers that are now available. Remember that, in general, unless it is a pigeon, starling, English sparrow, or domestic bird, it is probably protected, meaning that that it is illegal for you to possess body parts or live animals without the proper permits. I recommend exploring your state's game and fish or environmental conservation website to find out what the laws are in your area, which may differ slightly from the major federal legislation listed below.

Bald and Golden Eagle Protection Act. This piece of legislation prohibits the taking, possession, sale, purchase, bartering, or offering to sell, purchase, or barter, export or import of the bald eagle at any time or in any manner. Amendments in 1962 added protections for Golden Eagles and special permits for Native Americans.

Endangered Species Act of 1973 (ESA). This act provides a means whereby the ecosystems upon which endangered species and threatened species depend may be conserved, to provide a program for the conservation of such endangered species and threatened species, and to take such steps. Keep in mind that there are both federal and state endangered and threatened species.

Migratory Bird Treaty Act of 1918 (MBTA). This measure governs the taking, killing, possession, transportation, and importation of migratory birds, their eggs, parts, and nests for educational, scientific, and recreational purposes.

The Illumination of Fire-in-Water

by Mary Pat Lynch

The elements earth, air, fire, and water are associated with the four directions of the world and of sacred circles, the tarot suits, magical tools, healing systems, and models of the psyche. With the fifth element of spirit, space, or ether, these elements form the basis of spiritual and magical systems in many cultures.

In Aristotle's model of the elements, earth, air, fire, and water arise from the opposites hot and cold (primary), and dry and wet (secondary). Air and fire, the masculine yang elements, are hot. Earth and water, the feminine yin elements, are cold. Earth and fire are dry; water and air are wet.

Classical ideas of compatibility, the elemental dignities, are based on this model. Elements with the same primary feature naturally go together, combining easily. Elements sharing a secondary feature are neutral. Elements that share neither feature—earth and air, and fire and water—are not considered compatible.

Do the elemental dignities always work this way? Can we expand our view?

The Fire-in-Water Motif

Fire and water combine in another ancient, compelling motif called fire-in-water. The idea that creative fire is carried in water can be traced back to the Indo-European tradition that underlies many cultures of Europe and Asia.

Tales from Iran, India, Ireland, and Wales tell of a mysterious, glowing light found in water. This fiery essence carries magical and poetic inspiration. Seeking it involves a dangerous quest.

In Vedic myth, the fire god Agni arises from the waters. Messenger of the gods, invoked in all sacrifices, Agni's three forms are fire, lightning, and the sun. Agni is the illuminator, bringer of knowledge. Water is associated with goddesses, seen as cleansing, renewing, and also quickening.

Agni's arising from the waters mirrors the sun's journey across the sky each day, diving into deep waters at night and rising renewed each morning. Fire and water together are the undifferentiated ground of all being, which is Brahman. The emergence of fire from water is the primary act of creation.

The idea that fiery power is hidden in magical water fits Celtic tradition. Rivers, lakes, and wells are sacred to Celtic peoples, sources of healing and inspiration.

In his book *The Fairy-Faith in Celtic Countries*, Evans-Wentz shares this tale from an Irish mystic:

> In the world under the waters—under a lake in the West of Ireland in this case—I saw a blue and orange coloured king seated on a throne; and there seemed to be some fountain of mystical fire rising from under his throne, and he breathed this fire into himself as though it were his life.

The tale continues as the mystic sees gray figures approach the throne, who "placed their head and lips near the heart of the elemental king, and, then, as they touched him, they shot upwards, plumed and radiant, and passed on the other side, as though they had received a new life from this chief of their world."

Now listen to Scott Cunningham (*Earth Power: Techniques of Natural Magic*) describe a sea spell he created and his experience with it. The spell involves drawing a circle in the sand above the waterline just as the tide begins to rise. This is followed by a rune or image within the circle drawn while visualizing "blue liquid flames." You then visualize your need and wait for the tide to carry away your spell.

> "One day, while performing this spell on the beach during a light rain, I stood waiting for the wave to wash it away. As it did, I felt a bolt of energy shoot up from the

rune I'd sketched on the sand and hit me in the chest. It was an actual physical sensation. The energy went forth and did indeed bring into manifestation my need."

This is a direct experience of fire-in-water. In Western ceremonial magic, the cup is the receptacle, ready to receive energy that comes from a divine, outside source. In contrast, fire-in-water portrays a cosmos in which the divine spark is already held within the water, originating there, ready to be released to enliven and illuminate. The cyclic interplay of fire arising from and returning to water balances yin and yang, God and Goddess.

Powerful Waters

In Celtic lore, water is numinous, magical, and sacred. Wells and pools are in-between places where waters from the other-world enter our world. Nechtan's Well at Segais, the head of the Boyne; Connla's Well under the sea; Bec's Well; and Fec's Pool are only a few of these magic places.

Nechtan and his three cupbearers guard the well at Segais and only they are allowed to approach it. One day, Nechtan's wife, Boann, decides to visit the well. As she draws near, three waves arise and take from her an eye, a hand, and a thigh. The waters overflow, carrying Boann away with them to the sea, creating the Boyne River.

Notice that the well belongs to Nechtan, and Boann's presence is forbidden, yet she is the one whose presence unleashes the waters. The new river is named for her.

This mirrors the stories of sacred waters in Arthurian lore. Magical lakes and wells are guarded by fairy women or priestesses until they are attacked, and sometimes raped or killed, by knights who wrest control of the waters away from their female guardians.

The Shannon River is created in similar fashion when Sinend, another forbidden woman, decides to visit Connla's Well under the sea to gain its knowledge. At Connla's Well, the hazels of wisdom grow, the sacred trees that bring out foliage, flower and fruit together. The hazelnuts, full of wisdom, drop into the well to be carried in water throughout the land.

Do you know the bodies of water closest to you? Do you visit and work with them? In this time when waters everywhere are threatened by dams, diversions, and pollution, connecting with water sources near our homes becomes important on many levels. The work of healers like Sandra Ingerman show that water nourishes the soul as well as the body, and that we can partner with water to heal the Earth and ourselves.

Find out where your water comes from. Can you visit its source? Learn what threatens the purity of the watershed where you live. Can you take action, in the magical and the mundane world, to protect and heal the water?

Scott Cunningham offers his sea spell (on page 282) as an all-purpose spell, one that could easily be adapted to a river, lake, spring, or even a reservoir. Make friends with sources of water; they are sources of power.

Magical Fire

At Connla's Well, the hazelnuts drop into the pool and become imbued with magic. These hazelnuts are objects of quest, sought after by poets and Druids. Patience and preparation are needed, for they are only available once every seven years.

The Salmon of Wisdom eats the magical hazelnuts, becoming the wisest of creatures, displaying an outward sign of this wisdom in its speckled skin. Finn Éces, the poet, waits seven years to catch the ancient salmon. He knows that when he eats off its flesh, creative inspiration will be his.

Finn Éces prepares a fire, then sets his young apprentice Demne to watch as the magical salmon cooks. Finn the poet must be the first to eat the salmon to gain its gifts, and he warns the boy not to taste the fish as it cooks.

But magic can be wayward, and a bubble forms on the speckled skin. The bubble pops, splattering oil on the young boy's hand. He puts his fingers in his mouth to cool them. Instantly Demne gains the wisdom the old poet waited for all those years.

The elderly poet is disappointed but not vindictive. He gives Demne a new name, befitting his new status, and the hero Finn mac Cumhal begins a life of magical adventures.

In another version, Finn mac Cumhal gains his visionary powers by being splashed with water from a pitcher held by a fairy woman as she slips through the doorway of a sidhe mound. Finn sucks the water from his fingers, and receives illumination. Finn mac Cumhal is a great warrior, but throughout his life, he also has the gift of prophecy, dropping into visionary states and gaining information about events in his world.

In Ireland, poets waited seven years for the hazelnuts of wisdom to gain the creative fire called *imbas*. In Wales, it was called *awen* and figures in the tale of Cerridwen's cauldron and the initiation of the great poet Taliesin.

This tale tells how Cerridwen, a powerful sorceress, had a very ugly son. Concerned about how her boy would get on in the world, she decided to give him great powers of prophecy and poetry. Cerridwen gathered magical ingredients and set her cauldron simmering over a fire that must burn continuously for a year and a day.

A year and a day is a long time, so Cerridwen set the serving boy Gwion Bach to tend the fire. For long weeks and months, Gwion Bach stirred the cauldron. As the fateful day approached, Cerridwen positioned her son nearby, ready to catch the first drops that would spring forth when the potion was ready. Those first drops would contain the magical power.

At the moment of power, the cauldron bubbled up, sending drops of hot liquid into the air. The burning drops fell on Gwion Bach's fingers, which he shoved in his mouth, tasting the magic potion.

Gwion's first realization was that Cerridwen would kill him if she could, and he ran. As he ran, he changed into a hare coursing through the fields. Cerridwen became a hound snapping at his heels. Gwion jumped into a river and changed into a fish; Cerridwen followed as an otter. Gwion took to the air as a bird; Cerridwen swooped down as a hawk. Seeing a threshing barn, Gwion thought to hide himself as one grain of wheat among many. Cerridwen became a small black hen and swallowed him up.

Cerridwen found herself pregnant with the transformed boy, and after carrying him in her womb for nine months was unable to kill him outright. She put him in a tiny boat in a river, returning him once again to magical water.

There he was found by a courtier, who was struck by the beauty of this child. He took the child to court, where the king adopted him and gave him the name Taliesin, which means shining brow. His hard-won illumination showed even in his face. Over the years, he grew into the most famous of poets.

The Search for the Grail

In the Arthurian tales, the search for illumination carried in water is the search for the Grail. In the elemental associations of the tarot, Knights are fire and the suit of Cups is water. It is intriguing that the Knight of Cups, Fire of Water, is often related to the figure of the Grail Knight.

In these tales, the power of the Grail conveys spiritual gifts as well as healing for the land. Goddesses of Sovereignty, mysterious women of magic, guard these gifts, often hidden in water. The sword Excalibur, held by a woman's hand over the still waters of a lake, is a striking image of fire in water.

The Grail legend takes on Christian values and the theme of worthiness: Only a virtuous knight can gain the grail. In earlier tales, this notion of virtue does not appear. Only the courage and strength to succeed in the quest are needed.

The theme of virtue is also injected into other tales. In the tale of Cerridwen, for example, many versions say Gwion Bach just happened to be standing by, and was accidentally (or synchronistically) chosen for the gift. Patrick Ford's translation states clearly that Gwion had learned during his months of tending what the cauldron contained. At the opportune moment, he shoved the hapless son out of the way to claim the magic for himself.

Perhaps worthiness in the conventional sense has little to do with imbas and awen. To attain the highest levels of poetic inspiration, we must be willing to take risks, place ourselves in danger, open to experience, and reach out our hands for something we know might burn.

~

Rituals invoking the gifts of fire-in-water might include a candle set inside a holder deep enough to be placed in a shallow bowl of water. Floating candles can also combine fire and water on the altar. Cerridwen and Taliesin, Finn mac Cumhal, the Salmon of Wisdom, and the Ladies of the Lake—any might be woven into ceremonies to explore this motif and invite illumination.

Fire and water, in these traditions, are not incompatible. They are powerful and unpredictable; choosing to work with them calls for courage, strength, and opening to magic.

For Further Study

Cunningham, Scott. (2002) "Earth Power: Techniques of Natural Magic." Excerpt printed online in *The Llewellyn Journal*: www.llewellyn.com/journal/article/1613

Evans-Wentz, W. Y. (1911) *The Fairy Faith in Celtic Countries*. Available online at: www.sacred-texts.com/

Ford, P. (1974) "The Well of Nechtan and 'La Gloire Lumineuse,'" in *Myth in Indo-European Antiquity*, ed. Gerald James Larson, co-ed. C. Scott Littleton and Jaan Puhvel. University of California Press, 67–74.

Ford, P. (1977) *Mabinogi and Other Medieval Welsh Tales*. University of California Press.

Water Magic

The Masks We Wear

by Kristin Madden

In Act II, Scene VII of Shakespeare's play, *As You Like It*, Jacques says, "All the world's a stage, and all the men and women merely players. They have their exits and their entrances, and one man in his time plays many parts …" On some level, we all realize this is true. In order to interact cohesively with society, we play roles for which we wear masks. Very few people see us for all that we truly are on all levels of being. Our masks serve several needs that make life easier for us and for our communities.

First and foremost, our masks protect us. They allow us to go about our lives without showing too much. They may cover fear and prevent others from seeing us as prey. They may cover strength, protecting us from conflict with dangerous individuals. They hide aspects of us that would not in our best interests to show everyone.

The masks we feel we need also help us meet our needs in this world. As children, we learned that our caretakers responded to our needs depending on certain behaviors we exhibited. Some people learned to cry, whine, or yell for attention. Others learned to be silent and fade into the background to avoid negative attention. The masks we crafted to help us play our roles assured our survival and, to some extent, our happiness. Sadly, society imposes some masks that do not support certain freedoms, and the true self is dramatically suppressed.

These masks often change over time. As Shakespeare wrote, each of us plays many parts throughout life. In many ways, I am the same person that I was as a child.

But I have changed dramatically over the years as well. The masks I wore as an infant, a girl, a teenager, and even a young adult no longer serve my needs or truly represent me. In truth, some of the masks I wore last year no longer fit. As we get older, we craft new masks to serve our needs for work, friendship, and romantic relationships.

We also wear masks to help us explore different personas, interests, and ways of being. The job-interview mask is usually very different from the religious or neighbor mask. Speaking for myself, I am not quite the same person when I am teaching as I am when I am off in the wilderness alone on a wildlife survey. I know many Pagan priests and priestesses whose families have no idea about their religious roles. I have friends who are drag queens in some situations and very buttoned-down businessmen in others.

The masks we wear frequently represent real aspects of self, allow us to safely explore new roles without losing ourselves in the process, and they facilitate interactions in many different situations. As such, they are beneficial, healing, and fun. However, masks can also alienate us, from true relationships with others and from living life as a whole and complete individual. It is not uncommon for an individual to layer on so many masks that uncovering the true self can take years of peeling back layers. This can cause us to forget that we are not the roles we play—that *we* created the masks in the first place. Too many people don't believe they can change their masks, and they lose the ability to access the unlimited multidimensional beings that they truly are beneath the masks.

Crafting a New You

Whether you have become stuck in your masks or are exploring something new, you can use tangible, crafted masks to break free and facilitate shapeshifting. The shamanic mask, possibly one of the oldest forms of shapeshifting and ritual art, is also an extremely beneficial healing tool. The mask can externalize feelings, identities, illnesses, and behaviors that the individual in need is not fully aware of or is repressing. Simply through creating and wearing the mask, these issues are brought out into the light of day where they can be handled.

Mask-making can also be used to bring in the gifts of spirit allies, deities, or people we admire and respect. Simply wearing a mask allows us to pretend to be that role. Working with this magically solidifies the embodiment of those energies and creates a way to access that persona even when the physical mask is not worn.

Before you can work with masks, you need to decide which mask to craft. This time-honored practice is something that anyone can do well. My son made his first mask at eight years old with only a small bit of assistance placing the plaster strips. If a child can do it, so can you! Your mask may be determined in a very individual way through dreaming, meditation, or shamanic journeying. It may be something that you uncover through talking with trusted loved ones or by freely writing in your journal. This is also an excellent time to use your divination methods or your pendulum.

Masks need not be perfect, realistic representations of a spirit guide, deity, or individual. In fact, it is preferable if they are more symbolic and mystical. You are not going to eliminate your identity entirely and become what you make the mask of. Your intent is to access similar energies within your Self and bring those through, so your mask needs to allow for personal freedom in manifestation. To be honest, some masks are wholly symbolic and are not meant to represent any specific person or being.

I recommend making a rough sketch of your mask first, keeping in mind that the creation may later take on a life of its own, but your rational mind needs a place to begin. If possible, do this in sacred space with a minimum of distractions. Choose meditative music to play in the background or have a friend drum while you focus on the image and feeling of the energy you intend to create.

Mask-Making Ceremony

Once the intent is established, a mask-making ceremony can be held. Set up your ritual as you normally would for any spiritual ceremony and have all necessary items for the creation of your mask within the ritual space. Masks may be constructed out of any material, even paper bags and magic markers. Collect anything you feel you may want to use. Bear in mind that you may end up evoking

lost soul fragments or shadow aspects. As a result, you may want to be prepared for an emotional release during the ceremony. Having a box of tissues on hand is highly recommended.

Consecrate sacred space in your preferred manner. During your invocation, be sure to invite any spirits involved in the creation or expected use of this mask. Begin by speaking aloud what you hope to eliminate or create in your life and what brought you to this point. Remember that this is safe, sacred space and allow yourself to step out of your comfort zone. Follow that up with a grounding and centering exercise to focus your heart, mind, and spirit on the task at hand.

Allow the mask-making to be as lighthearted or serious as it needs to be. Allow enough time to discard and re-create as necessary, but do not permit the focus to get stuck on the aesthetics of the end result. The process is at least as important as how the mask looks.

Crafting the Mask

Petroleum or vegetable jelly

Plastic wrap or shower cap

Rolls of pre-plastered strips, found in hobby stores

Scissors
Towels or newspapers
Bowl of warm water
Paper and pencil
Sandpaper
Craft knife
Velcro® strips
Optional: gesso (primer found in hobby stores), paper cup or plate, markers, acrylic paint, glue, feathers, fur, other decorations

1. Lay towels or newspapers down on the couch or floor where you will be laying back to craft the mask on your face.

2. Prepare the pre-plastered strips, scissors, and bowl of warm water. Cut the strips into sections ranging from 2 to 5 inches long.

3. Liberally cover your entire face with petroleum or vegetable jelly, smearing extra on any facial hair. Cover your hair with a shower cap or a layer of plastic wrap and smear some jelly over your hairline for added protection. Alternatively, cover your face and hairline with plastic wrap (Cut breathing holes for your nose and mouth.)

4. Dip one strip at a time into the warm water and smooth it onto the area to be cast, rolling off excess water with your fingers as you remove each strip from the water. Apply three to four layers of strips over your face. If you would like to fasten Velcro straps to hold the mask on your face, cover the area back toward your ears with plaster strips so that so that straps may be attached without interfering with the face of the mask. If you would like to paint animal eyes, cover your eyes with plaster.

5. Use additional plastered strips, a paper cup, or a paper plate to shape the mask. Paper cups can eas-

ily become bird beaks or elongated animal noses. Paper plates can be cut to form ears. Plastered strips can be rolled or balled up to exaggerate eyebrows, cheekbones, and jaws.

6. In about 15 minutes, the drying plaster will begin to pull away from your face. Let it dry for at least 5 minutes after completing the final layer. When you are ready, simply stretch and scrunch up your face under the mask as you gently pull it off. It should come off easily if the plaster is dry enough. Allow it to dry for 48 hours before decorating.

7. If you covered your eyes, use the craft knife to bore two small holes for you to see through.

8. Smooth out any rough paper edges with sandpaper. If you want a very smooth surface, paint the dry mask with gesso.

9. Glue the Velcro strips to the temple areas of the dry mask.

10. Decorate with feathers, paint, fur, and other items to bring through the energy you seek.

Once complete, the mask should be dedicated to your goal and worn for a meditation or journey during that initial ceremony. This is likely to add depth and power to the experience. Discussion or journaling can be an essential part of understanding, integrating, and manifesting the experience.

Placing the mask on an altar or anywhere you will see it regularly will help keep this process present in your conscious mind. Seeing it and working with it, through meditation and ritual, on a consistent basis will deepen your experience and aid you in embodying the new persona.

In time, this new mask will become as comfortable and solid as masks you have worn for most of your life. Once this occurs, you have two options for the mask. You may choose to keep the mask as a reminder of your success and focus for further work. Alternatively, you may ritually dispose of the mask once you personify what you intended. This is a common choice and people will ritually burn or bury old masks, releasing the energy and prayers to the multiverse.

~

Whatever masks you wear, take the time to examine them. Be sure that these are masks you choose consciously and with full intent. Keep those that ensure your survival and happiness, but find ways for them to also allow for the full beauty of your true identity to be preserved and accessed. Masks can, and should, be joyful explorations of Self.

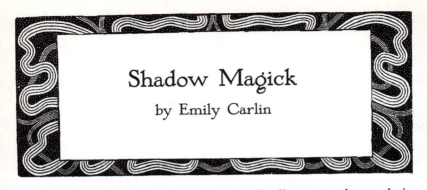

Shadow Magick

by Emily Carlin

A lot of popular spiritual practices teach adherents to better their lives by creating a positive mindset, generating positive energy, and so forth. This is great for most people most of the time, but it isn't so easy for some. Perhaps you're stuck in a spiritual rut and your practices aren't giving you the desired results. Perhaps you've had experiences that have rocked your foundation so hard that the gentle path just isn't cutting it. Or perhaps you look at all that love and light and just feel a little nauseated. Sometimes the only way forward is not to look at the bright side, but instead to examine the shadows—to stare in the abyss. Having a desire to look into the darkness doesn't mean that you're a negative or bad person; it just means that you need to travel a different path to spiritual growth.

The essence of shadow magick is taking a hard look at yourself, determining what things aren't working, the things that are broken, and changing them. For many, the hardest part of shadow magick is seeing what those shadows really are. The shadows that dog our steps are rarely the bogeys people expect—ghosts, goblins, and the like. Shadow magick works with our internal shadows: our fears, insecurities, incorrect assumptions, weaknesses, pettiness, and irrationalities. Everyone has traits they wish weren't there. Some people deal with these by bringing so much positive energy into their lives that there's no room for shadows. However, that doesn't work for everyone. Instead, some of us look to shadow magick to teach us to dive deep into the darkness and keep going down until we punch out the other side.

The fundamentals of shadow magick begin with looking into our shadow; a practice I call Looking in Dorian Gray's Mirror. For those of you who are unfamiliar with the story *The Picture of Dorian*

Gray, by Oscar Wilde, it is about a young man who wishes that a portrait of him would age instead of his body. Magically, this wish comes true, and the portrait ages and bears all the scars of Dorian Gray's soul. Over the course of time, Gray becomes more and more depraved and the portrait becomes so terrible and twisted that Gray locks it away. In the end, Gray is confronted with the portrait, looking at everything he has become—being able to see with his eyes every twist of his soul—and he takes his own life. Shadow work is about looking into that portrait every day. It takes time, discipline, and courage to look at oneself so honestly. If you cannot see what you really are, how can you ever really change and grow?

Looking at your shadows is only the beginning. Once you've identified the things you don't like about yourself, you're not allowed to just sit there and moan about them—you have to do something about it.

This is where shadow work gets tricky, because some of those things you don't like are genuine problems that need to be fixed, and some of them are things that you've merely been taught to dislike that aren't true shadows (though the feelings that keep you from accepting those traits may be). No one can tell you whether something you detest about yourself is something you need to change or if it's just your way of looking at it that needs to change. There is no easy answer for how to understand your shadow; it's something you have to determine for yourself in whatever way works for you. Some people use meditation, divination, or communication with spirit guides or trusted friends to examine their shadow. For you it could be any, all, or none of these things. Only you can see into your own soul.

Once you've leapt that hurdle, it's time to forgive yourself for your weaknesses. Don't laugh—it's important. Most people who are actually motivated enough to do something about changing their lives and dark enough to do it through shadow magick are really hard on themselves. Whenever I find a new flaw in my image of myself, I tend to spend a goodly chunk of time wallowing in depression, bemoaning how horrible/useless/bad/etc. I am. It's normal and healthy to allow yourself a bit of time to roll around in self-pity as long as you then pick yourself back up and forgive yourself.

The next step is to do some working focused on "fixing" the problem. This is often a ceremony in which you own and embrace whatever the shadow is. Embracing a shadow means allowing yourself to have whatever feeling or thought it is, but to then think about it reasonably and not act on it unless it's truly rational and correct to do so. It's really just a stylized way of reminding yourself to think before you act and to not get too mad at yourself for not being perfect. Sometimes the shadow is bad enough to really need to be excised rather than embraced, in which case a more focused banishing ritual would be appropriate.

~

Shadow magick is about being really, really honest with yourself and never being afraid to look in the dark. Do it long enough and you end up knowing yourself very well indeed. Sure, there are kinder, gentler ways of growing, but sometimes you need a good drop kick to move forward.

Looking in Dorian Gray's Mirror

These days, people are not encouraged to examine themselves deeply, if at all. We breeze through our days playing a part: the student, the grunt, the boss, the teacher, the wife, and so on. How often during your day do you batten yourself down so that the real you isn't exposed? Do you do it because it keeps you safe, because you think who you are is unacceptable, because it would crack your mask? Living masked day in and day out can make it very difficult to see oneself clearly. Wear those masks long enough and sooner or later you'll start to forget the person you really are and then you'll be nothing but the hollow mask of the character you play. Shadow magick breaks through the lies, most especially the ones you tell yourself. This simple ritual will introduce you to shadow magick and the practice of looking deep within.

Materials:

A black candle

Insight Oil*

A small mirror

Incense, if desired (dragon's blood or a mixture of frankincense and myrrh both work well)

Paper

Pen or pencil

    * To make Insight Oil, grind 1 teaspoon each of dried mugwort, sage, and yarrow into a fine powder. Mix with 3 tablespoons of jojoba oil in a jar with a tight fitting lid. Let steep for three to four weeks. Strain and it's ready to use. For the most potent oil, make this on the dark moon and let it steep until the next dark moon.

Perform this ritual at night in a quiet, private place where you won't be disturbed. This is most effective during the waning and dark moon. Also, make sure you have enough time to both perform the ritual and to decompress afterward. Looking at the shadow is emotionally taxing and can leave you wrung out. Give yourself time to deal with whatever comes up without other responsibilities pressing on you.

    Gather your materials, shut the door, close the drapes, turn off your cell phone, and turn down the lights. Sit comfortably on the floor (or on a chair at a table) with your materials in front of you.

Take a few minutes to simply breathe and let go of the stresses of the day. Ground and center as you normally do. If you find that your mind has difficulty pushing away the thoughts of the day, perhaps you need to deal with them before performing this ritual.

Light the incense if you're using any. Anoint your third eye with a drop of the Insight Oil. Think for a few minutes about why you want to see yourself more clearly. Think about what you hope to gain. Think about what challenges you expect the exercise to present. Are you really willing to see yourself without bias, warts and all? Take some time to write down these thoughts until you feel that you really understand why you're doing this.

Anoint the black candle with the Insight Oil and light the candle. Pass the mirror just above the candle flame (just far enough out that the heat doesn't hurt your fingers, but you can feel it). Envision the heat and light of the flame passing into the mirror, cleansing its energy and empowering it. If you're using incense, pass the mirror through the smoke while envisioning the smoke imparting its energy to the mirror.

Hold the mirror to your third eye and either think or say out loud:

I will see myself clearly. I will see who and what I really am. Show me my strength. Show me my weakness. Show me all that I am. Show me joy and sorrow, pride and folly, success and failure. I see clearly. I see who and what I really am.

Look in the mirror. Look at yourself, really look at yourself. Look beyond the face you present to others, look beyond your flesh. Look deeply into your own eyes. See the kernel of "you" that lives deep within your soul. What do you see?

Take a few minutes to write down what you see. Write down your strengths, your weaknesses, everything. Who is the person that lives deep inside your true heart? What in your life needs to change in order for that person to thrive?

You may find this easy or difficult. If it's difficult, don't worry, you're on the right track. If it's easy, either you're a near bodhisattva or you just aren't ready to see what lies below—that's okay too. Shadow magick only works when you're ready for it to work, so it's okay to put it aside and come back later.

When you feel you've seen all of yourself that you're able to process now, turn over the mirror and say:

Thank you for showing me my deeper self.

If it's short enough, let the candle continue to burn—snuff it out if it isn't. (The candle can be reused the next time you do this exercise.) Stand up and turn on the lights. Allow yourself some time to process the experience.

A Real Balancing Act

by Alan Lucia

If we can conceive of light in all of its modes of existence, including the majority of its vibrating states unavailable to our limited human sight, we can begin to understand the ancient teaching that proclaims: "Light is knowledge." And with this proclamation, we can most likely agree that the strongest source of this knowledge within the region of space we share is our good friend, the Sun.

This fireball has long been, and is still believed to be, a *god* by many cultures around the world—a spiritual being of untold powers and inherent masculine overtones. To others, however, our central star is thought to be nothing more than a physical life force, a means of energy—just one space furnace among trillions throughout the known universe.

Modern scientific studies concerning this massive body of heat and light have given us important information regarding its physical makeup. For example, the Sun's inner creative dance between atomic particles and intense gravity is thought to produce the light we enjoy each day. And aspects of the Sun, such as its electromagnetic field, its layered surface structure, the effects of sunspots, and the vast power of outward-traveling "solar winds," have been explained in ever-greater detail.

This life-giving source utterly dwarfs all of the planetary bodies it is thought to have spawned. Science accepts its existence as ... well ... just the way things are—normal fare for the entire universe. Otherwise, beyond careful observation of the physical state of things, considering the possibility that *anything* other than high-pressure, high-temperature subatomic bonding (fusion) is going on within the core of our central star is currently rejected by most scientists. Fortunately for us, though, many metaphysical and quasi-scientific thinkers have been striving to incorporate myriad ancient teachings, and at times newly channeled teachings from discarnate entities of differing stripes, in with today's physical discoveries.

Many of these teachings (both old and new) are centered on the concept of Creative Consciousness and how it plays a part in the establishment and continued nurturing of each planet's physical environment. It is taught that without some kind of preexisting exercise of cognitive awareness (intentional design), by default, all physical existence would have to materialize out of a process of unguided, random chance. Many wholly scientific thinkers are fine with this scenario. Yet most spiritually minded people of numerous paths find this hard to accept.

And who can blame them? After all, scientific hypotheses are in reality nothing more than educated guesses—just as much a shot-in-the-dark as many spiritual teachings tend to be. Not that scientific theories should be shunned or ignored. On the contrary, they should be celebrated for the general betterment they've helped our world realize. By obtaining more knowledge about the physical nature of our world, and our solar system at large, we've begun to notice a meeting place between scientific observation and metaphysical traditions.

Certain scientific beliefs once thought to be infallible are now being updated. Olden Newtonian ideas having to do with the concrete nature of physical matter and gravitational interplay between cosmic bodies have given way to more ethereal teachings due to quantum physics, and its undeniable mystical shadings set squarely upon today's scientific community. This development would probably have pleased Mr. Newton, given that he was a strong advocate of alchemy as it was understood in his time.

Alchemical symbolism is often depicted the fine balance between the Sun and Moon, light and dark, male and female creative energies, and so forth. Newton, a brilliant mathematician, would have immediately appreciated our newly developed understanding that on quantum levels all matter is essentially coming from "nothing" (inconceivably minuscule disconnected subatomic particles). He would likely fully embrace today's newest ideas that the balance of continuously interacting positive and negative (masculine/feminine) charges on a subatomic level are the best explanation of manifested physicality—with much, if not all of these minute, "fuzzy" items having no mass (traceable physical property) at all!

This kind of thing can get fairly complex, fairly quickly. So suffice it to say that the more our concrete world of olden scientific reality dissolves within the ever-growing body of newer quantum discoveries, the more the idea of pre-physical, intentionally creative consciousness presents itself as a viable explanation concerning the initial design, and following outward expression of planetary environments located throughout our family of eight planets and hundreds of moons.

As we all know, each of our planets exhibits unique environments. Obviously, the conditions we find here on Earth are absolutely essential for life as we know it. The richly varied climates we find on this planet are delicately balanced and carefully attended, or so it seems. Most people—magical thinkers and non-magical thinkers alike—agree that today's exceptionally complex environment has taken eons to create, having gone through many different incarnations, all the while supporting countless, long-extinct species of flora and fauna.

Generally speaking, based on recent interpretations of global fossil and rock strata records, each episode in time seems to show evidence of long periods of slow adaptation within ancient species, interspersed with *sudden* periods of evolutionary upgrades—one period of extended life setting the stage for the next more complicated stage. A brief evolutionary chronology begins with trilobite instinctual minds that matured toward dinosaurs and primitive forestation, which eventually gave way to higher-functioning mammalian herd-like mentalities surrounded by incalculable rain forest and desert-adapted plant and insect life. Finally, we have reaching the kind of individualized consciousness capable of completing complex mathematical equations and traveling out into space. The creative process, having come full circle as that initial force of creative consciousness (Sun-based masculine design and feminine implementation), had discovered a way to express itself in bipedal human form—you and me, in other words.

To explain further, those who hold to the possibility of precognitive design often drop this part of a solar system's development straight into the lap of its respective sun—actually two suns in most solar systems! They use terms like "Logos" or some solar god name to better relate to this designing, overseeing, primordial mind. They find planetary traits, relationships, and movements to explain the seeding strategies of this creative being. They often, and perhaps rightly so, describe these actions as being motherly, nurturing, and feminine in expression from planet to planet. They see the need for these intricate plans to find fulfillment through caring, wise, and patient implementation: again—Sun-based, "masculine" design requiring "feminine" expression; one without the other incapable of existing in a creatively meaningful way.

This is not to say that world environments are not shot through with masculine counterbalancing energies, as are the very designing Logoi themselves with feminine energies. For balance between these creative forces is evident and necessary within both physical and preexisting nonphysical states, just as each of the higher mortal and animal minds of our world show potential toward both creative gestalts of consciousness.

Creativity is therefore a mutually supportive, mutually gratifying act. Without the feminine expression of masculine design upon all worlds, that is, without these physical manifestations of the unseen work of a given Logos through the loving hands of numerous cosmic expressions we occultists often call "goddess," only half of the story would be told. This diminished reality is thought to have been, or still to be, the condition of the universe wherever and whenever this balance fails to be embraced.

Within our star system, glad to say, it seems we have successfully struck this all-important life-engendering balance, resulting in wondrously created life forms showing up routinely on planet Earth. Here we are classified as carbon-based life forms. Some of the larger moons are thought to be capable of sustaining life forms like ours, however, other planets and moons could easily, and by as much exacting design, sustain all kinds of sentient life forms that are foreign to our way of thinking.

A Logos, expressed through its feminine energies, is not limited to creating life in only one way . . . our way. And why should She be? Simply because we don't know of these other environs and the lives they potentially nurture is no reason they can't exist. They too may be unaware of our existence. Perhaps such things are currently none of our concern. Then again, perhaps, as some occultists draw upon, we mortals are often in contact with these other worlds and races in many different ways . . . a matter for another article, one would think.

Speaking more of moons—146 according to NASA and many more unofficially: up to as many as 336 in our solar system as of 2011—it appears this traditional symbol of goddess manifestation is quite abundant across our solar plain. Here on Earth we've come to recognize our moon in numerous ways. At times, she represents powerful influences of magic and feminine creativity. At other times, this astrological body helps peoples around the world keep track of days and months, acting as a very practical calendar. Then again, in the modern Western world, using the "light of the silvery moon," has become a means of romantic expression. And in a recent Hollywood film, *Hancock*, starring Will Smith, our Moon has even been used as the solar system's largest billboard!

The fact is, without the physical presence of this space body, life on our planet would simply not exist as it does. Our oceans wouldn't be pulled from side to side causing cleansing effects along all saltwater shorelines. And the Sun is not to be outdone in this case either. Its evaporative effects upon our world's oceans ensure an uninterrupted amount of needed water is shifted from the saltwater bodies to the freshwater lakes and rivers of large areas of dry land. The two of them together do this essential work. Just as the two of them project

many spiritual influences our way for use as we see fit. Goodly cosmic parents as we seem to have find no fault in this kind of dynamic, continuous support of their creation. They obviously take some kind of pleasure in presenting us with all manner of challenges for personal and social growth.

It's hard to say whether all star systems have been so well governed. As with all things in this imperfect universe, chances are some are and some aren't. And since the old occult adage, "As above, so below" is every bit alive and well these days as history has shown it to be, we can safely say that we are who and what we are precisely because the creative minds (individuals and groups) that play a part in the successful continuance of this and all planets existing within this local God/Goddess creation have given greatly of their talents and energies, just as we often do for our children, friends, extended family members, and yes, of course our magical pets (familiars).

The various enviroments here on Earth offer almost endless chances for learning adventures—some communal and pleasant, others life threatening. Through it all, these creative forces and groups of associated dimensional beings work to give their sentient populations on every planetary abode a way to personally participate in the cosmic drama of balancing light and darkness in an inward game of physio-spiritual self-evolution. The masculine and feminine energies within each of us, as across our solar system, are eventually explored to their fullest through the mounting experiences of lifetime after lifetime, until all is personally known. Until the imbalanced creatures of creation become the balanced creators of new, as yet unforeseen cosmic adventures. A future we all have open to us, should we choose to learn to absorb the "knowledge" inherent in the light directly felt from our central masculine star, or the indirect light reflecting off the feminine, mystical moon(s) that brings us so much hope, comfort, and strong magic.

Together, across all dimensions, planets, and creative populations, *we are each learning* how best to utilize our innate masculine/feminine energies—the kind of creative energies it takes to evolve and maintain a *balanced* star system like ours.

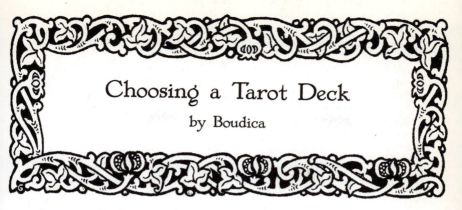

Choosing a Tarot Deck
by Boudica

As a professional card reader, I have many decks. Some are for my own amusement, others are working decks. Some of my clients prefer specific decks I have, while others like to see my latest or want to be surprised by a different deck. When you read for clients, try to use a deck that speaks to you and pleases your client visually. I think some of my clients have a personal attachment to specific decks, and that's probably why the decks resonate so well with them.

It's the same with you, the reader. While you may never read for clients, you still want a deck that resonates with your own personal self, and choosing a deck can be critical in making that connection to yourself.

Once upon a time not so long ago, there was only one popular deck—the Rider-Waite deck. The deck is rich in symbolism, the images simple yet elegant. It was influenced by the early occultist Eliphas Lévi, and the card's images were artistically done by Pamela Colman Smith, who was guided by A. E. Waite. The publisher was Rider Company.

There are volumes written about the meanings of this deck, the most complete was the book written by A. E. Waite himself, which guides the user through the symbols and the images card by card, in the upright and reverse positions. It only makes sense, as he designed the deck. The book also includes layouts and meanings of repeating numbers and certain echoing card draws. It was the book that I learned from on a deck I received as a gift and I highly prized in my early card-reading days.

The popular decks that followed were all "mostly based" on the same format—four suits and accompanying court cards (called the Minor Arcana) and the "trump cards" (called the Major Arcana). While there were differences—some changes in the meanings of the suits, symbols, or imagery—the decks still follow the same basic meanings and format as the Rider-Waite deck. Oh, there are decks that diverge considerably from the original, but they do not seem to be very sought-after and have become curiosities for collectors more than working decks. Today, most decks still follow the format of the Rider-Waite deck, so a good basic grounding in that deck and its meaning will assist any newcomer to the world of tarot. I highly recommend Rider-Waite for your first deck along with the accompanying book, as it will give you all the basics you need and enable you to interpret most any other deck with ease.

Part of one's ability to "read" cards originates from within. Depending on how intuitive and gifted you are, a deck can be immediately obvious or you may have to dig a bit to find the meaning. Know that many clients are the same way, and choosing just the right deck for client use can be as complicated as choosing a deck for yourself. There is the learning how to read, and then there is the learning how to interpret what you see. These are two very different steps, which is why I recommend a simple and well-documented deck first. If you make the reading easy and concentrate on the interpretation, the result will be a better reading overall.

However, should you be drawn to a particular deck and end up purchasing eye candy, you'll have to figure out the meanings from there. That's okay, but be aware that not all decks come with books, which can present a challenge to the new reader. Many decks come with the "Iddy Biddy Users Guide" in the box, and the interpretation of the deck is mostly sketchy and sometimes debatable. My advice in this instance is to find a deck that comes with a book written by the creator of the deck and/or the artist. They know best what they were looking to convey in the meanings of the cards. The new reader will find this very useful advice and a seasoned reader may discover meanings that they had overlooked or not considered. I find insights all the time in the books that accompany the decks. It is a worthwhile investment.

But in all things, we come to the point where you want a deck that says "you"! There are literally hundreds of decks out there. Which one is right for you? Well, maybe you need to look at decks before you purchase one. There are a few really good sites that offer a variety of decks for you to browse through. The major manufacturers are well represented: Llewellyn Publishing, Lo Scarabeo, and U.S. Games come to mind as major publishers/distributors who have a good-sized collection online for you to wander through. But the site that I have watched over the years is aeclectic.net. This site started as a review site of tarot decks exclusively. They received permission to reproduce a couple of cards from each deck reviewed, and then really excellent reviewers would examine the deck and list good points and not-so-good points. The images of the decks, however, were critical to the site's success. They have led many people to their decks of choice. And there are also some short-lived decks pictured there, which makes it a valuable resource for the collector as well. By the way, there is also a plethora of spreads on that site so you can find something in a spread that speaks to you as well.

There are stores that have decks on display. Some storekeepers will allow you to handle their display decks, others will not. Displays at some of the larger retailers have deck samples that you can look at. Any way you do this, I highly recommend you actually look at the deck before you purchase and do not make an impulsive buy. I know too many people who have been very disappointed with impulse purchases of decks, and I have acquired some decks very cheap because of it.

But what should you be looking at when you purchase a deck? Well, first, what appeals to you? Are you attracted to animals or to people? Do you like elements, or symbols, or designs? Decks are complex these days. Obviously, do not choose a deck with dragons if you do not like dragons. Likewise, if you are a springy and bubbly person, choose a deck that reflects your inner self, not something that is dark and ominous. Don't like cats? Well, then make sure your deck doesn't have any cats in it. There are even decks with toned-down symbolism for Death and the Devil if you are delicate in nature. And then there are decks that speak with lifestyles, God or Goddess centered, Goth, GLBT, nature-based decks, and more. There literally is something for everybody out there. Find one where the images appeal to you.

Carefully consider not just the images but also the symbolism. You will find a mix of suits, numbers, names and languages on the cards. From Roman numerals to Hebrew, from pentacles to gold coins, the images can be subtle or obvious. I would like to recommend that you steer clear of decks with very little or no symbolism. The images can be pretty, but what are you going to actually read in them? Symbols are very important as some may jump out at you during a reading that will be key to that reading. Again, I go back to a good grounding in symbolism. Choose a deck that has a variety of symbols in it as well as images that appeal to you.

Besides images and symbolism, there are some boring but important practical matters to consider. How well is the deck produced? Are the cards stiff, yet pliable? This will come into play with regular use. Can you shuffle the deck without seriously bending the cards? Does the deck fit comfortably in your hands? Are the colors appropriate for you? Bright colors, pastel colors, black and white; what appeals to you?

There are also "pop decks" that may be pretty or important at the moment, only to fade away along with the interest. The Harry Potter tarot deck immediately comes to mind. It may be cute, but it may not be usable for the long term. A pop deck is not something that will stand the test of time for usage, in my opinion. And while there is nothing wrong with collecting decks, even pop decks, you will want a working deck when you are starting. Collecting decks can come later.

Finally, choose something that very clearly speaks to you. It is important to learn how to read the deck, but it is more important to choose a deck that will also express itself to you. As I mentioned earlier, not only should you know how to read the deck, you should be able to interpret what the cards are saying. So choose something that resonates deep within you. Does the deck stand out in a crowd to you? Does it feel good? Do the images tell you something? No matter what the images look like, they still have to tell you something. A good way to check this is to choose a card that contains only symbols. The Ace of Cups is a good choice. What does the image say to you? Do you get "feelings" from the symbols, the images, the card itself? And pay attention to what it says! Sometimes you can hear the deck calling, or it may be telling you to pick another deck!

So to recap, it's not about walking into a store and purchasing a deck; it's all about the connection between you and the deck. Choose a deck that resonates with you, that is sturdy and constructed well, and that comes with a good book. Choose a deck that appeals to your lifestyle, that has meaning to you, and that contains enough symbols to make the deck easy to read but does not confuse or clutter the cards and their meaning. Choose a deck that says you! I believe if you do the research before you purchase you will be happier with the cards that you do buy and it will become a lifelong working relationship between you and the tarot deck.

Enchanted Tea Cup

by Mickie Mueller

Tea has a long and vibrant history in cultures all over the world. Consider the importance of the Japanese Tea Ceremony, the British passion for their national drink, or the constant consumption of tea by Tibetan monks in order to stay focused during meditation.

This simple infusion of leaves in water has become a way of life for many people. It has delighted the spirit, awakened the mind, and driven economies as well. Tea is a way to offer hospitality, heal the body, celebrate life, and ignite inspiration. Tea is technically a brew made from the tea plant, whereas herbal teas are actually herbal brews. With the popularity of herbal brews that don't include tea leaves, our culture has embraced the term "tea" for all consumable infusions or brews whether containing tea leaves or not. And why not? The ingredients in teas and herbal blends both have health benefits and can be used to create magic. Creating magic using tea is a very powerful and personal kind of magic. It is transformative in its very nature because you take the magic you make within you, for as you ingest the tea the magica becomes part of every cell in your body.

There's Just Something About Tea

All over the world, tea has become something of a ritual. Tea as a beverage has its roots in China. Legend has it that the second emperor of China, Shen Nung, discovered tea when the wind blew some tea leaves into a cup of hot water in 2737 BCE.

In Japan, the Tea Ceremony is a big event; the host spends days in preparation. The guests are first purified to

get rid of any dust from the outside world, and then the tea is prepared. Each move while preparing and serving the tea is intricate and precise. The Tea Ceremony is an important part of the culture and shows respect and appreciation for social interaction between the attendants and the host. It is also an opportunity to slow down and enjoy the beauty of simplicity.

Tibetans add butter or sweetened milk to their tea, and it is said they couldn't live without it. Everyone owns a personal tea bowl that only they may drink from. They use both hands while handling the bowl as a sign of respect. Similarly, it is important to never refuse tea in Tibet.

In the United Kingdom, tea is actually used to describe more than just the drink. We've all heard of afternoon tea. "High tea" and "low tea" are two versions of teas. Many people in modern times think of high tea as being the elegant version of afternoon tea, but these small meals are actually named after the tables on which they are traditionally served. Low tea is the fancy small meal of tea, cakes, biscuits, and scones that would be enjoyed in the afternoon in elegant sitting parlors, served on china at a low table like a coffee table. High tea was actually a working-class meal that takes the place of dinner. This was served at a high dinner table after the workday and would include staples such as cold cuts, steak and kidney pie, pickled salmon, and hearty bread.

In the Indian sacred text Ramayana (750–500 BCE) tea was clearly mentioned, but commercial production of tea didn't come to India until the arrival of the British East India Company in the 1820s. India is now one of the largest producers of tea in the world. The word for "tea" in India is *chai*, the favorite preparation of tea is Masala Chai, sweetened spiced tea with milk. In America, we call it chai tea, which is redundant since *chai* means tea. Every culture in the world seems to have its own tea traditions.

Make the Perfect Tea

There are some tricks to brewing the perfect cup of tea. The first and most important thing to know is that a cup of tea is actually a little tea and a lot of water, so the water you use is very important. The more pure and free from chemicals your water, the better. If you have a water purifier, use it for you tea. If not, you can use bottled spring water to get the best health benefits and the best flavor from your tea. Heat your water to just boiling and then turn it off; overboiling water depletes the oxygen from the water, and oxygen is what extracts the flavor from tea. Many teapots are designed for loose tea, which is the classic way to brew. If you prefer, you can use a tea ball or tea bags in a cup, mug, or teapot. Either way, be sure to warm your cup or pot with hot water from the tap. Always be careful not to overbrew or underbrew your tea. I've seen instructions to brew from 2½ minutes to 5 minutes depending on taste and variety of tea; check the tea package for exact times. After brewing is complete, remove the tea bag. You can then add sweetener of your choice, lemon, milk, or cream. For magical tea, natural sweetener is preferred over the chemical fake stuff.

Make Your Own Tea Magic

There are many ways to bring your own magical ceremony into your tea. First, choose tea with the magical properties you are looking to bring into your life. Here is a helpful list of many types of popular teas and their metaphysical properties. If you have tea ingredients that are not on this list, try looking them up in a book on herbalism, I recommend *Cunningham's Encyclopedia of Magical Herbs*. Some of the teas listed are made from tea leaves or are blends and will contain caffeine. I have labeled these with "caf." The herbal teas are caffeine free, and identified with "ncaf."

Black tea: invigoration, awakening of the spirit, prosperity, courage, strength (caf)

White tea: the least processed tea leaves, youth, gentleness, cleansing, removing negativity (caf)

Green tea: purity, finding self, balance, health (caf)

Oolong: beauty, grace under pressure, overindulgence or addiction (caf)

Chai: overall multipurpose magical tea, herbs and spices for love, power, protection, success, healing (caf)

Earl Grey: power and success (caf)

Jasmine tea: soothe the spirit, friendship (caf)

Blooming tea: inception, potential, manifestation (caf)

Yerba maté: strength through adversity, insight (caf)

Rooibos (redbush, substitute honeybush): relaxation and calm, well-being, joy (ncaf)

Mint: healing, prosperity, travel, transforms negativity (ncaf)

Chamomile: healing, calming, prosperity (ncaf)

Ginseng tea: passion, love, prosperity, vitality (ncaf)

Hibiscus tea: lust, passion, love (ncaf)

Ginger tea: protection, health, power, love (ncaf)

Tea Additive Magical Properties

Milk: nurturing, Goddess energy

Raw (unrefined) sugar: dispel evil influences, protection, friendship, love,

Honey: healing, energy, happiness, fulfillment

Stevia : balance, wisdom, love, love of self

Lemon: purifying, protection, longevity

Now that you have chosen your tea, you may want a special teacup, mug, or teapot to use just for making your magical brews. You might look for a lovely antique teacup and saucer in a secondhand store or you may have a special heirloom one of your own. Many people prefer a nice big mug. You might like a handmade mug from a local potter, one shaped like a Witch's cauldron, or a mug with your favorite god or goddess on it. Your magical cup should mean something special to you.

When making tea for magical purposes, it's recommended that you boil your water on the stove, don't nuke it in the microwave. If you want to and you have time, you can leave your water in sunlight for a day for spells dealing with success, prosperity, power, and happiness, or in moonlight for a night for spells dealing with love, wisdom, calming, and beauty. Think about whether you want lunar or solar energy and charge your water accordingly.

Transformative Tea Spells

You have your tea, water, and cup; now all you need is two to five minutes and you can charge your magical cup of tea and get some real transformative magic going! Tea spells are simple, quick, and amazingly powerful. Here are some spell ideas to get you started and give you some inspiration. Feel free to get creative and make these spells your own, or come up with new ones of your own invention.

Rooibos Tea Warm Comfort Spell

Brew a cup of Rooibos tea, and stir in some honey to taste. Hold the cup in your hands and as you gaze into the golden tea, breathe in the aroma. Picture a time in your life that you were truly happy; feel how you felt that day, hear the sounds, see the images, fill your heart with that feeling. Draw an "X" in the air above your teacup, capturing that energy in the teacup. Say the following charm:

> Bush tea; bring comfort in all that I do,
> I'll carry that feeling the whole day through.

As you drink the tea, feel joy wash over you.

Earl Grey Shining Success Spell

Earl Grey tea is made from black tea and flavored with bergamot oil, which is traditionally used for spells concerning money and success. If you can, use water infused with sun energy for at least several hours. Brew your tea and trace a pentagram in the cup with your spoon. Hold the brewed tea up so that the sun is reflected in the surface of the tea and say,

> Black tea and bergamot, I charge this brew,
> Power of the sun, I appeal to you.
> May all that I do today be a success,
> I step into the sun, the world to impress.

Drink all of the tea except the last few drops. Pour the last bit onto your palms and rub it in. Feel confidence brewing all through your body.

Chai Overall Magical Boost Spell

The variety of spices in Chai Masala make this tea really pack a magical punch. If you feel like you need an overall magical boost, this is the tea spell for you. Brew your cup of chai, then add sugar, stevia, or honey and milk if you like. Take in the aroma—you can already feel it filling you with magical energy. Hold your tea in both hands and say:

> *In tea leaves I release courage and strength,*
> *Cinnamon promote my healing and success,*
> *Clove bring me wealth of both abundance and love,*
> *Ginger bring protection and power from above,*
> *Cardamom awaken my passionate heart,*
> *As this warm cup of chai all its gifts to impart.*

Enjoy your cup of chai and feel its energy running through you, filling you with blessings of love, success, and protection.

Blooming Tea Flower New Project Spell

Tea flowers are a really unique method for brewing tea. Each serving of this tea starts as tea leaves bound with flowers, and the whole thing blooms in hot water. This can be a solitary ritual or could be a really dramatic part of an Ostara ritual for a small coven. While you boil your water, hold the flowering tea ball in your hand and focus your energy on your new project and what you want to manifest with it. Focus on the actual goals that you want to reach. Drop the tea into a clear glass mug, jar, or even a wine glass. Pour the hot water over the tea ball. Say the following charm:

> *Flower bloom and open wide,*
> *Release your magic from inside.*

Watch the bloom open as it changes from just a nugget of an idea into something beautiful and magical. As you drink the tea, you will also drink into yourself all your potential for your new project.

~

A variety of traditional and herbal teas can be as useful as a whole cabinet full of herbs if you know how to use them. Have fun working with magical tea and find new ways to incorporate their magic into your life while creating your own tea rituals and ceremonies.

A Sip of Summer
by Andrea Chavez

Lemons. From rare aphrodisiac to ubiquitous garnish, this exotic fruit should be a mainstay in every cook and magic-user's cupboard. Lemon's citrusy goodness can enhance a meal, clean a bathroom or a magical circle, and with a little patience and time, can become a little sip of summer in a glass.

Lemons: A History

One would think that the noble lemon would have a clearly defined history, but it is actually shrouded in some mystery. One reason for the inconsistent stories one reads could be that lemons and limes were considered to be the same fruit. They are not. True, unripe lemons are green and truly ripe limes are orangey-yellow and the two fruits are closely related, but they are indeed different species. The lemon is a *Citrus x limon* and the lime is *Citrus x latifolia*.

Most histories concur that the lemon originated in Northern India in the Indus Valley where artifacts in the lemon shape were found indicating that the fruit was important enough for people to create examples of them, but why they held such importance is unclear. Perhaps they discovered lemon's wide array of uses.

By 1900 BCE, the fruit had made its way to China, where it was known as the *limung*, a variation of the Persian name *limun* from whence we get the word lemon.

The Egyptians used lemons in their embalming process as one of the ingredients used in the scents, oils, and herbs rubbed on the body and in the linen and straw stuffing used to fill the body cavity. This might be where we get our use of lemons for purification and cleansing rituals in our magical world today. Stuff your next poppet with some lemon peel!

A Prized Treasure

Some of lemon's most amusing history comes from the Renaissance in Europe. Lemons were rare, exotic, and therefore pricey. The farther north they went, the more they were worth. In parts of Britain and the northern countries, they were literally worth their weight in gold. This treasure garnered the attention of the Catholic Church and got a racy reputation as a result. Church officials considered the unfamiliar lemon and concluded that it was the work of the devil. While the juicy orange was round and sweet—obviously the work of God—the lemon was oddly shaped and sour. After little debate, the lemon was actually excommunicated.

The lemon dealt with this shame by becoming a treasured aphrodisiac used by the rich and famous. Even notorious playboy Giacomo Casanova used the lemon in his pursuits of the fair sex. If one thinks about it, lemon's racy reputation becomes more clear. It has many qualities that excite the libido: It was exotic. It was expensive. It was dangerous to the point of being banned by authorities. On the physical side, it looked, well, not unlike part of the female anatomy. It smelled fantastic, and the sensation of popping the juicy little cells into a lover's mouth was enough to send even Casanova running to the nearest black market lemon shop.

Today we might use this history of lemon's titillating side to help increase our own magical love spell. Try adding a slice of lemon to your chalice on a Friday, the day of Venus, for a little something extra in your ritual. For a more direct route, keep a few by the bed for a little lemony squeeze with your partner.

Conquering the New World: Lemons Go to Sea

Columbus brought the lemon from the Old World to the New World during his second voyage in 1493 when he landed in

Hispaniola. Sea voyages like that one became a defining moment for the lemon because it became a medicine.

Scurvy is a nasty disease caused by a lack of vitamin C in the diet. Vitamin C is most often found in fruit, and lemon is packed full of the stuff. Sailors from the Middle Ages through the height of the Age of Sail in the 1800s were often at sea, where fruit does not grow, for many months. Explorer Vasco da Gama lost half of his men on a cruise to India in 1497 due to scurvy.

Eventually, someone made the connection that a sailor who kept and ate lemons did not get the disease. In 1753, naval surgeon James Lind discovered lemon's antiscorbutic properties and put it all together. He started the requirement that ships must carry lemons for the crew since lemons will last up to three months if kept in a cool, dark place like the hold of a ship. That was usually long enough before landfall was made and new supplies gathered. While the rest of the world laughed at the British sailors' dedication to their lemons, the British sailors stopped getting scurvy.

The term "limey" for a sailor comes from this practice. But why "limey" and not "lemony"? Remember, most people didn't know that lemons and limes were two different fruit. They thought that limes were just unripe lemons. Even today, that belief is still prevalent, if untrue. Fortunately for maritime wellness, either fruit will help ward off scurvy.

Correspondences: Magic from the Mundane

With any area of magical correspondences, one should investigate the connection between the correspondence and the item and not just accept the word of others. Looking to the history of the lemon highlights some potential magical uses, such as love spells or healing work. With just a little more digging, further magical correspondences are apparent in the lemon's chemical make-up. The so-called constituents are all hiding in plain sight.

Citric acid: Citric acid makes up about 6 to 7 percent of the lemon (an orange is only 1 percent citric acid). It is used to help strengthen bones when combined with calcium oxide to make calcium citrate. Citric acid is used in anti-acids and helps make soda pop sparkle. It improves blood circulation and can alleviate many illnesses if taken in small doses but be warned, too much citric acid will cause mouth sores.

Hesperitin: Hesperitin is good for the blood, vascular health, and keeping cholesterol in check. Here is an example of when it is good to know the origin of the word. The Hesperides were Greek nymphs who tended the garden of the goddess Hera. The same garden that grew the Golden Apple, which looks like—a lemon!

Citral (or lemonal) and limonene: These volatile oils make the lemon smell like a lemon. Lemon myrtle and lemongrass have even more citral then the lemon itself. Limonene is used in manufacturing insecticides, perfume, cleansers, some medicine, food, and most lemony things. Lemon oil is such a powerful cleaner that it is being studied for its ability to kill viruses and even cancer cells, but more research is needed in this area before it becomes the wonder-cure.

From Science to Altar

As you see, the scientific constituents of lemon can lead to many magickal ideas to harness the power of the lemon. Spells involving cleansing, healing, the Goddess, increasing passion in the blood, and just making things work better may all call upon the lemon.

Think of the culinary uses for lemon—the juice is often squeezed into a sauce, over fish, into the stir-fry, or into a plain glass of water. It creates something greater than its parts. The lemon gives the whole a boost—a kick of energy, power, taste, without taking away the original taste of the food. Just as the lemon enhances food, it can enhance magic.

The lemon is considered to be a feminine fruit and is associated with the moon despite its sunny complexion. Lemon is cooling in nature. It is the yin energy from the East, and in the West the signs of Cancer, Pisces, and Scorpio all claim the lemon. The moon's day, Monday, is a great time to do magical work with lemons. But, as I suggested earlier, Friday and Venus could be good correspondences with lemon, as they too are feminine in nature and have the added attraction of the inspiring feelings of love that the lemon can bring to a table.

Some Quick Magical Ideas

Use lemon juice as a spritz or straight from the fruit to cleanse your magical circle.

Pop a piece of lemon under the chair of a visitor. Folklore claims that will create a lifelong friend.

Use lemon-scented soap or shampoo as part of your pre-ritual wash.

Use lemon essential oil in an infuser to brighten a room and promote the working of any spell.

Add lemon peel in a sachet for a quick whiff of the essential oil as a pick-me-up.

If the stone or crystal can handle water and citric acid, diluted lemon is an excellent addition to the cleansing process of magical crystals or, indeed, any magical tool.

For an uplifting altar display, add a bowl of lemons by your goddess statue. They will keep for a long time and can be used as needed.

A small glass of limoncello and lemon cookies used for "cakes and ale" can provide a final boost of magical power to the end of magical circle work.

The Italian Connection

I first discovered the lovely liqueur called limoncello while on a trip to Italy, where to the tourist it appears that they drink the stuff like we might drink lemonade. Rest assured this is not the case. Limoncello can pack a punch and is meant to be drunk in small, chilled, tasty amounts as an after-dinner *digestivo* or drink to help with digestion. A small sip of this potent lemon-infused alcohol will warm even the coldest toes on a dark winter day, invoking feelings of summertime.

If a trip to southern Italy is not in your bank account, you can make your own limoncello with just a bag of lemons, a little preparation, and some patience.

Ingredients
10–12 lemons (organic)
750 ml vodka or other neutral alcohol
4 cups water
3 cups sugar
A glass pitcher or large Mason jar
Plastic wrap or lid
Bottles with stoppers for final product
Time and patience

Peel the zest of 10 to 12 washed, organic lemons in long strips. Any type of lemon will work. The Italians use Sorrento, but the standard grocery store lemon or even the Meyer lemon (a cross between a lemon and a mandarin orange) will work too. The lemons should be organic as you are using the peel, and pesticides will stay in the peel of any fruit. I use a standard vegetable peeler to remove the zest. Try to avoid the white pith, which is bitter.

Place the peeled zest in the glass pitcher or large Mason jar and add the 750 milliliter bottle of vodka (or any neutral grain alcohol). Buy what you can afford; the lemon will do the rest.

Cover and store in a cool place for as long as you like, but at least a week. Stir the mixture once a day to help agitate the peels and extract the oil.

Recipes vary on the amount of time needed to infuse limoncello. Some will claim it can be done in a week; others say it isn't really limoncello unless it has steeped for over six months. I say, whatever looks and tastes right to you is perfect. I infuse mine for two to three weeks or until I have a moment free to finish it off. The liquid will be a pretty yellow and smell like a vodka lemon drop.

Measure four cups of fresh, cool water and three cups of white sugar and place over low heat. Yes, use sugar; honey would be, well, just wrong! You can stir it once or twice just to get the sugar and water mixed, then leave it alone! Additional stirring will create sugar crystals, which you don't want. Allow the mixture to reach a slow boil and let it boil for about fifteen minutes without stirring it. This forms what is called a "simple syrup." After fifteen minutes, turn off the heat and let it sit until completely cooled. Do not rush this; just let it cool all the way to room temperature. It will take a few hours. This is where the patience comes into play.

Remove the lemon peels from the alcohol and pour in the syrup. Cover it up again. Store it in a cool, dark place; keep shaking it once a day, for as long as you wish—several days, several weeks, three months. It won't go bad; it will just get smoother and smoother.

When you are ready to bottle it, pour the limoncello into bottles with stoppers and label it, as you should always label everything made in the kitchen.

Limoncello is meant to be sipped ice cold. You may keep it in the refrigerator or, indeed, in the freezer. It will not freeze totally due to the alcohol content, but it will get nice and slushy. Sometime limoncello will turn cloudy or milky white as it is cooled—do not be alarmed, that is perfectly fine. It is also fine if it stays crystal clear. It depends on the lemons used and other environmental factors, but both are considered to be good limoncello.

It should be sipped in small quantities. Use those cute after-dinner glasses you've always wanted to use! Feel free to mix it into a tonic, seltzer, with champagne, pour it over ice cream, or splash it in a tea. Your imagination is your only limit.

The Gift of Summer All Year Long

Limoncello and other lemony gifts can make beautiful Yule presents for both your magical and non-magical family and friends. Add some tales from the lemon's exotic past to make a great conversational gift they won't forget. But remember to keep a little bottle for yourself so on those dark, cold winter days, you can open up the stopper and take a sip of summer in a glass.

Energy Healing Basics

by Deborah Blake

You may think of energy healing as some mysterious ability that only gurus and unusually magickal people have, but the truth is, all of us have the potential to use energy to heal. You've probably used the most simple of healing techniques without even realizing it. When we hurt ourselves and instinctively hold on to the place that hurts, we are doing rudimentary energy healing. The mother who kisses her child's boo-boo and makes it feel better is doing it, too.

Like any other skill, some people have more natural ability than others. After all, everyone can take art classes, but only some people are truly gifted. But that doesn't mean we can't all paint. In the same way, everyone can do energy healing on one level or another. Who knows? You may have a gift for healing and not even know it. In fact, that turned out to be true for me.

Energy healing is the use of some kind of natural energy (rather than medicine, acupuncture, or other external tool) for the purpose of healing. No one really knows how it works, although there are many different theories and approaches. It is generally agreed that the practitioner somehow taps in to the energy of the universe (or of God, spirits, etc., depending on what you believe) and uses that positive force to encourage the body to heal faster than it would on its own. Sometimes the results are minor but noticeable, and sometimes they can be downright miraculous.

Different Types of Energy Healing

There are a variety of energy-healing techniques, although from what I have discovered, they are all the same at the core. I'll explain more about that in a minute. Here are three approaches that most people are likely to be familiar with.

Reiki

Pronounced *ray-key*, Reiki is a form of energy healing based on a spiritual practice developed by Japanese Buddhist Mikao Usui in 1922. It has since been changed and adapted by a series of different teachers, some of them Westerners. In theory, Reiki practitioners are trained to channel "ki" or "chi" energy through the palms of their hands. Through classes taught as degree levels (first, second, and master), the students are given various secret symbols and gestures that are intended to help them better transfer this energy from themselves to their patients, or use it to heal themselves.

Therapeutic Touch

Therapeutic Touch was developed by two women, a nursing educator and a natural healer, in the early 1970s. Dolores Krieger (Ph.D., RN) and Dora Kunz were interested in creating a form of energy healing that could be easily taught, and Therapeutic Touch has since been used by many in the nursing world. They used the laying on of hands in a professional setting, something completely unheard of at the time. (www.therapeutictouch.com)

Ironically, considering its name, those who use Therapeutic Touch often work about an inch or so off the patient's body, and never actually touch the other person. Instead, they use their hands to sense the aura, or energy field, of the patient's body, and detect any abnormalities or blockages. They then manipulate that energy to increase healing and calmness.

Natural Healing or "the Healing Gift"

There are those folks who just have a natural ability to heal. This isn't something they were taught or learned in a class-

room—it just came to them. My own healing ability is one of these, and I like to call it intuitive healing because it is a matter of listening to the intuitive voice in the back of my head that tells me what to do for my clients. Other people call it psychic healing, or simply "the gift." Those who come from more traditional (i.e., Christian) religious backgrounds sometimes refer to this as the laying on of hands or faith healing. They believe that the gift comes from God and that God is the one doing the actual healing. Pagans are more likely to credit the healer or some universal energy that the healer is able to tap.

My Experience with Energy Healing

I discovered that I had a gift for healing after taking an introductory class on energy work. I'd been seriously ill for years, and many other folks had worked on me, often for a reduced rate or even for free. It is my belief that the gods gave me the gift of healing so that I might "pay it forward." I have always been a psychic, so the ability was probably lying dormant all along, but once I started tapping into it, it was quite amazing.

Out of curiosity, I took a Reiki Level One class and a day-long class on Therapeutic Touch to see if there was any difference between these approaches and my own natural gift. There were certainly variations in how the energy healing was done—Reiki tends to be taught as a more rigid approach, although longtime practitioners may stray from that—but as far as I could tell, the energy at the root of all three healing styles was the same; only the method of use was different.

Since that time many years ago, I have learned many helpful techniques from a variety of energy healers using a multitude of systems, but I simply integrate them with my own intuitive gift, using whatever works best for each individual client. If you decide to follow one of these paths to energy healing, my best advice is to be flexible and to listen to your own inner wisdom—sort of like anything else in witchcraft!

Getting Started: A Simple Exercise

You can always take a Reiki class (although they can be very expensive) or look for someone who teaches Therapeutic Touch; sometimes a nursing school will have a practitioner who also accepts students from the outside. But there is no reason why you can't do a few simple exercises on your own.

Remember, everyone has the ability to do simple energy work. If it makes you more comfortable, you can do your experimentation within a magickal circle, but it isn't necessary to do so. You may also want to light a candle to one of the healing gods or goddesses (Apollo is a good one) and ask for whatever help that deity may wish to give.

Start by grounding and centering. Take a few slow, deep breaths. If you are sitting, feel your tailbone connecting with the energy of the earth. If you are standing, connect through the soles of your feet. Feel the energy of the earth coming up into your core (around the area of your

belly button). Then open yourself to the energy of the sky, and feel it entering the top of your head and moving down to meet the earth's energy in your core. Close your eyes, breathe deeply, and feel your core growing full and warm.

Don't worry if things don't happen dramatically the first time you try this; sometimes it takes practice.

Rub your hands together briskly, back and forth a few times. This helps the energy start flowing down your arms and into your palms. Then move your hands so that they are about shoulder-width apart, held out in front of you with your elbows slightly bent and your palms facing each other. If it helps, visualize yourself holding a giant invisible beach ball between your two hands.

Stay in that position for a minute and see if you can feel the energy moving between your palms. Then slowly move your hands toward each other, palms facing. See how close your hands have to get before you feel the energy. It will feel like a small, round ball or maybe just like a slight resistance to forward movement. When you reach the point where you can feel that resistance, try pushing your palms gently toward each other and then pull away and do it again. The more you practice, the more sensitive you will become to the energy, and the farther away your hands will be from each other when you start to sense it. It may help to visualize the energy as a glowing light.

Once you have formed the ball of energy between your hands, tip your left hand up over your right, as if you were pouring the energy into the palm of your right hand. Then hold your left arm out and run your right hand slowly down it, starting at the shoulder and ending at the fingertips. Keep your right hand about an inch away from the other arm as you move very slowly down. You should be able to feel the energy moving with the hand, and the fingertips of your left hand may tingle after you get to the end. Then make the energy ball again and switch hands.

As with everything else, this will become easier with practice, but you may be surprised by how rapidly your skill develops. Remember that you should never work on anyone else without their permission, and be sure to ground before you start so that you don't pick up any negative energy from the person you are working on. Especially in the beginning, it is a good idea to visualize anything you take in going back out of you through your feet and harmlessly into the earth.

Energy healing isn't a substitute for standard medical care, but it is a wonderful way to tap into the positive power of the universe to help yourself and others—and what could be more magickal than that?

Private Ritual for the Death of a Parent

by Lisa McSherry

We don't do grief.
—Joan Didion, author

For most of us, talking about how we feel is difficult, and doubly so when we are grieving. We are in pain, often combined from sorrow and anger to varying levels, and we are alienated from others because of that pain. We may feel guilty because of unfinished business we didn't take care of in our relationship. Or we may not feel much of anything at all; it's too distant. People avoid us or are deeply awkward in our presence. Social niceties encourage us to make it easier on them, which is exhausting, so instead we project a sense of calm, an air of not needing sympathy or of having "moved on"—as if the death of a love one was a minor part of our lives.

As I write this, my grandmother is dying, and my mother and I are having long conversations about how she is processing—or not—her grief. My grandmother was not a very nice person for most of my mother's lifetime, which damaged my mother in many ways. Not surprisingly, my relationship with my mother was influenced by this damage. These issues are actively being presented to us in the here and now.

The death of a parent has a profound influence on us. With their death, we become the oldest in the family, we become the adults, we become the next in line to die. This article began as a straightforward ritual: outline, words, symbols; but as I am working with my mother, I realize that grieving takes place in stages, and so our rituals must also take place in different places and times.

You think that their
dying is the worst
thing that could happen.

Then they stay dead.
—Donald Hall "Distressed Haiku"

We grieve in the moment, we grieve while making funeral arrangements and arguing over who gets the tea towels. We grieve when we are alone, we grieve at the funeral. But it's not enough. Grief is truly what happens when everyone has gone home; when you've thanked everyone for their help. Grief begins when we are once again alone, asking "now what?"

~

I had the privilege of seeing Sir Ian McKellan play King Lear several years ago. This play is about a man who has everything and then loses it all. There is an iconic moment in Act V when Lear walks on stage carrying his dead daughter in his arms. He staggers under the burden, almost falling, but refusing to drop her until he lays her gently down. Grief is heavy; it is unbearable; it is different for every one of us. Some people find losing a parent bearable—sad but not devastating. Others are crippled by their pain.

They make adjustments in their life to cope with the burden of grief. Life is details: the stories that families tell come from growing up together, sharing meals and experiences. Death wrenches those details away. What is left is pain.

The Five Stages of Ritual

I didn't write a single ritual, I wrote five, each designed for a different stage of the grief cycle. You may wish to alter their form or content, or repeat one or several, or never do another. As I said, grief is individual and you know your needs best.

To create sacred space, physically clean the area you are going to use and then set it up with the items you will be using in the ritual. Cleanse yourself, consciously relaxing and letting as much of your negative emotions go as possible. (Showers are great for this.)

Face east and imagine a door opening. Say: "*I call upon the powers of air to guide me and inspire me.*"

Face south and imagine a door opening. Say: "*I call upon the powers of fire to give me the energy to complete this task.*"

Face west and imagine a door opening. Say: "*I call upon the powers of water to support me emotionally and help me understand my psyche.*"

Face north and imagine a door opening. Say: "*I call upon the powers of earth to strengthen and ground me.*"

See a sphere forming around you, enclosing you and your ritual space completely. Say: "*As above, so below, I stand between the worlds and beyond the bounds of time.*"

To open the circle, bow to the four directions, and imagine the sphere dissolving while saying: "*I thank the powers of air (fire, water, earth) for their presence here. Go if you must, stay if you will. Blessed be.*"

Accept Your Grief

Part of every misery is, so to speak, the misery's shadow or reflection: the fact that you don't merely suffer but have to keep on thinking

about the fact that you suffer. I not only live each endless day in grief, but live each day thinking about living each day in grief.
—C. S. Lewis

Grieving can be frustrating. It is upsetting to be so upset; it's hard to be discombobulated by something as intangible as emotions. Thus a major component of the grieving process is learning to accept that we are grieving and allow it to run its course. I'm a firm believer in praying "Please let me learn this lesson quickly so I can move on" and the loss of a parent is definitely a Cosmic Lesson. There is no use in your feeling terrible because you feel terrible; this ritual can help you accept that you are grieving.

Process

Choose a time when you will be alone and uninterrupted. Have a good-sized mirror nearby, as well as tissues and a glass of water.

Create sacred space. This can be done formally or informally, with as much detail as you require.

Meditate on the quality of your grief, of your pain.

When you are ready, look at yourself in the mirror. Say "I am <name your feelings>." If it seems appropriate to shout it, do so. If you want to curse, or ramble on, go ahead.

Do your best to name as much of what you are feeling as possible. (You may want to journal this. If you do, make sure you also talk aloud—you need to hear how you feel.)

Promise to take care of yourself.

Promise not to let anyone tell you how you should feel.

Promise to respect your feelings.

Create a self-care plan to support you through this time. (You know best what you need, but I suggest making sure your plan includes extra sleep, quiet time, and plenty of distractions [jigsaw puzzles are ideal] when you need them.)

When you are ready, take several deep breaths. Drink your water.

Open the circle.

You may want to hold a stone during the ritual, and then carry it around with you to help you remember to respect your feelings. Good stone types include amethyst, apache tears, jasper, and sodalite. Some people may prefer to use rose quartz or hematite.

Forgive Others

Long after your parent is laid to rest, you'll be dealing with the awkwardness and insensitivity of others. During the emotionally draining period near the end you will find yourself extra-sensitive to the emotional wobbles within the people around you. It is a time when many decisions must be made, and that leads, almost inevitably, to disagreements. Much of the tension will arise from poor communication, but it will also come from the need of others to do something—anything—to fix the situation, rather than letting your grief run its course. To help you forgive:

Choose a time when you will be alone and uninterrupted.

Create sacred space. I strongly recommend having an image of Buddha or Tara to contemplate—their loving compassion is the energy you want to manifest.

Sit comfortably in a chair, with your back upright, and your feet flat on the floor. Breathe slowly, deeply and rhythmically for at least five minutes. Don't hurry this exercise. Let your body and breath slow to a peaceful, comfortable rhythm before going further. You want to be as relaxed as you can be.

Imagine yourself surrounded by a thick, warm blanket or shawl. Let it settle softly about you, comforting and protecting you within its thick folds. Feel yourself snuggling into it, feeling safe and warmed.

Visualize that the person that you are having difficulty with is sitting across from you. They are not allowed to speak to you or touch you without your permission or an invitation to do so. As clearly as you can, tell them your truth. Tell them about your anger, your pain, the hurt that you feel. Stay as centered on your own feelings and pain as you can. Say everything you need to say, leaving nothing back. End by saying:

<Full name>, I forgive you for the pain you brought to me, whether real or imagined, deliberate or unintentional.

Breathe deeply and release your hurt. Give yourself permission to feel hurt in future situations, but promise to let it go so it doesn't stagnate within. You may wish to offer a personal prayer to Buddha or Tara.

Stay within this feeling of safety as long as you wish.

When you are finished, imagine the blanket melting into your body, becoming an invisible shield to support you from the idiocy of others.

Open the circle.

Dealing with the Pictures in Your Head

The death of a parent is usually accompanied by many difficult scenes—hospital room tableaux, arguments, quiet time spent looking at their face, last requests, bad news, smells. Even if you weren't present when mom or dad died, your brain will make an image of it, perhaps one that is even worse than reality. Many of us in the grief process will also be reluctant to talk about the dead, either because we don't want to remind others of our grief or because we don't want

to speak ill of the dead. This keeps the images in our head strong and vibrant.

For this ritual, you want to do some research and preparation. Find out as much as you can about how your parent died (if you weren't there); write down in as much detail as possible what you can remember about the difficult scenes. Write it all out.

Choose a time when you will be alone and uninterrupted.

Have a fireproof container, matches, and be prepared to put out a fire (just in case).

Have a bunch of cheap paper, a pen (perhaps a nice one), and a bunch of beautiful paper.

Create sacred space.

Document everything you can about the pictures in your head. What evokes them? What don't you know? What is the worst thing about them? Use the cheap paper.

Spend as much time as you need documenting the worst you possibly can.

When you are ready, burn the pages.

Think about that scenario and reframe it in a more positive light. You don't have to make it sweetness and light, but a few changes will often make a big difference in how awful the scene made you feel.

Write that new scenario on the gorgeous paper.

Releasing Anger

For those of us who were abused by or had extremely difficult relations with our parents, their death comes with particularly mixed emotions. Eventually, you may settle on rage as your primary emotion. Anger can be cleansing and supportive, but rage tends to be destructive. I offer this ritual as a way to process that emotion.

Choose a time when you will be alone and uninterrupted.

Have at hand a red candle, cheap writing paper and pen, very nice writing paper (and perhaps a really nice pen), a white candle, a fireproof container, and matches.

Create sacred space: face the east, and call upon air to help you express your rage clearly. Face the south, and call upon fire to help your rage burn up and out of you. Face the west, and call upon water to help your emotions flow freely within the circle, cleansing your spirit and restoring yourself. Face the north, and call upon earth to allow you to safely ground your rage, and to sustain and support you through the releasing process. As you call the directions, visualize a circle of white light forming around your working space, shielding you and protecting you with the elements you've called in.

The Goddess Kali is particularly appropriate for this ritual, but if you haven't worked with her before, then I recommend Sekhmet, Nemesis, or Lyssa.

Light the red candle and begin to write or draw your rage on the cheap paper. Focus on making the issues clear and how what happened made you feel; avoid paying attention to the other person's guilt or motivations. Using "I" statements helps here.

Next, hold the paper between your hands, focus your awareness on the red candle, and begin to chant, shout, scream, or make whatever sounds help you to feel the rage come up and leave you. Send the rage into the red candle, watching the flames burn brighter and hotter as the force of your anger fuels them.

When you feel you've released as much rage as you can, burn the papers.

Light the white candle.

Shift your focus to feeling calm and at peace. As you do so, write or draw on the fine paper your strengths, those qualities which are wonderful about your self.

When you are finished, read or describe those qualities aloud. Speak in the present tense and acknowledge your strength, your beauty, your intelligence.

Open the circle (let the candles burn out).

A really quick and dirty (non-ritual) version of this (with thanks to the authors of *About Grief* for the idea) is to turn on your vacuum cleaner and scream and shout while cleaning up. This is an excellent cathartic mechanism if you just need to blow off some steam.

Ritual Script:
The Conversation You Never Had

Many of us have difficult relationships with our parents. Many of us don't get the chance to heal those relationships or even find a sense of being able to move on and past those problems. Death is the final barrier to closure, and our grieving process can be prolonged by guilt and a re-emergence of memories of those long-buried pains. We may find ourselves fiercely angry or deeply ashamed. As hard as it might seem while we are feeling this way, the keys to integrating our emotions lie first in expressing, then in understanding, and finally in forgiving.

Choose a time when you will be alone and uninterrupted.

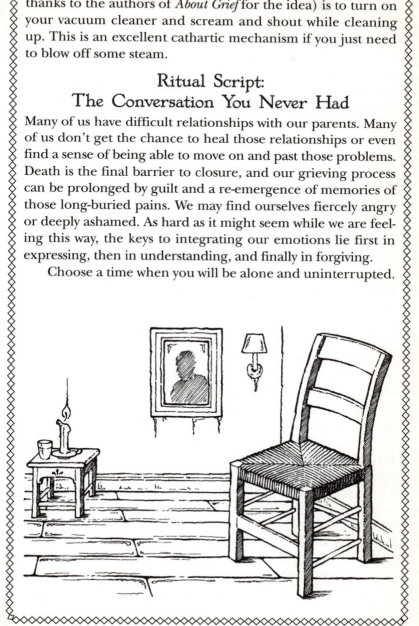

Place an extra chair and a picture of the deceased across from you. (You may also want to have a glass of water. You're going to be talking a lot.)

Create sacred space.

Start talking. Explain what happened. Tell them how you feel. Tell them what they did wrong. Go ahead and express whatever emotion seems appropriate in the moment. Mock them. Cuss them out. Really get into it.

At some point you'll realize you are repeating yourself. When you do, take a break. Stand up, walk around, do jumping jacks or anything that gets your blood moving a bit.

Sit down again, and tell the story again, only this time talk about what you learned from it. Try to avoid being cynical—you want to find the positive and bring it into the circle.

Now tell a story about a shared experience that makes you laugh and regard the deceased fondly. This is as much a part of your experience as the negative.

Say aloud ,"<full name>, I forgive you for the pain you brought to me, whether real or imagined, deliberate or unintentional."

Open the circle.

I find myself drawn to specific rituals within the larger world, most notably those from the Jewish tradition. I offer them to you to incorporate into your own rituals as you see fit. Upon hearing of a loved one's death, grief is expressed by tearing one's clothing. That torn clothing is worn for the seven days following (shiva is the term, Hebrew for "seven"). During that time mirrors are covered and mourners grieve intensely by not going to work, not wearing shoes, sitting on low chairs, and not watching any entertainment. For the thirty days after that, the mourners begin to re-enter society, but continue to refrain from attending parties or celebrations, they do not shave or cut their hair, nor do they listen to music. These practices recognize that when a major change in life has taken place, the survivor needs to step out of everyday activity for a while. A year after the death of a parent, the family gathers again at the grave site and unveils the grave marker. This ritual marks the end of the mourning period for the family.

~

Grieving is hard work, and it is not accomplished in anything like a linear fashion. You will need time to rest and gather your strength for the next round. Go ahead and take that sleeping pill; one won't turn you into an addict, and you need the sleep. Whatever you choose to do, I know your way of dealing with your grief is exactly what you need to do.

> *Give sorrow words. The grief that does not speak*
> *Whispers the o'er-fraught heart, and bids it break.*
> —Malcolm in *Macbeth*

For Further Study

"Jewish Mourning Rituals" found at: www.religionfacts.com/judaism/cycle/mourning.htm

Lewis, C. S. *A Grief Observed*. New York: Harper Collins, 1961. pg. 22

Marasco, Ron, and Brian Shuff. *About Grief: Insights, Setbacks, Grace Notes, Taboos*. Chicago: Ivan R. Dee, 2010.

Nuland, Sherwin. *How We Die: Reflections of Life's Final Chapter*. New York: Vintage Publishing, 1995.

Pinsky, Robert. "'The Year of Magical Thinking': Goodbye to All That," *New York Times*, October 9, 2005. found at: www.nytimes.com/2005/10/09/books/review/09pinsky.html?pagewanted=all.

Safer, Jeane. *Death Benefits: How Losing a Parent Can Change An Adult's Life—For the Better*. New York: Basic Books, 2008.

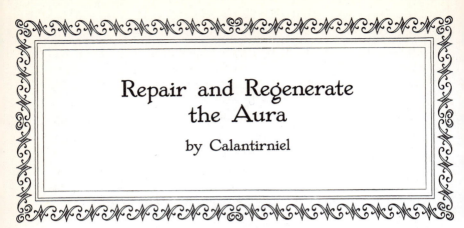

Repair and Regenerate the Aura

by Calantirniel

An aura, simply described, is the active energetic body that permeates and surrounds our physical bodies. It is part of us rather than separate from us. While not visible to our physical eyesight, it is often described as egg-shaped and can extend on average (for humans) about an arm's length from the body all around and even farther if the person is spiritual, vital, and aware. We are more expansive if we feel safe and happy, and we pull the aura in closer if we feel the need to protect ourselves. Plants, animals, and even inanimate objects also have auras. There are a number of different ways of seeing and defining the aura, and descriptions for various layers that go beyond the scope of this article. Anyone can use these techniques to work with these unseen energy bodies for uplifting their spirits, revitalizing their health, and improving their connection to source.

If you have access to a metaphysical vendor that provides Kirlian photography or other comparable technology, you may wish to have your aura photographed and even interpreted. Keep in mind that while these machines can provide very useful information, an experienced human aura reader will likely be more accurate, so it is good to choose someone who provides this service with the photograph. Since our auras are always changing, you may wish to date this photograph so you can later see patterns that were developing, patterns that are leaving, and changes you decide to make with this knowledge.

If you don't have access to this technology, An easy and inexpensive way to define the auric field is to use dowsing rods or even

a pendulum. With dowsing rods, start some distance from the person and walk toward them, with the rods being parallel. When you start to approach the person's auric field, the rods will come together and touch at the point that the aura of that person ends. When using a pendulum, approach the person with it swinging forward and backward, and upon reaching the aura's border the pendulum will instead swing left to right, at the aura's border. Do this several times in different places because the aura field may not be perfectly egg-shaped and could need some energy work.

As you dowse and define the aura, you may notice other senses starting to work, perhaps senses you did not know you had. It cannot be overemphasized: your intuition, or your inner sense of knowing, sometimes described as your inner guidance or "compass," is the most important of these senses. If you can see the aura at this point, that is wonderful—but not necessary. It is much more important to "sense" it, and not just the feel of it, but even to somehow sense colors (which are visually defined as different levels of frequency or vibration). Some of you who will study the layers of the aura can then use this technique to determine each layer, including the electromagnetic layer that is the closest to our physical bodies, most often appearing white and sticking out from the body about one or two inches. Whether you see or sense these colors, please know that no one color is better than another, as we all have different purposes in our lives at any given time.

Here's a basic rule of thumb: If the colors are clear, light, bright, and vibrant, the aura is healthy in these areas. In areas they appear or feel dull, dingy, muddled, or murky, energetic healing techniques will be needed to restore the aura's vibrancy.

These areas can be holes or tears, which can allow undesirable energies to enter as well as allow a person's energies to leak out. For those who feel sensation, these areas can feel like a "draft." The person can often feel drained. This type of damage is really common because when we go into the world, we inevitably "brush" our auras across other people and things, which can inadvertently tear them. This is also the case when we physically injure ourselves and can see the area of the injury needing energetic healing. Interestingly, like a cloth that gathers dust, this is also the way we pick up residual energies, some of which can weigh our energies down and deplete our vital force. We can even do this to ourselves by not getting enough sunlight, fresh air, exercise, good foods, and water, and can overdo it with processed foods, alcohol, drugs, and other influences (like anger and depression) that weaken our aura.

While most of this damage happens accidentally, sometimes the causes of damage are rather deliberate, since many people who live in a fear-based paradigm believe it is easier to steal, threaten, or disempower another rather than to build and empower themselves. This is certainly most unfortunate.

It is common for more than one color to be present in the aura, and the differences you notice usually have a valid explanation. For instance, I had my aura read many years ago right after a Reiki I attunement. While much of it appeared to be a clear peridot or apple-green color, there appeared to be a beautiful light warm purple color on the top of my head (signifying good intuition at the time). If a color you see is in between two other colors, it will often have qualities of both of the colors that create that color.

Another thing to keep in mind: Colors on the left side are usually future energies being received, and colors on the right side are usually passing or past energies being given into the world or

COLOR	CLEAR, VIBRANT	DULL, DINGY
Purple	Very good intuition, active interest in spiritual matters	Can be conflict between logic and intuition, prone to headaches, tension
Blue	Communication, honesty, a good sense of fairness and justice, calm, reflective	Overcaregiver, sensitive, may experience loneliness, feeling low, prone to sinus, throat, or mouth sensitivities
Green	Nature lover, often healers or teachers, true friendships, warm, giving, open-hearted	Closed-off heart to others (green with envy), may feel lost, uncertain, heart/ blood/ circulatory ailments
Yellow	Sunny, optimistic, may be learning new knowledge, curious, focus and intellect work in sync with willpower	May take on too many projects and not finish them; can lack focus, appear indecisive, nervous, fear, stomach/digestion issues
Orange	Creative, warm personalities, nurturing, intelligent, positive, self-knowledge	May overanalyze, feel blocked, emotionally drained, deny needs, lower digestive or female reproductive problems
Red	Physically active, passionate, deliberate, purposeful, practical, strength and vigor	Can have quick temper, impulsive anger, overwhelmed by desire, control issues, letting go, survival, colon or male reproductive-area problems
Brown	Lover of the countryside, traditional values, down to earth, family ties to farming, banking, mining	May feel hemmed-in, restricted, energy may need cleansing and recharging
Pink	Inner child, self-love, purity, innocence, compassionate	Being too hard on self, not loving or nurturing the inner child, relates to the heart area
White	Purity of purpose, can be spiritual or religious, can look light golden	Usually a light cleansing needed
Black	Not usual; as a temporary measure, it means strong protection and almost appears invisible	Old issues (karma, past lives, ancestral) that need to be cleared, usually old anger, feeling stuck, blockage, holes, healing energy and repair needed

projected, and even things being released. During that same aura reading, I had some orange energy on my left side near my arms and hands, and shortly after the reading I went into a highly creative cycle. If I had already gone through this highly creative cycle, my aura would have reflected this orange color on my right side.

The main qualities you can expect from these colors in auras are listed on the chart on page 351. Upon review, you may notice a similarity to the chakra system—indeed, they are interrelated.

Restoring Your Aura

Now that you know what an aura is, and how to define it by seeing or sensing it, you can learn a technique to restore it to its proper working order.

Create protective spiritual workspace with the method you usually use. Some may simply ask to be surrounded by protective and loving white light, while others may call on their spirit guides and/or a deity like Jesus, Buddha, Isis, or Odin. If you like working with an angel, Archangel Michael is highly recommended. If you are working on another's aura, ask these spiritually protective forces to determine and reinforce healthy, balanced working boundaries.

Cleansing the aura: Use a scanning or sweeping motion either downward or counterclockwise with your hands alone, and either actual or visualized tools like a crystal (black tourmaline with citrine works well here), a crystal or oak wand, a golden or crystal comb, even your fingers. Many people don't think of this, but using an actual raw egg as a crystal is one of the best auric "vacuums" around. Please dispose the liquid contents of the egg by flushing it down the toilet, and the shells are best placed in outside trash, preferably away from your land (if the egg cracks before you are done, immediately get a new egg, and dispose of all used eggs properly).

Repairing the aura: After cleansing, you may notice those murky-colored areas or places that feel like a draft still exist. I like "darning" or sewing the aura together with an astral needle and healing thread at the hole to patch it. I also like "filling" and smoothing as if you have wood putty to fill in the holes or rough spots in wood. If you are attuned to Reiki or another healing energy method, use symbols to call healing energies along with these techniques. To extend this repair work, the person can regularly take a flower essence designed to tighten the aura and provide protection. Two great choices in the single flower formulas are Yarrow from Flower Essence Services (FES), and Fringed Violet from Australian Bush Flower Essences. Two flower/gem blend formulas that work very well are the Yarrow Environmental Solution formula from FES, and the Guardian blend from Alaskan Essences.

Regenerate the aura: Begin by rubbing your hands together briskly while visualizing "breathing" energies from the top of your head and the bottom of your feet into your body from the sky (including Sun, Moon, stars) and through the Earth and all of her life (imagine you have roots that move). Now feel this strong energy between your hands, then while breathing deeply in and out, arms moving in crisscross fashion, surround your body as if it were in a cocoon, top chakras first, allowing this energy to fill the large egg-shaped space (any color that feels right is good as long as it is a clear, light, "sparkly," or bright color). When reaching your feet, breathe in deeply and "grab up" the energy, tossing it above your head and allowing it to fluff and fill out your area in a natural, unforced way. Intend that your energy now replenishes through spirit working through you, rather than from you, which will lessen the tendency to allow others to deplete your energy. In fact, you may find yourself replenished instead of drained when others need energy from you!

Maintain your renewed aura by regularly smudging with sage, using crystals like black tourmaline and citrine, taking cleansing baths, spraying around you with rosewater, and regularly taking the flower essences mentioned in aura repair section above. Keeping your aura clean and strong can also lead to better physical health over time.

If you find yourself in a pinch when you are really drained and low on energy—hug a tree! May you always feel vital and re-energized!

Dark Moon Meditations

by Autumn Damiana

In "Wicca 101," we learn about the different phases of the moon (waxing, full, and waning) and how they relate to the three faces of the Great Goddess (Maiden, Mother, and Crone.) We are also taught that the moon determines when and how to go about doing our witchy business. Technically, the "dark" moon refers to the very end of the waning moon, right before it becomes new again and cannot be seen in the sky. However, the phrase "dark moon" has come to include the entire waning moon phase. This is traditionally a time when only banishing spells are cast, and the focus is on more introspective work such as divination, study, and meditation. Most magical folk have little trouble with divination and study, but for some reason, many of us don't meditate regularly. Some of us have never been taught or don't realize that we already know how. Others are unaware of the importance of meditation, and may also not realize how useful the practice can be.

Why Meditate?

Many believe that the whole point to meditation is to find "inner peace." This is an attractive idea but also quite a challenge, considering that adepts may dedicate their entire lives to this goal. However, that doesn't mean that you should completely abandon your quest for inner peace. The beauty of meditation is that it can provide you with all sorts of other benefits that will help you find whatever you ultimately want out of life. These benefits can manifest in a variety of ways, from reduced stress to greater emotional stability to an overall feeling of better health and well-being.

As a Pagan, Wiccan, or Witch, there are also a few other reasons to meditate. One reason is the health advantage. Magic and ritual can overtax the system, and meditation is a good way to balance and recharge the body. Another good reason is that meditation is a way to train the mind. Because we often use visualization in our Craft, it is important to practice visualization techniques. It is also a good idea to learn how to focus, which can only be accomplished when you figure out how to deal with or ignore distractions. Meditation can help in both of these areas. Lastly, most spiritual traditions or disciplines stress the importance of knowing the Self. You can easily explore this inner terrain through meditation, which can boost your intuition, enhance your psychic abilities, deepen your awareness and understanding, and bring you into harmony with Universal Oneness.

Basic Meditation

Stereotypes of meditation abound, such as the idea that you must empty your mind completely or that you need to remain absolutely still while holding unnatural or unfamiliar poses. No wonder so many of us find meditation so mystifying! In fact, there are hundreds of meditation styles and techniques, and while these stereotypes stem from actual practices, they are of an advanced nature and can take years to master. Effective meditation does not have to involve complicated or hard-to-learn methods, nor does it have to be formal or ritualized, unless you want it to be. Here are a few sample meditation exercises, which you may be familiar with:

1. Breathing slowly and purposefully.
2. Listening to the sound of your breath or your heart beating.
3. Grounding and centering.
4. Using prayer or meditation beads.
5. Repeating or chanting of a sound, word, mantra, or phrase.
6. Conscious relaxation; letting go of worry, stress, and tension.
7. Participating in a guided meditation or journeying exercise.
8. Walking or following a labyrinth or other circuitous path.
9. Spending a few moments in quiet contemplation of something specific.
10. Engaging in stretching, yoga, dance, or any body movement.

The secret to getting the most out of meditation is to decide what you would like to accomplish, and then choosing the method best suited to help you achieve that goal. This way, you won't ever have to be frustrated that you are "forcing" the practice or feel that you are not doing it right. Start with any of the above meditation ideas that seem easy to you, and practice just relaxing or listening to your inner Self. Experiment and see what happens. Everyone is different; while some may be able to meditate sitting still in silent reflection, others will prefer to move around, chant, or engage in freeform meditation just "zoning out."

Any kind of meditating during the dark moon is appropriate because of the moon phase's emphasis on introspection. However, if you really want to take advantage of the dark moon's specific energies to give your meditations extra oomph, tailor your meditation topics and goals accordingly. Just as with spellwork, the dark moon is a good time to concentrate on anything that you would like to banish. You can meditate to relieve stress or anxiety, decrease time spent loafing in front of the computer or TV, or work on letting go of grief, resentment, anger, addiction, illness, or any other form of negativity. A meditation can even take the form of an actual spell. You can also use the dark moon to meditate on subjects such as completion of a cycle, death and rebirth, endings, the shadow self, or why disintegration and destruction are sometimes necessary.

Working with Dark Goddesses

The Great Goddess has many different aspects, and one of the ways we work with, worship, and understand her is through Her many identities. Here is a short list of some goddesses that embody a "heavier" energy compatible with the dark moon phase. You might want to say a prayer to one of these goddesses before a meditation, or establish an ongoing dialogue with one or more of them during the dark moon.

Sekhmet: The Egyptian lioness-headed goddess Sekhmet once wielded the scorching heat of the sun against humankind because they had lapsed in their worship of the gods. A goddess of war and vengeance, Sekhmet also represents loyalty, the healing arts, and the fiercely protective nature of a mother lioness. Call on Sekhmet to help "tame" you when you feel out of control or to help discover, understand, and heal the imbalances within you.

Kali: One of the most complex and often misunderstood goddesses in India, Kali has a fearsome reputation as a bringer of death and destruction. However, Kali destroys only what stands in the way of new creation. She represents the conquering and yet transformative power of time, which marches ever onward, bringing necessary change whether we like it or not! Kali is the perfect goddess to call on to overcome fears or other obstacles blocking you on your life's path or impeding your personal progress.

Morrigan: A powerful and ferocious Celtic warrior goddess, Morrigan is a favorite among modern Pagans. Known as "the Phantom Queen," she is the goddess of battle, strife, the circle of life and death, and prophecy. Often represented as a raven or a crow flying above the battlefield and feeding on the dead, Morrigan can also appear as a beautiful young woman or an old hag. Because of this, she has a reputation as a shapeshifter. Morrigan can teach you how to adapt when necessary, but she can also show you how to take control and change your fate. Her most valuable lesson is in recognizing which approach is the right choice.

Lilith: This is a controversial figure from ancient Jewish legend. Purported to be the first wife of Adam, Lilith was created at the same time and out of the same earth as he was. As a result, she felt she should be regarded by Adam as an equal and refused to be ruled by him. When Adam continued to assert his dominance, she left both him and the Garden of Eden behind, instigating "the first divorce" and causing herself to be replaced by the more submissive Eve. Today, Lilith is considered an archetype of a strong, confident, determined, and independent woman. Work with Lilith to build these traits in yourself or to overcome adversity from others.

Hecate: A Greco-Roman triple goddess, Hecate is synonymous with sorcery, the night, and the moon. In recent times, Hecate has been identified with the moon's waning phase and is usually depicted as the Crone or Wise Woman. And yet, because of her threefold aspect, she has been worshiped in times past as embodying all the phases of the moon and all of the stages of life. Regarded as the patroness of Witches, you can ask Hecate to aid you in any form of divination or magic. Call on her to help you understand the Mysteries or to gain wisdom of the Self through introspection.

Specific Meditations for the Dark Moon

A General Meditation for Letting Go

Lie down outside under the waning Moon (or hold an image of it in your mind). Breathe in and out, slowly and deeply, until you start to relax. Speak to the moon, and ask it a question such as "what do I need to cut out of my life?" or "how can I let go of what is no longer serving me?" Continue to breathe deeply, concentrating on the image of the moon, and let your mind wander until an answer comes to you naturally. Whatever the answer is, even if it seems silly or makes no sense, meditate on it for some time and see what else surfaces. When you are satisfied that you have accepted the answer and given it serious consideration, thank the moon and allow your consciousness to return to normal.

Breaking Bad Habits or Behaviors

For this meditation, you need to obtain a long stick that you can break in half with your hands. (Don't do it yet!) You will also need a small ball of black yarn or a skein of black embroidery floss.

The string represents the bad habit, behavior, pattern, or just general negativity in your life. The stick represents the platform supporting this negativity. You will meditate on whatever you want to change while you wind the yarn around the stick.

For example, say I want to meditate on quitting smoking. In this instance, the black yarn would represent everything negative about smoking, such as the health risks, the cost, and the smell. The stick would represent whatever has been supporting my smoking, like addiction, stress, and stubbornness. As I wrap the stick with the yarn, I will meditate on all the ways that smoking has affected me, the reasons I want to quit, the relationship between my habit and the behaviors that justify it, and all of the other thoughts, ideas, and emotions that come up during the meditation.

Whatever ideas you choose as your focus, take your time winding the yarn, and really think about the symbolism between it and the stick. When you have finished, look at the stick and see how tangled up it is. Now, will yourself to change and break the habit or discontinue the negative behavior or pattern, and at the same time, break the stick in a few places. Finish the meditation by unraveling the yarn off the broken stick, symbolizing that if you break the support structure for your bad habit, you can also break the habit itself. Save the yarn, and repeat the meditation with a new stick as needed.

Contemplating Death and Other Endings

On the full moon, select a single cut rose, carnation, tulip, or other ornamental flower in full bloom. Place the flower in a vase full of water where it will not be disturbed and that will be comfortable for you to meditate. This meditation lasts the entire two-week period of the dark moon, and involves observing the flower every day as it fades.

The directions are simple: set the flower in its place on the day of the full moon. Sit in front of it for at least a few minutes, and note its exact size, color, scent, texture, overall appearance, and anything else of interest. Write these observations down, if you wish. Revisit the flower every day, and mark its changes. These may not be apparent right away, but over time, it will be obvious that the bloom is dying. Resist the urge to clean up the petals or pollen, and refrain from changing the water, even if it becomes stagnant or the flower starts to mold. (I know it can be smelly or gross, but this is part of the natural cycle.) Continue to meditate on the flower every day for at least a few minutes, witnessing the changes taking place as it degenerates.

During these times, keep in mind the idea that eventually everything ends or dies. This is not meant to be a harsh or depressing view of life, but rather a reality check that can be used constructively to help understand that death is simply the precursor to rebirth. Ask yourself, what has recently ended in your life, is ending now, or perhaps needs to come to an end? Why? How does this affect you? What will be the next step or stage? Meditate on these questions and ideas, and know that there are no right or wrong answers. Every thought or feeling you have on the subject is valid and should be acknowledged. Again, write these in your journal if you wish. On the last day of the meditation (the new moon), think about what you have learned from the flower and thank it for sharing its lessons with you. You may then clean it up by putting the flower in a compost pile, a yard waste bin, or somewhere outside to continue decomposing.

~

These meditations are just a few of the many suitable ideas for the dark moon phase. Naturally you should feel free to change them to fit your particular needs, as well as make up your own meditations—the more personal and meaningful, the better. Like many things in life, meditation will become easier and more enjoyable with practice, but because there are so many different ways to meditate, it should never be boring or feel like a chore. Now that I have shared a little bit about meditation and why I believe it to be such a worthwhile pursuit, I hope that you will be inspired to start a regular dark moon meditation practice. After all, this is exactly what the time of the dark moon is for.